The English Question

MANCHESTER
1824

Manchester University Press

DEVOLUTION series
series editor Charlie Jeffery

already published

Beyond devolution and decentralisation
Alistair Cole

Between two Unions
Europeanisation and Scottish devolution
Paolo Dardanelli

Territorial politics and health policy
UK health policy in comparative perspective
Scott L. Greer

Devolution and electoral politics
Dan Hough and Charlie Jeffery (eds)

Devolution has established new political institutions in Scotland, Wales, Northern Ireland, London and the other English regions since 1997. These devolution reforms have far-reaching implications for the politics, policy and society of the UK. Radical institutional change, combined with a fuller capacity to express the UK's distinctive territorial identities, is reshaping the way the UK is governed and opening up new directions of public policy. These are the biggest changes to UK politics for at least 150 years.

The Devolution series brings together the best research in the UK on devolution and its implications. It draws together the best analysis from the Economic and Social Research Council's research programme on Devolution and Constitutional Change. The series will have three central themes, each of which are vital components in understanding the changes devolution has set in train.

1 **Delivering public policy after devolution: diverging from Westminster**: Does devolution result in the provision of different standards of public service in health or education, or in widening economic disparities from one part of the UK to another? If so, does it matter?

2 **The political institutions of devolution**: How well do the new devolved institutions work? How effectively are devolved and UK-level matters coordinated? How have political organisations which have traditionally operated UK-wide – political parties, interest groups – responded to multi-level politics?

3 **Public attitudes, devolution and national identity**: How do people in different parts of the UK assess the performance of the new devolved institutions? Do people identify themselves differently as a result of devolution? Does a common sense of Britishness still unite people from different parts of the UK?

The
English Question

edited by Robert Hazell

Manchester University Press

Manchester and New York

distributed exclusively in the USA by Palgrave

Published by Manchester University Press
Oxford Road, Manchester M13 9NR, UK
and Room 400, 175 Fifth Avenue, New York, NY 10010, USA
www.manchesteruniversitypress.co.uk

Distributed exclusively in the USA by
Palgrave, 175 Fifth Avenue, New York,
NY 10010, USA

Distributed exclusively in Canada by
UBC Press, University of British Columbia, 2029 West Mall,
Vancouver, BC, Canada V6T 1Z2

British Library Cataloguing-in-Publication Data
A catalogue record for this book is available from the British Library

Library of Congress Cataloging-in-Publication Data applied for

ISBN 0 7190 7368 5 *hardback*
EAN 978 0 7190 7368 7

ISBN 0 7190 7369 3 *paperback*
EAN 978 0 7190 7369 4

First published 2006

15 14 13 12 11 10 09 08 07 06   10 9 8 7 6 5 4 3 2 1

Typeset by Servis Filmsetting Ltd, Manchester
Printed in Great Britain
by Biddles Ltd, King's Lynn

Contents

List of boxes, figures and tables   *page* vi
List of abbreviations   viii
List of contributors   ix
Foreword   xi

1 Introduction: what is the English Question?   *Robert Hazell*   1

PART I   ENGLAND IN THE UNION

2 England and the Union since 1707   *Iain McLean and Alistair McMillan*   24

3 The challenges to English identity   *Arthur Aughey*   45

4 The government of England by Westminster   *Meg Russell and Guy Lodge*   64

5 Whitehall and the government of England   *Guy Lodge and James Mitchell*   96

6 What the people say – if anything   *John Curtice*   119

PART II   THE GOVERNANCE OF ENGLAND

7 From functional to political regionalism: England in comparative perspective   *Michael Keating*   142

8 The idea of English regionalism   *John Tomaney*   158

9 Facts on the ground: the growth of institutional answers to the English Question in the regions   *Mark Sandford*   174

10 A very English institution: central and local in the English NHS   *Scott L. Greer*   194

11 Conclusion: what are the answers to the English Question?   *Robert Hazell*   220

Bibliography   242
Index   259

Boxes, figures and tables

Boxes

1.1	Institutional solutions	*page* 6
4.1	The territorial extent of the Higher Education Bill	85
5.1	Adams *et al.* territorial breakdown of Whitehall departments	100
5.2	Whitehall departments represented in the government offices for the regions as of 2002	112
5.3	Regionalism in Whitehall departments	115
11.1	Institutional solutions to two versions of the English Question	221

Figures

8.1	Schematic history of regional bodies in north-east England	163
10.1	Structure of the NHS, 1948–74	200
10.2	Structure of the NHS outside of Northern Ireland, 1974–82	201
10.3	Structure of the NHS in England, 1991–96	202
10.4	English NHS, January 2005	203

Tables

4.1	House of Commons ministers in UK government departments, by location of constituency	67
4.2	Membership of departmental select committees, by location of constituency	68
4.3	Written parliamentary questions to departments, by location of constituency	69
4.4	Election results 1945–2001 in UK and England	71
4.5	Election results 1945–2001 in Wales, Scotland and Northern Ireland	74
5.1	Whitehall's 'regional' turn	111
5.2	Central government spending on regional development agencies	115
6.1	Attitudes towards how England should be governed	121
6.2	Attitudes towards regional government	122
6.3	Attitudes towards Scottish MPs	123

6.4   Regional variation in attitudes towards how England should be governed   123

6.5   Regional variation in attitudes towards regional government   124

6.6   Attitudes towards English devolution in 1970   126

6.7   Perceived impact of devolution on how Britain is governed   129

6.8   English attitudes towards devolution in Scotland and Wales   130

6.9   Trends in forced-choice national identity   131

6.10 Trends in Moreno national identity   131

6.11 Attitudes towards how England should be governed, by forced-choice national identity   132

6.12 Trust in the UK Government   133

6.13 Regional variation in regional pride   134

6.14 Attitudes towards regional government by regional pride   135

6.15 Attitudes to English regional government by perceptions of government bias   136

6.16 Perceptions of the impact of regional chambers/assemblies   137

6.17 Attitudes towards regional government by perceptions of impact of regional chambers/assemblies   137

6.18 Attitudes towards public service standards   139

9.1   A chronology of institutional regionalism   177

10.1 Member states in federal constitutions   195

10.2 Staffing of the four NHS systems   198

11.1 Summary evaluation of institutional answers to the English Question   222

Abbreviations

AHA	area health authority
CNR	(Cabinet) Committee of the Nations and the Regions
CEP	Campaign For an English Parliament
CFER	Campaign For the English Regions
DCA	Department for Constitutional Affairs
DCMS	Department for Culture, Media and Sport
DEFRA	Department for the Environment, Food and Rural Affairs
DETR	Department of the Environment, Transport and the Regions
DfEE	Department for Education and Employment
DfES	Department for Education and Skills
DGH	district general hospital
DHA	district health authority
DTI	Department of Trade and Industry
DTLR	Department for Transport, Local Government and the Regions
EC	European Community
GLA	Greater London Authority
GLC	Greater London Council
GO	government office for the region
HP	Hospital Plan
LSC	Learning and Skills Council
MAFF	Ministry of Agriculture, Food and Fisheries
MOH	medical officer of health
NEDA	North-East Development Association
NEDB	North-East Development Board
NEIDA	North-East Industrial Development Association
NEPC	Northern Economic Planning Council
NHS	National Health Service
ODPM	Office of the Deputy Prime Minister
PCT	primary care trust
PR	proportional representation
PSA	public service agreement
RCU	regional co-ordination unit
RDA	regional development agency
REPB	regional economic planning board
RSA	regional selective assistance
SHA	strategic health authority
UKIP	UK Independence Party

Contributors

Arthur Aughey is Senior Lecturer in politics at the University of Ulster, where his research includes work on Northern Ireland's politics with special reference to unionism, British politics with special reference to the politics of the constitution, and Conservative political thought. His recent publications include *Nationalism, Devolution and the Challenge to the United Kingdom State*.

John Curtice is Deputy Director of the Centre for Research into Elections and Social Trends and professor of politics at the University of Strathclyde. A particular interest of his has been the impact of devolution on public opinion across the UK, evinced most recently in his co-editing of *Devolution: Scottish Answers to Scottish Questions?*

Robert Hazell is Director of the Constitution Unit and professor of government and the constitution in the School of Public Policy, University College London. Originally a barrister, he spent much of his working life at the Home Office. He left Whitehall to become director of the Nuffield Foundation and founded the Constitution Unit in 1995. He was director of a five-year research programme into the Dynamics of Devolution funded by the Leverhulme Trust, 1999 to 2004.

Scott L. Greer is Assistant Professor of Health Management and Policy at the University of Michigan's School of Public Health and a member of the Constitution Unit, University College London. His publications on health and territorial politics include the monograph *Territorial Politics and Health Policy*; he was a co-editor of *Questioning Geopolitics* and the editor of *Territory, Justice and Democracy* (forthcoming).

Michael Keating is Professor and Head of the Department of Political and Social Sciences at the European University Institute, Florence, and professor of Scottish politics at the University of Aberdeen. At present he is working on nationality questions and European integration, and on devolution in the United Kingdom. He is co-director of the ECPR Standing Group on Regionalism, co-editor of *Regional and Federal Studies*, editor of the book series 'Regionalism and Federalism' (Presses interuniversitaires européennes).

Guy Lodge is Research Fellow in the democracy team at the Institute for Public Policy Research (ippr). His research interests include constitutional reform, civil renewal and political engagement. Previously, at the Constitution Unit, University College London, he worked on the ESRC-funded 'Devolution and the Centre' and the Leverhulme-funded 'Devolution and Westminster' projects.

Iain McLean is Professor of Politics and Official Fellow, Nuffield College, Oxford University. His research interests include public choice, electoral systems, public administration and public finance, UK government and Enlightenment political thought. Among his recent writings are *Rational Choice in British Politics* and (with Martin Jones) *Aberfan: Government and Disasters*.

Alistair McMillan is a Research Fellow of Nuffield College, Oxford University. His research interests include Indian politics.

James Mitchell is Professor of Politics at the University of Strathclyde and the author of numerous book and articles on Scottish and UK politics and devolution. He was the principal investigator of the ESRC funded 'Devolution and the Centre' project.

Meg Russell has been Senior Research Fellow at the Constitution Unit, University College London, since 1998. She is the author of various reports and briefings on Parliament and its reform, including *Reforming the House of Lords: Lessons from Overseas*, and of *Building New Labour: The Politics of Party Organisation*. She was seconded full time as an advisor to Robin Cook in his role as leader of the House of Commons, June 2001–March 2003.

Mark Sandford is a Research Fellow at the Constitution Unit, University College London, where he leads research on regional government. He has published several reports and articles on aspects of strategy-making, network governance and civic engagement in the English regions, and the Government's policy on elected regional assemblies; he is the author of the monograph *The New Governance of the English Regions*.

John Tomaney is Professor of Regional Governance and Co-director of the Centre for Urban and Regional Development Studies at the University of Newcastle upon Tyne. His main research interests are the political economy of regional development, the politics of devolution in the UK and all aspects of the development of north-east England.

Foreword

This book is one of three which bring together the findings of a five-year research programme 'The Nations and Regions: The Dynamics of Devolution', led by the Constitution Unit and funded by the Leverhulme Trust. The other two books are *Devolution and Power* and *Has Devolution Worked?*, also published by Manchester University Press. We are extremely grateful to the Leverhulme Trustees for their foresight in funding a major research programme at the dawn of devolution in the UK, and to our twenty-five research partners in the programme from a dozen universities spread across the UK.

Chapter 5, by Lodge and Mitchell, on the government of England by Whitehall, is the product of the research project 'Devolution and the Centre' which was funded under the ESRC's 'Devolution and Constitutional Change' programme (project no. L21925 20–26); we are grateful to the ESRC and to their Devolution Programme Director Professor Charlie Jeffery for allowing it to be included in this book. Chapter 10, by Scott Greer, received support from the Nuffield and Leverhulme Trusts.

Like many Constitution Unit projects, this has been a major collaborative effort. We thank first the contributors to the book, for the quality of their own chapters and for attending a series of meetings in which we discussed each other's contributions and the book as a whole. Within the Unit I should like to thank in particular Dr Scott Greer, who has been my major collaborator in planning and editing the book. Akash Paun was both conscientious and crucial in putting the book together and editing the final manuscript. Thanks also go to our excellent research assistants Roger Masterman and Guy Lodge, and to Corinna Matthews and Laura Venning who helped, as interns, in the final stages of putting the book to bed. As always we owe a great debt to our able and committed administrators, Helen Daines and Matthew Butt.

Robert Hazell
School of Public Policy
University College London

1

Introduction: what is the English Question?

Robert Hazell

The English Question is a portmanteau heading for a whole series of questions about the government of England. These have been thrown up as a result of the Labour Government's programme of devolution to Scotland, Wales and Northern Ireland, and of regionalism in England. Because England was initially left out of that programme, devolution has provoked a bout of questioning and self-questioning on the part of critics and commentators at a range of distinct levels, questions that vary from existential issues about identity (Who are the English? What is Englishness?) to cultural issues (How does Englishness find expression?), to political questions about the place of England in the Union and the need for devolution within England.

This book is about the political questions. Scotland, Wales and Northern Ireland have a stronger political voice, thanks to their new elected assemblies. England and the English regions risk losing out – in the distribution of government funds, in competition for inward investment, in voting on English laws. Do the English care? Do they want any devolution for themselves? And what should be the Government's response? These concerns lie at the heart of the political versions of the English Question.

England is the gaping hole in the devolution settlement: some believe that devolution will not be complete, and the settlement will not stabilise, until the English Question has been solved; others believe that England can be left out indefinitely and devolution confined to the Celtic fringe. Opinions vary not only about the answers, but about the nature of the question. This book aims to explain the different formulations of the question and to set the answers in a proper historical and constitutional context.

At the core of the book lies a strongly institutional approach. This is not another quest in search of Englishness, the English and their national or cultural identity; although we cannot ignore the links between national identity and political representation (discussed in chapters 2 and 3). But our central focus is on politics and political representation for England and the English regions, and what institutional form that political representation should take.

The political versions of the English Question relate both to the place of England as a whole within the Union (United Kingdom) and to regionalism within England. The book therefore tackles the English Question at the macro, all-UK, level, and at the regional and local level within England. The English Question consequently can be divided into the following groups of sub-questions:

England's place in the Union

- Does England need to find its own separate political voice to rebalance the louder political voice accorded to Scotland, Wales and Northern Ireland?
- Could this be supplied by: an English Parliament; 'English votes on English laws'; independence for England?

Regionalism in England

- Does England, too, need devolution – to break from the excessive domination of central government in London, as an alternative or as a supplement to all-England solutions?
- Can this best be supplied by elected regional assemblies, functional regionalism, stronger local government or elected mayors?

Continuation of the status quo

Is it, alternatively, that the English want none of the above, with no separate representation or political voice and no share in devolution either?

These questions have come onto the political agenda as a result of devolution to Scotland and Wales. Some go back a long way and were questions with which Gladstone grappled when seeking to deliver Home Rule for Ireland. They are big issues, issues which will determine the future shape and nature of the Union as much as the future government of England. Devolution has already profoundly changed the UK's system of government, but it extends only to 15 per cent of the population. England, with 85 per cent of the population, for the moment is left out. But if the English choose to opt in, the choice they make will have huge consequences not only for the government of England but for the whole future of the Union.

Different versions of the English Question

Is the English Question about England's place in the Union or is it about improving the government of England?

The English Question has gained prominence as a consequence mainly of devolution. But interest in regionalism in England long predates devolution to Scotland and Wales, as shown in chapter 8. There is an English Question which is purely internal to England, and would be posed regardless of devolution elsewhere. It springs from longstanding concerns about the poor performance of many of England's regions: the North–South divide, persistent low economic growth, an economy which is excessively dominated by London and the South East (Adams, Robinson and Vigor 2003; Office of the Deputy Prime Minister Select Committee 2003). This version of the English Question arises, not in reaction against devolution in Scotland and Wales, but from the same motivating force which inspired devolution in other parts of the UK: resentment against London and the centralism of government based in Westminster and Whitehall.

This *purely English* version of the English Question asks: how can we improve the government of England? Recent answers have included administrative decentralisation, elected regional assemblies, city–regions, elected mayors. The Government has experimented with three of these measures, with regional government in England being the policy solution, addressed mainly in Part II of the book, which shows how different answers in terms of policy prescription stem from different versions of the English Question. Regional government is not intended to rebalance England's place in the Union, but to improve the government of England: to improve poor economic performance in the English regions by giving them greater autonomy and reducing the dominance of the government in London (Cabinet Office/Department for Transport, Local Government and the Regions 2002).

The *UK version* of the English Question, addressed in Part I of the book, asks about England's place in the Union, and raises issues of political representation and political voice for the English post-devolution. It is epitomised in calls for an English parliament, or English votes on English laws. Made in a wider, UK-level, context, these calls are for a rebalancing of the Union by strengthening the place of England following devolution to the smaller nations of the UK: they demand that England be recognised as a political unit to match the stronger recognition which devolution has accorded to Scotland and Wales. These calls appear sometimes to be more of a protest vote than a policy prescription, a reminder that the English, too, need to be heard now that the Scots and the Welsh have a louder voice. The protesters are not interested in decentralisation within England; indeed they are strongly opposed to it, because they regard measures such as regional assemblies as fragmenting England, when the country needs to speak with a stronger not a weaker political voice (Campaign for an English Parliament 2001; Knowles 2004).

Is the English Question static or dynamic?

Answers to the English Question can vary, depending on whether the respondent takes a static or a dynamic view. The *static* view responds that the English do not seem to care. Chapter 6 shows how the English are quite relaxed and tolerant about devolution in Scotland and Wales, but do not seem at present to want any devolution for themselves. In the 2001 election English voters remained indifferent to calls from William Hague for English votes on English laws. The static view concludes that the Government can muddle through, with no further changes in the government of England, and that devolution in the UK can remain lopsided *ad infinitum*.

The *dynamic* view, in contrast, looks ahead, and warns that the English may not remain relaxed and uninterested for ever in devolution. Countries like Spain show that asymmetrical devolution, confined initially to the historic nations (Catalonia, the Basque Country and Galicia), can spread over time to other regions which originally showed no interest. The English may awaken only slowly to the realities of devolution and be slow in demanding their share of the benefits. Pressures may build up gradually, and come from without and within: from the demonstration effect *without* of devolution in Scotland and Wales; and from growing dissatisfaction *within*, with the centralised way in which England is governed.

Is the English Question an elite- or mass-level question?

Answers also vary depending on whether the English Question is asked of the general public or of political elites. There is as yet little awareness of these issues among the general public in England, giving rise to the static view outlined above: the English masses have little interest in devolution elsewhere in the UK and make no demand for devolution for themselves (see chapter 6). In November 2004 that was dramatically confirmed by the 'No' vote in the North-East regional referendum. At elite levels there is greater awareness, more sense of the anomalies and the potential political dynamic unleashed by devolution, with a desire to find solutions. But there is a clear political divide, with Labour in favour of and the Conservatives against regional assemblies. Given the mainly technocratic arguments advanced for regional assemblies in England, the debate may remain confined to elite levels for some time to come. The 2004 referendum in the North East was the first big test of whether the elites could make the case for regional government in terms which appeal to the masses.

Is the English Question about structures and territory or about powers, functions and budgets?

This is one of the distinctions which is difficult to explain, because it is seldom articulated. It is a measure of how inchoate much of the debate around the English Question is, so that it seldom moves beyond rather simplistic arguments about the territorial division of England. The Campaign for an English Parliament (CEP) is vehemently against dividing England into regions. It argues that, following devolution to Scotland and Wales, England itself should be recognised as a unit and level of government. By contrast, the Campaign for the English Regions (CFER) argues for regional government with boundaries based on the eight standard English regions. (As noted above, the two campaigns are answering different versions of the English Question: the first, a UK version; the second, an English-only version).

This is not the only issue to divide the two campaigns. The CFER has been involved in a vigorous debate about the powers, functions and budgets to be devolved to elected regional assemblies (Campaign for the English Regions 2002). There have been fierce battles within government, between John Prescott and the main Whitehall departments, all reluctant to give up their powers (see chapter 5). The upshot was a weak model, of slimline, strategic assemblies with limited functions and relatively small budgets: bodies, some argued, that were not worth voting for (Sandford 2002a; Stevens 2004). Chapter 9 reminds us that alternative and stronger models are on offer through which, if ever they get launched, regional assemblies may accrue further powers.

By contrast there is no parallel debate about the powers, functions and budget of an English parliament. It is an indication of how the CEP is more of a protest movement that it has not drawn up a prospectus or blueprint for the parliament it hopes to create. It has not moved beyond copying out the powers of the Scottish Parliament and proposing the same for England. There is no detailed constitutional design, no equivalent of the reports produced by the Scottish Constitutional Convention, to say what size it should be, by what system it should be elected, how it should be financed and what its relationship would be to the Westminster Parliament.

Institutional answers to the English Question

Following the analysis at the beginning of this chapter, institutional answers to the English Question can be grouped into two broad sets. There are responses which strengthen England's place in the Union, to give England a louder voice; and responses which strengthen regional or local government in England, to reduce the dominance of the central government in London. The second set of measures, to strengthen regional or local government, are reasonably familiar. They are briefly mentioned here to explain where they belong in the argument, but not discussed fully until chapters 9 and 11. The first set of measures, to strengthen England's place in the Union, are less familiar and need a little introduction before we explain the overall structure and argument of the book.

Box 1.1 Institutional solutions

Solutions to strengthen England's voice in the Union

- An English parliament
- English votes on English laws
- English independence

Solutions to decentralise the government of England

- Elected regional assemblies
- Functional regionalism
- Revival of local government
- Elected mayors

Strengthening England's voice in the Union

AN ENGLISH PARLIAMENT

An English parliament would in effect create a federation of the four historic nations in the UK. To counterbalance the Scottish Parliament and the Welsh and Northern Ireland Assemblies, the English would have their own parliament to make laws for England. It is the solution propounded by the CEP, a pressure group founded in the late 1990s in response to devolution in Scotland and Wales. The CEP is not a political party,[1] but is a voice for English nationalism and the protest that with devolution the Scots, the Welsh and the Northern Irish will have a louder political voice and the English risking losing out. The introduction on the homepage of the CEP's website gives the flavour:

> Devolution has brought about major constitutional changes within the United Kingdom. Scotland now has its own parliament, Wales its own assembly . . . Devolution however has not been extended to England and the English people at all. England has neither a parliament nor an assembly. Constitutionally and politically it still does not exist because, by the express intent of the UK govern-

ment, it is being denied any national political institution of any sort to make the statement that the people of England are a distinct nation.[2]

ENGLISH VOTES ON ENGLISH LAWS: WESTMINSTER AS A PROXY FOR AN ENGLISH PARLIAMENT

If England cannot have its own separate parliament, the English could yet find a louder political voice within the existing parliament at Westminster. Westminster could provide a proxy for an English parliament within the wider shell of the Union Parliament. Prior to devolution we had a three-in-one Parliament, and it was clear when Westminster was operating as the legislature for Scotland, Wales or Northern Ireland (for which it has distinct structures and procedures). The suggestion has been made that following devolution we could develop a four-in-one Parliament, and Westminster could develop distinct structures and procedures to operate in English mode (Hazell 2000a).

Most discussion of this issue has focused on Westminster as a legislature and 'English votes on English laws'. The issue was first raised in the devolution debates of the 1970s by the veteran Scottish Labour MP Tam Dalyell, and it was named after his constituency as 'the West Lothian question'. More recently it has been addressed by the Commons Procedure Committee, in an early inquiry into the procedural consequences of devolution (Procedure Committee 1999); and by the Conservative Party's Commission to Strengthen Parliament, chaired by Lord Norton of Louth (Conservative Party 2000). Both inquiries proposed referring English bills to special committees restricted to English MPs, but provided for the final stage to be back on the floor of the House where all MPs can vote.

Legislation is not the only English business conducted at Westminster. English business is also transacted through the work of departmental select committees; through questions to ministers on English matters; and through the revived Standing Committee on Regional Affairs (open only to English MPs). Chapter 4 shows that in the early years of devolution there has been little recognition or formalisation of English business at Westminster, and little evidence of a burgeoning English consciousness among MPs. Westminster may have the latent capacity to operate as a proxy for an English parliament, but there is little sign of much political will in favour of it doing so.

INDEPENDENCE FOR ENGLAND

It may come as a surprise that anyone has seriously advocated independence for England; but that solution has been propounded by certain academics and by fringe political parties. Among the academics, the best known is Tom Nairn, who has been predicting the break up of Britain for twenty-five years. Independence for England would be the result of Scotland and Wales separating from the UK, which he predicts as the inevitable consequence of devolution (Nairn 1981: 2000). Similarly but less splenetically Richard Weight (2002) has forecast the dissolution of the UK, arguing for English separation from Scotland to enable England to find a new sense of national identity as an independent nation state. The journalist Simon Heffer (1999) has also argued that England should break the union with Scotland: if the Scots do not first separate from England, England should break loose from an over-dependent Scotland.

The main political party advocating independence for England is the English Independence Party (formerly the English National Party). Members are opposed to a federation, which they see as a recipe for conflict, with England subsidising the rest of the UK, and are in favour of England withdrawing both from the United Kingdom and from the European Union. They claim to support a 'moderate, democratic and enlightened nationalism' in order to distinguish their brand of nationalism from that of the British National Party and the National Front.[3]

In contrast to those advocating a strengthening of England's voice within the UK or outright independence, there are many who view the decentralisation of government within England as a more appropriate response to the post-devolution constitutional anomalies that this volume analyses. This alternative approach to the English Question is discussed in the section which follows.

Decentralising the government of England

ELECTED REGIONAL ASSEMBLIES

Regionalism is an old idea (see chapter 8) which was given fresh impetus by devolution. The Campaign for the English Regions (CFER), founded in 2000, derives its inspiration from devolution to Scotland and Wales in much the same way as the CEP, even though their policy prescriptions are very different. Thus the CFER's website opens with the following statement:

> Citizens of the English regions are now waking up to the implications of the unprecedented constitutional reform project of the Government. Scotland has a Parliament; Wales, Northern Ireland and London all have Assemblies: all democratically elected. As a first step to devolving power in England the Government has established Regional Development Agencies in each English region. Each RDA is scrutinised by an unelected regional chamber of local representatives.
>
> While we welcome these developments they are widely seen as not going far enough. Campaigns now exist in five English regions to establish *elected and representative regional government*. Our campaign's aim is to find local solutions to local problems. We aim to develop organic models for English regional government from within our own regions.[4]

The CFER was formed to co-ordinate a national campaign on behalf of the constitutional conventions springing up in the English regions to develop plans for elected regional assemblies and to ensure the Government delivered on its manifesto promise to extend devolution to England. Labour's 1997 manifesto had included a commitment to legislate to allow people, region by region, to decide in a referendum if they wanted directly elected regional government. This manifesto pledge remained unfulfilled in Blair's first term. Deputy Prime Minister John Prescott was blocked by his cabinet colleagues from going that far, but allowed instead to establish regional development agencies (RDAs), with non-statutory regional chambers providing a weak line of accountability in the region. The manifesto pledge for directly elected regional assemblies was repeated in the 2001 Labour manifesto, and was acted on in Blair's second term.

Following the passage of the Regional Assemblies (Preparations) Act in 2003, the Government announced that the first three referendums would be held in the North East, the North West and Yorkshire & The Humber in autumn 2004. Then, in a surprise development, John Prescott announced in July 2004 that only one referendum would be held, in the North East. The reason given was that there had been difficulties with all-postal ballots in the North West and in Yorkshire & The Humber in the June 2004 elections, and all-postal ballots were due to be used also for the referendums. The *real* reason, many commentators observed at the time, was that Labour was deeply divided over the issue in the North West and seemed likely to lose the referendum there and in Yorkshire & The Humber: a defeat the party could ill afford in the run up to a general election. In the event, Labour lost the one remaining referendum: in the North East the Government's proposals were rejected by 78 per cent of those voting, on a 48 per cent turnout.

FUNCTIONAL REGIONALISM

Despite this decisive rejection in the November 2004 referendum, the regional agenda in England is not dead: political regionalism has suffered a setback, but functional regionalism will march on. It is the shorthand term for the regional tier of government that has long existed in embryonic form, but which in recent years has grown in importance.

Labour's commitment to establish elected regional assemblies dates from 1992. John Major took the first steps in regionalising the structures of Whitehall by bringing together the regional outposts of four Whitehall departments in 1994. The government offices for the regions (GOs) have steadily grown as the voice of Whitehall in the regions, also reflecting regional views back to Whitehall, and now include representatives from nine government departments.

The pace of regionalism quickened with the election of New Labour to government in 1997. Although its nerve failed when it came to establishing elected assemblies in the first term, New Labour did move swiftly to establish RDAs in 1999. The RDAs' budgets have been steadily increased, and their powers and flexibility have also grown since the creation of a 'single pot' in place of the initial separate funding streams. They are shadowed by regional chambers, non-statutory bodies of local authority leaders and representatives of the private and voluntary sectors, which have also been given budgets of £0.5m apiece to scrutinise the RDAs and other regional bodies. Taken together the triumvirate of GOs, RDAs and regional chambers is beginning to provide the building-blocks for a regional tier of government.

This functional regionalism will continue even though elected assemblies have been rejected. The Government recognised as much in the 2002 White Paper on elected regional government, which devoted a whole chapter to ways in which the existing voluntary regional chambers might be strengthened (known to regionalists as the 'Chapter 2 Agenda'). Mark Sandford shows (chapter 9) how the fledgling regional institutions have taken on a life of their own, with more effective joint working, specialist forums and partnerships, leading to a stakeholder–network model of regional government, with a host of policy networks around the core of formal institutions.

STRENGTHENING LOCAL GOVERNMENT AND ELECTED MAYORS

The main alternative advanced as an answer to excessive centralisation in the government of England is to revive local government. Much of the agenda is familiar, consisting simply of restoring to local government the powers and functions which have been steadily removed over the last twenty-five years; some of them to the regional tier. There is also New Labour's own agenda for reviving local government. This includes elected mayors, which seemed briefly in competition with regional government as Labour's 'big idea' for the revitalisation of government in England (see chapter 9). There is also a series of lesser reforms in the Local Government Act 2000. None is likely significantly to reduce the centralism in the way England is governed, but they are mentioned for the sake of completeness, because opponents of regional government sometimes assert that the answer is to revive local government.

The dynamism of devolution: pressures for further change

Having established the range of institutional answers to the English Question, we turn next to the forces in play which may favour one set of answers rather than another. We noted at the start how pressures may build up gradually in England, coming from without and within: from growing dissatisfaction with the centralised way England is governed; and from rivalry and emulation of the effects of devolution in Scotland and Wales. The next section summarises the pressures from within, to decentralise the government of England, and the following one the pressures from without, to strengthen England's place in the Union.

Pressures for further change to decentralise the government of England

Pressures to decentralise the government of England have so far been mainly technocratic rather than democratic, pressures from political and bureaucratic elites rather than from public opinion. The hiving-off of central and local government functions to new public bodies and quangos has led to a form of 'creeping regionalism' which Jack Straw defined as a *de facto* regional tier of government when New Labour started rethinking its policy on regional government in 1995 (Labour Party 1995). 'Creeping regionalism' continues in a haphazard, incremental way, with recent candidates being the Environment Agency (following the Haskins–DEFRA review: Haskins 2003) and the Fire and Rescue Service. It is driven partly by economies of scale: many public bodies need a field service, but operate on too big a scale to match the boundaries of local government.

Since Labour came into power in 1997 the architecture of English regionalism has been greatly strengthened. It is built around three main pillars: the GOs, the RDAs and the voluntary regional chambers. In Labour's second term all three regional pillars have been given extra powers and functions. Grouped around these regional bodies in each region is a growing policy community, seeking to influence the policies and priorities of the GOs and the RDAs and their spending decisions. Regional chambers are still developing as forums for the voluntary and business sectors to influence central and local government policies in their region. As they develop in a stakeholder–network model of regional government, the stakeholders themselves develop a vested interest in their continuance.

The final source of elite and technocratic pressure for regionalism comes from Gordon Brown and the Treasury. In the run up to the 2001 election the Chancellor began to support the case for stronger regional policies to reduce the growing divide between booming London and the South East and the poorer regions of the North (Tomaney 2001: 108–11). The North–South divide has been more openly acknowledged under the second Blair Government (Balls and Healey 2002; Adams, Robinson and Vigor 2003; Office of the Deputy Prime Minister Select Committee 2003), and the

Government has committed itself to use regional policy as a corrective measure. The 2002 Spending Review contained a chapter on the English regions, and a new target committing the Government and the regional bodies to reducing disparities in regional growth rates (HM Treasury 2002). The 2004 Spending Review placed an even stronger emphasis on the regional dimension (HM Treasury 2004a). The regional growth rates target was repeated and the Treasury published a document setting out its regional policy strategy (HM Treasury 2004b).

Pressures from the general public in the English regions are less easy to discern. There is a small demonstration effect from devolution in Scotland and Wales. Five English regions have established 'constitutional conventions', in direct imitation of Scotland, and it is no coincidence that they are the regions which border on Scotland and Wales, and are farthest from London: the North East, North West, South West, West Midlands and Yorkshire.[5] But the general public remains largely unaware. In polls in the spring of 2003 for the Government's 'soundings' about readiness for regional government, half had heard nothing about the Government's proposals, while one-third had heard something but could not say what (Office of the Deputy Prime Minister 2003). In focus groups in the West Midlands, not a single respondent was aware of either the GO or the West Midlands Regional Assembly, leading the researchers to conclude: 'the current infrastructure of regional governance does not provide a base in the public mind on which to build representative institutions' (Jeffery and Reilly 2002). Just how wide is the gulf between elite and mass opinion finally emerged in the North-East referendum, when initial indications that the 'Yes' campaign would win a narrow victory turned into a massive four to one defeat.

Pressures for further change to rebalance England's place in the Union

Pressures arising out of devolution in Scotland and Wales might be expected to fuel English resentment and the demand that England be granted parity – especially if the differences are exploited by politicians or the media. But to date the English seem well disposed towards devolution, and there is little evidence of an English backlash (see chapter 6). Over time, as the benefits of devolution sink in, that disposition may become more grudging. Devolution confers additional benefits on the favoured position accorded to Scotland, Wales and Northern Ireland, in terms of political representation and political voice. If the English do not regard themselves as under-privileged by comparison, in time they may ask themselves whether following devolution the Scots and Welsh should continue to have their cake and eat it.

Prior to devolution, Scotland, Wales and Northern Ireland enjoyed treatment that in three respects was special in comparison with the treatment of England:

- they had a separate voice in Cabinet, through the three territorial Secretaries of State;
- Scotland and Wales were over-represented in the House of Commons; and
- all three territories enjoyed significantly higher levels of public expenditure.

These benefits had been allowed to accrue in order to fend off demands for devolution. Following devolution, they have been left in place, but are beginning to fray at the edges.

In 2003 the post of territorial Secretary of State became a part-time incumbency, and Scottish (but not Welsh) over-representation is to be corrected at the 2005 general election. These are niceties of which the English public remains largely unaware. But the generous financial treatment of Scotland and Wales has become a matter of public comment, especially in the North East where people can see the difference in public services immediately across the border. The generous levels of spending in Scotland also featured in the London mayoral campaign in 2000. In an opinion poll of English citizens in February 2004, two-thirds said they were bothered that the English were subsidising the Scots; 44 per cent wanted Scotland to have relatively fewer MPs than England now that Scotland has its own parliament.[6]

There is an interaction here between elite and mass opinion: the English become aware of these issues only when they are publicised by politicians or the media. Columnists in the national media occasionally attack the Scots for continuing to whinge while doing well out of devolution.[7] Solidarity between the nations and the regions may come under strain, in terms of continuing public support for inter-regional transfers. Another area where English tolerance may become strained is in the allocation of Cabinet portfolios to non-English MPs. There has been occasional grudging comment about the number of Scots in Blair's Cabinet. This became sharper in 2003 when John Reid (an MP from a Scottish constituency) was appointed Health Secretary, responsible for running the health service in England, but the Government rode out the opposition and media criticism.[8]

These are the kinds of issues which might be exploited by the CEP, but the campaign appears to have attracted little public support. It is essentially *poujadiste*, having many retired members with little flair for PR, whose weekly demonstrations in Parliament Square in 2003 gained almost no media coverage. Nor has it attracted any heavyweight political support: in the 1997 parliamentary session a small group of Conservative MPs, including David Davis (later appointed party chairman) and Eric Forth (subsequently shadow leader of the House), supported the idea of an English parliament.[9] William Hague as Conservative leader flirted with the idea in 1999, but backed away when he found it commanded little support in the party or the country (Hague 1999; 2000). The English regard Westminster as their Parliament, and see no need for another one.

As one would expect, political elites have wrestled harder with the consequences of devolution for England, but have not got much further in terms of finding acceptable or workable solutions. After dropping the idea of an English parliament, Hague called instead for 'English votes on English laws', but evoked no response from the English public in the 2001 election. Even among the political elite, proposals to experiment with English votes on English laws, floated in the report of the Commons Procedure Committee (1999) and the Conservatives' Norton Commission (Conservative Party 2000), have gained no ground at Westminster.

English MPs appear to remain largely unconcerned, but with big variation between the parties, with over 90 per cent of Conservative MPs, but less than 10 per cent of Labour MPs, supporting English votes on English laws.[10] But, as chapter 4 shows, the critical comments are mounting. The Commons votes on fox-hunting in 2000 attracted comment that Scottish MPs should not be voting for England and Wales on the issue. There was more comment in July 2003 when the vote on foundation hospitals in England was carried thanks to the support of Scottish and Welsh Labour MPs. The Government's response on these issues is that there are not and can not be two classes of MP at Westminster: all MPs are equal and are equally entitled to vote on all matters coming before the House of Commons.

Strangely, the issue of English votes on English laws gets far more coverage in the Scottish press than in England's. Opinion polls show that the Scots think it is wrong for their MPs to vote on English business (Curtice 2001: figure 10.4; YouGov 2004: table 2).[11] So do the English, when asked by pollsters, but they seem not to care enough to make it an election issue. The issue will not come to the crunch until there is a government at Westminster with a very small majority which depends regularly on support from Scottish and Welsh MPs, rather than very occasionally as now.

Outside observers seem puzzled that the English remain so passive. It might be that the English quietly recognise that they are already dominant and have no need of an extra voice, despite the louder voice now granted to Scotland and Wales. As Disraeli observed, the English are governed by Parliament, not by logic. They might become more interested in voting rights at Westminster if Scottish and Welsh MPs were regularly seen to be inflicting unpopular measures on the English (such as university top-up fees) or blocking popular ones. But in the 2001 Parliament the Government's majority was such that the votes of the Scottish and Welsh MPs got lost among the larger numbers.

The structure of this book

Part I: England in the Union

The final section of this chapter explains the structure of the book and its argument. Part I is about England's place in the Union and how that may need to be adjusted in the light of devolution. The UK is a union state, of which England was the founder and has always been the dominant partner. Union with Wales was formally recognised in the Act of Union of 1534, with Scotland in the Treaty of Union of 1707 and with Ireland in the Act of Union of 1800. The nations joined the Union at different times and on different terms, but England has been the dominant partner throughout, through its greater size, wealth, population and power.

Iain McLean's chapter, which opens Part I of the book, explains the origins of the Union from England's point of view and the ideology of unionism which then developed to underpin it. But perhaps because the English were so easily dominant, and unreflective in their political character, the ideology was not clearly articulated or adapted by subsequent generations to meet changing circumstances. That may be why the passionate, or 'primordial', unionism described by McLean, in the reign of Queen Victoria, could not adjust to accommodate Irish Home Rule, and it may be why the ideology of unionism now seems a little threadbare after the abandonment of high unionism with the passing of the empire.

Arthur Aughey's chapter builds on the historical analysis developed by McLean. English self-confidence following the success of the Union and then of the empire produced a historic English narrative of integration which helped integrate the other nations of the Union into England's constitutional traditions and political institutions. Parliamentary sovereignty was translated from an English into a British doctrine. The development of a specifically English nationalism was not only irrelevant, but would have been counterproductive. England became Britain, and Englishness was fused into Britishness as a method of multi-national integration, embracing the Scots, Welsh and Irish.

In the last fifty years, loss of empire, economic decline, entry into the European Community (EC) and devolution have given rise to a narrative of disintegration. The English began to feel insecure in the face of external pressures from Europe for closer integration and internal pressures from Scotland and Wales for devolution. Aughey describes how English loss of self-confidence found expression in two related narratives of disintegration, one Conservative (Powell, Heffer, Scruton), the other radical (Nairn, Weight). Neither provides the basis for a clear or credible political programme. Conservative elegies about the decline of England and threats to Englishness offer no answers to the English Question and very little in terms of constructive proposals; nor do the promptings of radical critics like Nairn, in willing the break-up of Britain – and the English to cease being British.

Aughey is particularly interesting in his discussion of English nationalism. The conventional wisdom is that the English are in need of a stronger sense of national identity and should stop confusing Englishness with Britishness. Crick (1991: 104) has argued in answer to the narrative of disintegration that, like the Scots, the Welsh and the Irish, the English should develop 'a self-confident and explicit national feeling': 'We English must come to terms with ourselves.' What Aughey shows are the benign consequences of English identity being intermingled and conflated with Britishness, and of English nationalism being low-key and understated, which helps explain why there has been no English backlash against devolution and why English dominance has on the whole taken tolerant rather than triumphal forms.

English tolerance will be tested increasingly at Westminster as non-English MPs continue to vote on English laws, even though English MPs cannot vote on equivalent measures which are now devolved to Scotland and (less often) Wales. In chapter 4, on the government of England by Westminster, Meg Russell and Guy Lodge show that this is an old conundrum. It dogged Gladstone through all the Irish Home Rule debates, and the Unionist position has always been that there cannot be two classes of MP, so that all MPs are equally entitled to vote on all issues, regardless of territorial application. Prior to devolution there was a degree of reciprocity, so that English MPs were able to block Welsh disestablishment repeatedly between 1880 and 1914, but Scottish and Welsh MPs then contributed to the defeat of the 1928 *Book of Common Prayer*. But since devolution the anomaly cuts one way: Scottish and Welsh MPs can still vote on English measures, but the converse no longer applies.

This has led the Conservative (and Unionist) Party to abandon its unionist stance and to propose 'English votes on English laws'. Again this is not a new proposal: Gladstone toyed with it as the 'in and out' rule, and Harold Wilson wanted such a rule to prevent Northern Irish MPs voting down laws applying only in Great Britain. His Attorney General deemed such a rule unworkable, and Russell and Lodge explain the technical difficulties involved in identifying an English law. Many statutes contain a range of distinct provisions of varying territorial application, and even those provisions which apply only in England may have cross-border implications (as will top-up fees for English universities, which have knock-on effects in Scotland and Wales).

But there are statutes which apply only to England, such as the Greater London Authority Act and the Regional Assemblies (Preparations) Act. Both the Procedure Committee in 1999 and the Norton Commission in 2000 proposed half-way-house procedures for such bills, with a committee stage conducted by a committee consisting only of English MPs. The difficulty with such proposals is that ultimately the bill comes back to the floor of the House, where the Government can exercise its majority. The alternative, to insist that only English MPs may vote at every stage of an English bill, would amount to the creation of a parliament within a parliament. As Russell and Lodge argue, if that stage ever were reached it might be better to create a separate English parliament; but that proposal commands little support among the English public, to judge by the opinion polls, and has not been embraced by any leading politician.

The final two chapters in Part I provide a bridge to Part II of the book, since they deal with England's place in the Union and regional government in England. Guy Lodge and James Mitchell, writing about the government of England in Whitehall, show how Whitehall is still organised on a functional basis, with no England-only departments. Some are all-UK departments; others have a mix of Great Britain, England and Wales or England-only responsibilities. Devolution has required greater territorial sensitivity, but has not led to any major reorganisation of Whitehall.

Although there has been no reorganisation around *English* departments, Whitehall has reorganised in the English regions. Regional outposts of 4 Whitehall departments were first brought together by John Major in 1994, and since then the GOs have gradually expanded so that they now include representation from 9 departments. There is also a greater consciousness of the regional dimension in Whitehall and Treasury thinking. But when it comes to real devolution, most Whitehall departments remain strongly opposed to devolving any of their powers or budgets to elected regional assemblies.

The final chapter in Part I, by John Curtice, reports on public attitudes to the English Question. In the five years since devolution was introduced for Scotland and Wales, in 1999, the English have consistently rejected devolution for themselves, with a steady proportion of between 50 and 60 per cent supporting the continuation of England's present governance. Support for an English parliament is much lower, at between 15 and 20 per cent. Support for regional assemblies is also low, but crept up from 15 per cent in 1999 to 24 per cent in 2003.

Curtice goes on to explore why support for English devolution is so low. The English lack a strong sense of regional identity: even those who have an affinity with their region show little support for regional devolution. In terms of instrumental reasons, the English do not perceive that devolution has improved the way Britain is governed, and so are unlikely to seek it for themselves. One possible driver of regional government in future may be a strong public perception that London and the south east are advantaged over other regions.

Despite the steady growth of regional institutions and networks described by Mark Sandford in Part II, this remains an elite-level activity of which the public are largely unaware. The final tables in chapter 6 show that having a regional chamber/assembly is not perceived as making much difference. Curtice concludes that in the absence of any clear connection in people's minds between their affective link with their region and regional government institutions, little enthusiasm can be expected until people believe that regional government would be better than the status quo.

Part II: the governance of England

In Part II we shift the focus from rebalancing the Union and the State following devolution to Scotland and Wales to improving the governance of England. England so far is untouched by devolution. With its population of 50 million England is still governed as a unitary state, with a strongly centralised system of government, causing serious overload at the centre. Scott Greer's chapter on the English health service is a case study of the effects of excessive centralisation, and the vicious circle from which the centre cannot disengage. The English NHS is the largest health service in the developed world, with a huge concentration of power, accountability and blame at the centre. It used to have regional health authorities, but these have been dismantled in successive reorganisations which have aimed instead to distance the centre through the creation of quasi-markets. But these attempts have proved counter-productive, as the central effort first to create and then to regulate quasi-markets is so great that the centre is drawn in yet further. The addiction to 'functional' solutions – and their repeated counter-productive centralising outcomes – increase the likelihood that a government will use its vast power to do something drastic and make a major mistake.

In most other West European countries responsibility for the health service is shared with local or regional government. Michael Keating's chapter shows that all other West European countries with a population of 50 million or more have developed a regional tier of government. In countries like France, which began with indirectly elected corporatist bodies at the regional level, it proved difficult to avoid the politicisation required to resolve policy differences, leading ultimately to the creation of elected regional bodies. England seems to be heading down the same path, leading from functional to political regionalism.

John Tomaney (chapter 8) shows that the idea of regionalism in England has a long intellectual pedigree, which in the North East goes back 100 years. Academic and political actors have been prominent in developing it, and in creating structures like the North East Development Board in the 1930s – precursors of the development corporations and regional economic planning councils of the 1960s and 1970s, and the RDAs created in 1999. The North East was also quick to reject the idea of an English parliament, floated by the Speaker's Conference in 1919, because it would not meet the desire for local autonomy and would replicate the failures of the existing Westminster Parliament, which was already perceived as over-burdened.

Despite its long pedigree regionalism failed to capture the political imagination for most of the twentieth century and began to gather momentum only in the 1990s. Mark Sandford (chapter 9) shows how the fledgling regional institutions have taken on a life of their own, with more effective joint working, specialist forums and partnerships (such as the sustainable development round tables and the regional housing forums), leading to a host of formal and informal regional networks which have grown up around the formal institutions. The capacity being built up around these shadowy regional structures is important for future developments, and the public, private and voluntary sector partners are strongly committed to their continuance. Imperceptibly they are developing regional answers to the English Question which will endure even though the North East returned a 'No' vote to a directly elected assembly in the November 2004 referendum.

English acceptance of lopsided devolution

The two versions of the English Question, as we present them, are not mutually exclusive: they do not demand an either/or choice. They represent two separate but related sets of issues: one about rebalancing England's place in the Union following devolution, the other about improving the government of England. The English could decide to pursue both sets of issues: they could press for England to have a louder political voice, and they could press for measures to decentralise the government of England. Or they could pursue one set of issues but not the other. Or they could pursue neither.

At present the English seem inclined to pursue neither. It is quite possible that the English will not opt for any of the institutional changes summarised above, either to decentralise the government of England or to give them a separate political voice. The people of the North East decisively rejected a regional assembly in the 2004 referendum. The English seem uninterested in a separate English parliament, and not sufficiently interested to vote for English votes on English laws. They are in effect opting for acceptance of the status quo: the new status quo, in which Scotland, Wales and Northern Ireland have their own political institutions, but England remains governed by the UK Government in Whitehall and the UK Parliament at Westminster.

For the moment the English seem broadly content with the status quo. But it is a fluid situation which could evolve in a number of different ways. The Government and most political actors tend to view it in rather static terms. But over time devolution will release a powerful political dynamic which will lead to greater tensions and competition between the nations and the regions. Politicians can guide and channel those forces in a number of different ways. This opening chapter has described the dynamics released by devolution and laid out the different dimensions of the English Question. Subsequent chapters explore the different versions of the question in much more detail, and in the final chapter we sum up and analyse the different answers.

Notes

1 Political parties which support the creation of an English parliament are the England First Party (www.efp.org.uk) and the English Democrats Party (www.englishdemocrats.org.uk).

2 www.thecep.org.uk.

3 www.englishindependenceparty.com.

4 www.cfer.org.uk (original emphasis).

5 Details of the constitutional conventions can be found on the CFER's website.

6 YouGov for the *Daily Telegraph*, available at www.telegraph.co.uk/news /graphics/2004/02/16.

7 E.g. Andrew Rawnsley, 'There'll be whingeing in the hillsides', *Observer*, 29 June 2002; Simon Heffer, 'Yes! Scots are racist, but only to the English', *Daily Mail*, 25 September 2002.

8 The leader of the Conservative Party, Iain Duncan Smith, described the appointment as a 'democratic monstrosity': *Independent*, 14 June 2003. See also Simon Heffer, 'The thug who's a symbol of this rotten Cabinet', *Daily Mail*, 13 June 2003; and comment in the *Daily Express*, 14 June 2003; *Independent*, 14 June 2003. In a poll six months later half of the English said they were bothered that the minister in charge of the health service in England was an MP representing a Scottish constituency: YouGov for the *Daily Telegraph*, 16 February 2004.

9 There may have been rather more closet supporters. A Constitution Unit survey in 2004 suggested that one quarter of Conservative MPs supported an English parliament.

10 See chapter 4, note 19.
11 The YouGov poll showed that 78 per cent of Scots agreed that Scottish MPs should not be allowed to vote on matters affecting only England and Wales, compared with 66 per cent of people in England and Wales: evidence that differential press reporting can make a difference to public attitudes.

Part I
England in the Union

2
England and the Union since 1707

Iain McLean and Alistair McMillan

The English, the English, the English are best
So up with the English and down with the rest . . .

It's not that they're wicked or naturally bad
It's *knowing they're foreign* that makes them *so mad*!
(From *A Song of Patriotic Prejudice*, Michael Flanders and Donald Swann, 1965)

Flanders and Swann's spoof anthem showed that symbols of *Englishness*, as opposed to Britishness, are remarkably hard to find. The best-known twentieth-century attempts were by Prime Minister Stanley Baldwin ('The sounds of England, the tinkle of the hammer on the anvil in the country smithy . . .': Baldwin 1926: 7); and literary lion George Orwell ('the old maids biking to Holy Communion through the mists of the autumn morning . . . *characteristic* fragments, of the English scene': Orwell 1957: 64).[1] Irish, Welsh and Scottish people are aware of their dual identities ('more British than Scottish' . . . 'more Scottish than British'); English people much less so (see Curtice, this volume). The purpose of this chapter is therefore to examine why the English political leaders of the day sought to expand the Union in 1707 and 1800; why they failed to introduce devolution to Ireland in 1886 and were forced to grant it independence in 1921; and how they coped with the resurgence of devolutionist and separatist politics that began with Plaid Cymru's by-election victory in Carmarthen in 1966.

We face an immediate paradox. In a book about the English Question, this chapter is largely about English attitudes to Scotland and to Ireland, rather than to England. That is because English people have been so unreflective about England as a unit (Aughey, this volume). The English politicians who made and partially unmade the UK between 1707 and 1921 were preoccupied not with England but with Scotland, Ireland and the empire. But they were characteristically careless in their terminology. For three centuries, political leaders in England, like most other English intellectuals, have confused 'national', 'English' and 'British'. Consider such books, all written by distinguished intellectuals, as:

- *The English Constitution*, meaning the Constitution of the UK (Bagehot 1867/2001);
- *The Oxford History of England*, meaning the history of the UK (e.g. Ensor 1936);
- *Politics in England*, meaning the political system of the UK (Rose 1980).

Each of these has insightful things to say about unionism and the UK; but their very titles display confusion as to what they are about. Arthur Aughey (this volume) argues that English confusion of 'England' and 'Britain' is benign because it has prevented a nastier, more xenophobic, English nationalism from emerging. But it exacerbates the paradox of this chapter: in order to intuit what English politicians thought about England, we have to examine what they did about Scotland, Ireland and the empire. As Rudyard Kipling, the pre-eminent poet of empire (and cousin of Stanley Baldwin), wrote: 'And what should they know of England who only England know?'[2]

This book deals with two interlocking themes: *England in the Union*, and *the governance of England*. This chapter is mostly about the first, but England's adaptation to the Union has always had implications for the governance of England, so it touches on the second as well.

Union with Scotland, 1707

Although England and Scotland had shared a monarch since 1603, there was nothing inevitable about the parliamentary Union of 1707. The Scots might have seceded; the English might have tried to conquer Scotland (whether or not it formally broke the Union of Crowns by choosing a different monarch) or to ignore it. They did neither, but negotiated a Treaty of Union.

The idea that Union was inevitable is partly just the bad history that we all fall into, viewing the past with 20/20 hindsight. It is also the fallacy of 'natural boundaries' – a fallacy that has played a very important part in Irish history, too. England (except for Lindisfarne, the Isle of Wight and the Scillies) and Scotland (except for the western and northern isles) share a land mass. Does that not make them a natural unit? Certainly not. In 1707 most transport was still by sea. By sea, western Scotland was closer to Ireland than to England. The Celtic Church had spread from Ireland to Iona, off the west coast of Scotland, then to Lindisfarne, off the east coast of England. Northern Scotland was closer to Norway than to England – all Scots, but few English people, know that the nearest railway station to Lerwick is Bergen. But then, the Orkneys and the Shetlands are either in a map inset off Edinburgh or omitted altogether. There would have been a union state of Scotland and Norway had not the Maid of Norway, chosen as Queen of Scotland by the Scots barons after the death of Alexander II in 1286, died in the Orkneys en route.

By contrast, land movement through the thinly populated Borders was awkward and dangerous. Travellers were likely to be mugged by those Border *rievers* celebrated in balladry as freedom-fighters. There were few links between the Stuarts' northern and southern kingdoms. And it was easier to invade rich England from poor Scotland than was the converse.

By the early 1700s, the dynastic union of 1603 had proven unstable. When King Charles I attempted to impose Anglicanism on Scotland in the 1630s, the resulting Scottish invasion of England in the 'Bishops' Wars' sparked off the English Revolution and Civil War, during which the Scots in return tried to impose Presbyterianism on England in the Solemn League and Covenant. Cromwell and the Scots were no friends either, and Charles II tried to regain his throne in Scotland. But by the 1670s he had in turn fallen out with Scots politicians and divines who believed he was on the road to popery. A low-level guerrilla war broke out in Scotland between Royalists and Covenanters, as the former tried to ban the latter's religious assemblies. In the last two decades prior to Union, a resurgent Scots Parliament had shown its independence by sponsoring a trading company in Darien (Panama) and by reserving the right to nominate its own successor to Queen Anne, who was already expected to die childless. The Covenanters were a threat from the '*left*' to the English State, and Jacobites a threat from its '*right*'. James II tried to regain his throne with campaigns in Highland Scotland and in Ireland, where people were Catholics if only because their local oppressors were Protestant. Scotland posed a considerable security threat, and at least a minor economic niggle, to England.

Why then did England not simply conquer Scotland? Because all previous attempts to do so had ended in blood and tears. Edward I and II had failed to conquer Scotland in the days of Wallace and Bruce. The Scots had certainly suffered defeats, especially at Flodden in 1513 and from Cromwell's army at Dunbar in 1650 ('The Lord hath delivered them into our hands'). But no English leader, not even Cromwell, had imposed military rule on Scotland. The country was too big, too indented and too unruly. It was also too poor for an invading army to live off the land. At Dunbar, Cromwell's starving army was about to evacuate by sea when the Scots disastrously attacked. Like Afghanistan in the nineteenth century, Scotland was a wild north west frontier.

Therefore the Treaty of Union was a genuine treaty. The final Acts of Union of 1706–7, passed in identical terms by the two Parliaments, incorporated Acts of each that protected their respective Churches. Ever since 1707, the monarch (that is, nowadays, the executive) has been bound to protect a different version of Protestant truth in England and in Scotland, even though one might think that there can be at most one set of religious truths. The Treaty also protects Scots law and Scottish universities. Classical Unionists, such as A. V. Dicey (Dicey and Rait 1920), whose views are discussed below, were left with the paradox of celebrating the Acts of 1707 both for being fundamental to the Union and for preserving the English tradition of parliamentary sovereignty. This view, although influential, was ahistorical and self-contradictory. It was ahistorical because the Union was a treaty, not a unilateral decision, therefore the institutions of one side (even supposing that parliamentary sovereignty was one such) cannot simply have been passed to the new body. It was self-contradictory because if Parliament is sovereign then the 1707 Act cannot be fundamental law because Parliament can repeal it as easily as any other (see below).

British unionism could therefore never be systematically Jacobin (cf. Keating, chapter 7, this volume). In the French Revolution, the Jacobins created a French Republic, 'one and indivisible', the purpose of which was to turn peasants into Frenchmen – preferably anti-clerical Frenchmen whose sole loyalty would be to the French State. But the British State could never be one and indivisible because it originates in a treaty. Unionists must accommodate to this or ignore it at their peril.

Union with Ireland, 1800

In the seventeenth century, Ireland supplanted Scotland as the most serious security threat to England: Irish Catholicism was more dangerous than Scots Presbyterianism. Most Irish people were defiantly Catholic because their tormentors were defiantly Protestant. Catholicism threatened the State more than Presbyterianism because it was not only a world religion but one with political muscle. 'How many divisions has the Pope?' asked Stalin. In the seventeenth century, he had more than Jean Calvin. Catholic politicians, most dangerously the King of France or his ministers, could clothe their land-grabs in religion; moreover, they could expect sympathy from their co-religionists if they invaded. Ireland, unlike Scotland, was in easy reach of France. Under Mary Queen of Scots and her French regent, the alliance between Scotland and France against England had been sentimental and conspiratorial, but not military. But a French army could land directly in Ireland, as happened in 1690 and 1798.

The Irish Union of 1800–1 was, like the Scottish Union, a bargained outcome. But the British executive, in the shape of the temporarily sane George III, broke the bargain as soon as it had been concluded. In 1801, after the Irish Parliament had been incorporated with the British to form the Parliament of the UK in the expectation that Catholics would then receive civic and voting rights, George III vetoed 'Catholic emancipation' on the grounds that it contradicted his coronation oath to protect the Protestant religion. Catholic emancipation came, bitterly contested, in 1829, but by then it was too late to save Irish Catholics' loyalty to the Union.

Home Rule and Irish independence 1886–1921

What fools we were not to have accepted Gladstone's Home Rule Bill. The Empire now would not have had the Irish Free State giving us so much trouble and pulling us to pieces. (King George V to Prime Minister Ramsay MacDonald, c.6 July 1930)

By 1930 the Unionist monarch believed that it had been wrong to reject Irish Home Rule in 1886. But when W. E. Gladstone proposed it for the second time, in 1892, Queen Victoria tried to block him, describing him as 'an old, wild, and incomprehensible man of 82 and a half'. To explain why Home Rule failed until it was too late to do any good, we need to understand English unionism in its most passionate period.

The Irish Party obtained a bloc of Home Rule seats in the 1874 general election which grew to eighty-five seats in the general election of 1885. In the Parliament of 1885–86, no party controlled a majority in the Commons, so the Irish Party was pivotal. Its leader, Charles Stewart Parnell, entered secret negotiations with the incumbent Tories, but the Prime minister, Lord Salisbury, repudiated the secret deal between Parnell and Lord Carnarvon. The latter's resignation would have led to a political crisis but for the appallingly timed 'Hawarden kite' of December 1885. The son of the Liberal leader W. E. Gladstone, trying to be helpful, revealed that his father had been converted to Home Rule, thus ensuring that the Liberals rather than the Tories would split over the issue. The Salisbury Government was defeated when Parliament met; Gladstone became Prime Minister and introduced the Government of Ireland Bill 1886, which he drafted entirely on his own. He lost several ministers, most dangerously Joseph Chamberlain, and the Bill was defeated in the Commons when ninety-three Liberals voted with the Conservatives against it. These became the nucleus of the Liberal Unionists, who allied with the Conservatives in the Parliament of 1886–92. In 1892, the Liberals again formed a minority Government with Irish Party support.

Home Rule passed the Commons in 1893 but the Lords rejected it by 419 votes to 41. Nobody else in government shared Gladstone's enthusiasm for Home Rule or for a constitutional challenge to the Lords. The Unionists returned in the Parliaments of 1895 and 1900 to 'killing home rule by kindness'. They bought out the Irish landed class with (mostly English) taxpayers' money in order to create a freeholding class of Irish peasants. This solved the Irish land question but not the Irish Question.

Home Rule returned with the next hung Parliament, that of January 1910. Only when the Irish Party held a veto would the British parties be forced to consider it. In January 1910, they first had to get rid of the Lords' veto, as the Lords' rejection of the 1909 budget imperilled any action of any non-Conservative majority in the elected house of Parliament. With the help of the Irish Party and despite the obstruction of George V and his advisers, the Lords' veto was modified by the Parliament Act 1911 to a two-year right to return bills for reconsideration. This 'suspensory veto' would therefore still be absolute in the last two years of a parliament. In order to get Home Rule enacted prior to the 1915 general election, the Irish Party therefore forced it to take precedence over all other Commons' business in the sessions of 1912, 1913 and 1914. Unionist resistance to Home Rule was as fierce as was Irish Party enthusiasm for it. Andrew Bonar Law, elected Unionist leader in 1911, said that he could imagine 'no length of resistance to which Ulster can go in which I would not be prepared to support them'. This clear encouragement to Ulster Protestant paramilitaries was matched by a 'large cheque' in support of a consignment of German small arms landed at Larne in April 1914. Or so Capt. F. H. Crawford, the chief Protestant gun-runner, said in 1915 (Jackson 2003: 133).

The leading intellectual Unionist, Professor A. V. Dicey, had written in 1885: 'Parliament . . . has, under the English constitution, the right to make or unmake any law whatever; and, further . . . no person or body is recognised by the law of England [*sic*] as having a right to override or set aside the legislation of Parliament' (Dicey 1915: 38). To Dicey's fury, Gladstone quoted him with approval when introducing the Government of Ireland Bill 1886. Among the things that Parliament could do was give Home Rule to Ireland. For thirty years Dicey strenuously insisted the opposite. By 1914 he was arguing that the Parliament Act and the Home Rule Bill were such fundamental alterations of the Constitution that they should be subjected to a popular referendum (*ibid.*: xci–c), a tool that Unionists were curiously reluctant to offer to the people of Fermanagh and Tyrone.

Home Rule was enacted in 1914, but immediately suspended because of the outbreak of the First World War. The Ulster Protestant leaders by then had had enough of Captain Crawford's rifles and credible threats of violent resistance that they would obviously have to be excluded. During the First World War three things – this, the bloody suppression of the 1916 Easter Rising (not the rising itself) and the extension of conscription to Ireland in 1918 – fatally undermined the Irish Party. The electoral system delivered the *coup de grace* in the 1918 election, when Sinn Féin won 72 Irish seats (71 per cent) on 47 per cent of the Irish vote. The Sinn Féin members refused to take their seats at Westminster and constituted themselves as the first *Dail Eireann* (Parliament of Ireland). Guerrilla war broke out and became increasingly violent until a truce in July 1921, which was followed by a Treaty in December. By the Treaty (McLean 2001: chapter 7), Ireland, excluding the North, became a Free State within the British empire. Northern Ireland had been constituted as the six counties of north-eastern Ireland, subject to possible later unification with Southern Ireland. The 1921 Treaty added a Boundary Commission to delineate its boundary. However, after a leak to the hard-line Unionist *Morning Post* in 1925, the Boundary Commission's report was suppressed and the border remained where it was.

Why was English unionism so passionate between 1885 and 1921? Some of the reasons are cultural; others were constitutional, imperial and military. The Acts of 1707 and 1800 had prescribed Union 'for all time'. As in Lincoln's USA, therefore, some Unionists argued that they were unalterable, and that secession or even devolution to Ireland within a continuing Union were unconstitutional. Dicey maintained in 1920 that 'the Act of Union which created Great Britain laid the foundation of the British Empire' (Dicey and Rait 1920: 321). But the doctrine of parliamentary sovereignty maintains that Parliament may do anything *except bind its successor*. A sovereign Parliament could of course repeal the Acts of Union or amend them. That was why Gladstone's appeal to Dicey's authority in the 1886 debates so infuriated the latter. The fundamental contradiction in Dicey's view did not blunt the emotional force of his primordial unionism.

Unionists such as Dicey and Rait linked the Union of the UK to the British empire. The Scots did not share the benefits of the English empire immediately after 1707, and when they did it was largely in the USA, lost in 1783. But as the British empire was rebuilt in India, Canada, South Africa, Australasia, Africa and the West Indies, the Scots supplied more than their population proportion of its white rulers. This is unsurprising. Many elite careers in Great Britain were closed to them. Until the 1870s, they could not attend Oxford or Cambridge unless they were Anglicans, which few were. Until the 1960s, they could not attend Oxford or Cambridge unless they were rich, as student grants from Scotland were not tenable outside of Scotland. In the intra-UK division of labour, therefore, middle-class Scots tended to specialise in the occupations for which Scottish university training gave them a comparative advantage. These included medicine, science, law and engineering. As to working-class Scots, although a lot of romantic nonsense is talked about the 'democratic intellect' (Davie 1961), the parish school system enabled some 'lads o'pairts' to become the builders and engine-drivers of empire.

Rudyard Kipling's chief engineer McAndrew epitomises the imperial Scot. He is musing on the last leg of a voyage from Britain to New Zealand and back:

> LORD, Thou hast made this world below the shadow of a dream,
> An', taught by time, I tak' it so – exceptin' always Steam.
> From coupler-flange to spindle-guide I see Thy Hand, O God –
> Predestination in the stride o' yon connectin'-rod . . .
>
> Not but that they're ceevil on the Board. Ye'll hear Sir Kenneth say:
> 'Good morn, McAndrew! Back again? An' how's your bilge to-day?'
> Miscallin' technicalities but handin' me my chair
> To drink Madeira wi' three Earls – the auld Fleet Engineer
> That started as a boiler-whelp – when steam and he were low.
> (McAndrew's Hymn, 1894)

The high noon of unionism coincided with the high noon of empire. The loss of Ireland was a disaster for unionists because it signalled the first contraction of the Empire since the loss of the USA.

Welsh and Irish people had some of the same motives to seek careers in the empire. Their school systems and universities were less well-developed than the Scots', but they suffered much of the same exclusion from the English elite. As non-Anglicans, most of them were also barred from Oxford and Cambridge. They may have suffered more from racist caricature (echoed by Flanders and Swann) than did the Scots.

The military roots of unionism were also deep. Scotland and Ireland (and, in remoter times, Wales) were routes for enemy invasion of England. The last invasion via Scotland was the Jacobite rising of 1745–46. Bonnie Prince Charlie got as far as Derby. The last invasion via Ireland was in the form of the German submarine that landed Sir Roger Casement at Tralee in 1916 to link up with the Easter Rising.

Unionists recruited regiments for the British Army from Scotland, Wales and Ireland. In the nineteenth and twentieth centuries, this worked best for the Scots and the Northern Irish. Scottish, including Highland, regiments became famous for their ferocity. In August 1914, Lord Kitchener received appeals from leading politicians in Wales, Southern Ireland and Northern Ireland to form divisions of the British Army from those parts. The petitioners from Wales and Southern Ireland were no less than the Chancellor of the Exchequer, Lloyd George, and the leader of the Irish Party, John Redmond.

With magnificent and tragic insensitivity, Kitchener turned down their requests, but accepted the request of Sir Edward Carson and James Craig to turn the Ulster Protestant paramilitaries into the 36th Ulster Division. In the first two days of the Somme, 1–2 July 1916, the 36th Ulster Division lost 5,500 men killed and wounded. Compare the 3,523 violent deaths in Northern Ireland from 1969 to 2001.[3]

In war, Scotland controlled much of the North Sea, and Ireland most of the Atlantic. Winston Churchill wrote the clause of the 1921 Treaty that gave the UK access to the Irish 'Treaty ports' of Brerehaven (in Bantry Bay), Queenstown (now Cobh, on the south coast), and Lough Swilly in the north west. In 1938, to Churchill's fury, the Chamberlain Government ceded them back to the Irish Free State under Eamon de Valera. All UK efforts to reclaim them during the Second World War failed: the Free State remained neutral. All allied ships and submarines in the Battle of the Atlantic had to sail from Scotland or Northern Ireland at a cost of thousands of allied lives.

The heyday of primordial unionism

There was not much popular unionism in the early eighteenth century. The 1707 Union came about for pragmatic reasons, and it did not immediately end the mutual dislike of English and Scots at all levels of society. The first change came with the Scottish Enlightenment, from the early writings of David Hume in the 1730s to its peak under Adam Smith and the building of classical Edinburgh in the 1770s–90s. Hume spoke broad Scots but wrote lapidary English, including a classic *History of England*. Smith celebrated the free trade that (albeit with a dash of imperial protectionism) had at last brought prosperity to his Glasgow via the tobacco and slave trades. Scots intellectuals spread to Northern Ireland and notably to America, where William Small passed on the values of the Scottish Enlightenment to his star student Thomas Jefferson, and John Witherspoon to *his* star student James Madison.

The English did not start to reciprocate until the nineteenth century. That great unionist Sir Walter Scott stage-managed the visit of King George IV to Edinburgh in 1822 – the first by a reigning monarch to Scotland since 1707. It bequeathed a statue at the apex of the New Town (the intersection of Hanover St and George St) and George IV Bridge, which spans part of the old town so that the new could spread southwards. Scott invented tartan and the Highland heritage industry. He turned Rob Roy into a harmless picturesque feature of the landscape.

The most successful English unionist was Queen Victoria. 'It is innocence itself', said W. E. Gladstone on reading the second volume of her *Journal of a*

Life in the Highlands (Matthew 1999: 515). It was anything but. The queen had found a safe outlet for her passionate unionism. By settling her country home at Balmoral she set the seal on the image of sanitised romantic Scotland that Scott had first conjured. It helped that she was impervious to cold. Imitation Balmorals sprang up by the hundred in every Scottish town, and it gave its name to a suburb of Belfast. Perth, where the trains to the Highlands were broken up and re-marshalled at the start and finish of the shooting season, acquired one of the largest railway stations in the UK, for a town of some 40,000 people. Queen Victoria stopped there for breakfast twice a year, on the way to and from Balmoral. Romantic Scotland was fully integrated with the Union. *Wild Wales* was as enthusiastically but less royally promoted by George Borrow (2002). Ireland remained a more alien place, populated by comical or sinister cartoon figures as detailed in Roy Foster's *Paddy and Mr Punch* (1995).

English political elites prized the Union in and of itself. At bottom, their only answer to 'Why is the Union a good thing?' was 'Because it is there.' It was a founding, baseline part of what it was to be a Unionist. This is what we mean by *primordial* unionism. It accounts for the passions of Bonar Law and Dicey, and the passionate hatred of Unionists from Victoria downwards for Gladstone and for Irish Home Rule. Opinion polls on attitudes to the Union go back only to the late 1960s, but we can measure the success of political unionism in the four countries of the UK prior to that.

As for England, Aydelotte (1963; 1967) shows for the 1840s and Wald (1983) for the period from 1885 to 1918 that the main issue dimension in electoral politics between 1832 and 1914 was a centre–periphery one. In *core* England south of a line from the Humber to the Severn, MPs tended to be protectionist: in favour of maintaining the privileges of the Church of England and of the Anglican Churches in Wales and Ireland; against parliamentary reform, which would remove seats from the south and redistribute them to the north; enthusiastic about the empire; and against concessions to Catholicism or nationalism in Ireland. In *peripheral* England, north of that line, most MPs were on the other side of the main issue dimension, i.e., free trading; less favourable to Anglican privilege; favourable to parliamentary reform, under which their territory would gain seats; less enthusiastic about the empire; and relatively favourable to concessions in Ireland. The former cluster of ideas was associated with the Tory Party, although the great split of 1846 fragmented party labels. When the Tories re-grouped under Disraeli and Salisbury, they became the distinctively more imperialist and unionist party. The latter cluster was associated with the Liberal Party, and at the very end of the period with the Labour Party. Median voter theory suggests, therefore, that the median voter in *core* England was more Unionist than the median voter in *peripheral* England.

One of the best windows into mass unionism is popular political propaganda. McKenzie and Silver (1968) produce some ripe examples of primordial unionism in the late Victorian and Edwardian period. In the 1892 Parliament a Unionist pamphlet entitled *Disciplining England*! points out that the Conservatives won a majority of seats in England and that the

> radical majority of 40 [for Irish home rule] was entirely due to Irish, Welsh, and Scotch votes. Since then every action of the radical Government has been directed against the greatness and power of England. The 'Home Rule' Policy for Ireland is a direct attack upon England and the English race. To Englishmen are mainly due the Union of the United Kingdom and the building up of the wonderful Empire of 340,000,000 people that stretches over every portion of the habitable Globe. The disruption of that United Kingdom and the dismemberment of that Empire of which England is the centre and the heart, would be a deadly blow to the English race. (National Union pamphlet no. 223, May 1894, in McKenzie and Silver 1968: 54)

A Primrose League lantern-slide programme of 1889 consisted of:

- John Bull offering his hand to downcast Erin;
- Erin looking up and taking his hand;
- John Bull and Erin at peace watched over by Britain;
- an Irish farm in prosperous times;
- the same under the Land League;
- inside a farmhouse under prosperity;
- the same under the Land League;
- moonlighting;
- the maiming of cattle;
- a meeting of loyalists in Belfast;
- tenants paying rent;
- the Royal Standard and the same flag without a harp;
- justice, law and order;
- Lord Salisbury with Balfour on his right and Hartington [the Liberal Unionist leader] on his left;
- Disraeli encircled by a huge wreath of primroses (In Pugh 1985: 90).

The whole of Wales and Catholic Ireland were part of the periphery and the Conservatives and Unionists won few seats there. Only the small Anglican and landowning minority had a material interest in unionism, and after the Second Reform Act (1867) there was no Commons' constituency in which they were numerous enough to win the seat. Irish landowners and Anglicans had more power in the House of Lords, even after 1911. The Church of England bishops in the Lords voted en masse against Irish disestablishment

(1869); Home Rule (1893 and 1912–14), and Welsh disestablishment (various occasions until 1914).

Scotland was more complex. Church politics in Scotland followed lines different from those in England, and English politicians did not understand them. The Disruption of the Church of Scotland in 1843 had several effects. It warned English politicians not to meddle in Scottish Church affairs, for which they would get no thanks and many brickbats, as did Sir James Graham in 1843. It created the material and spiritual basis for a two-party system, in which the Free Church interest voted Liberal and the Church of Scotland interest voted Unionist (MacLaren 1974). But that division lay unrealised until 1886, when the Liberal split actualised it. Scottish Catholics, mostly of Irish origin, were heavily Liberal and of course supported Home Rule, but their limited enfranchisement prior to 1918 meant that, although they were a fifth of the population, they were less than a fifth of the electorate.

Northern Ireland was the true home of primordial unionism, an ideology which English politicians never understood but sometimes exploited. It has cultural, religious and paramilitary strains. Culturally, Protestant Ulster is an offshoot of lowland Scotland. Whereas in Scotland, Presbyterianism is established by the Act of Union, in Northern Ireland the Presbyterian Church has never been established, and the Anglican Church of Ireland was disestablished in the whole of Ireland in 1869. Therefore, Northern Irish Protestantism retains an embattled quality that Scottish Protestantism has lost. The Catholic 'enemy' is larger (40 per cent of the population at the 2001 census, compared to about 17 per cent in Scotland and about 8 per cent in England). It owes allegiance to a foreign state, in Protestant eyes – no longer France nor the Papal state, but the Republic of Ireland.

Paramilitarism in Northern Ireland goes back a long way. In the rebellion of 1798, some Presbyterians and some Catholics fought together against the common enemy, the Anglican Ascendancy. But since then most paramilitary activity has been sectarian. Protestant paramilitary activity reached its peak between 1912 and 1914. The Ulster Covenant (what heavy symbolism of title) committed those who signed it to 'us[e] all means which may be found necessary to defeat the present conspiracy to set up a Home Rule Parliament in Ireland' (Stewart 1967: 62). Andrew Bonar Law, the leader of the Conservative and Unionist Party, was of Scots–Canadian Presbyterian extraction; the Andrew Bonar after whom he was named was a leader of the Free Church of Scotland at the 1843 Disruption. As noted above, Law openly encouraged sedition, at Blenheim and Larne. By speaking at Blenheim, Bonar Law was certainly calling up the ghost of its former inhabitant, Lord Randolph Churchill, who in 1886 had said that if Gladstone went for Home Rule, the Orange card would be the one to play. Pray God, said Lord

Randolph, that it would be the ace of trumps rather than the two. It was; so why has no UK Unionist since Bonar Law played it?

The decline of primordial unionism since 1921

The unionism just described was primordial. Unionism is primordial if it supports the Union as a good in and of itself. It is instrumental if it supports the Union as a means to other valued ends, such as a uniform welfare state or a militarily strong UK. The last primordially Unionist Prime Minister was Bonar Law; and much water had flowed under the Grand Bridge at Blenheim Palace between 1912 and Law's brief premiership ten years later. Law and Long had joined their bitter Liberal enemies in the wartime coalitions. The Unionist members of the postwar coalition Government drafted the Government of Ireland Act 1920, which created governments of Northern and of Southern Ireland, and a Council of Ireland designed to bring them together by consent. As Enoch Powell growled many years later when the idea recurred: 'Consent will not be forthcoming.' The Government of Southern Ireland, and the Council of Ireland, never came into existence. Northern Ireland was created with the boundaries it still has; the attempt to make them more defensible (in both senses) being suppressed after the 1925 leak. The primordial Unionists of Ulster had not wanted Home Rule for themselves, but once they had it they found it convenient. The Unionists from the rest of the UK vanished after the Irish Treaty of 1921, in which Great Britain recognised the independence of the Irish Free State.

As W. B. Yeats had foreseen, all was changed, changed utterly. The main point of resisting Home Rule had become the imperial one. There was no longer a British material interest in Ireland, now that the Unionists had killed Home Rule by kindness. There remained a military interest, but in 1921 only Winston Churchill and Lord Birkenhead worried about it. Ireland was now a Dominion: the most reluctant one, as George V grieved to MacDonald in 1930. Its allegiance to him was purely nominal, although surprisingly it did not declare itself a republic until 1949, in the same year as India.

The empire (Commonwealth) remained as the central destination of British emigration, exports and policy until the slow, painful, turn of UK policymakers to Europe and decolonisation, both in the 1960s. As late as the 1950s Australia (population 10 million) was the UK's largest trading partner. At that time, the

> unreality of so much of the discussion about the links between the Commonwealth and the United Kingdom was inherited by the Conservative Party from those Liberal Radical Unionists who had followed Joseph

> Chamberlain across the floor of the Commons in the 1880s . . . They took with
> them a deep sense of bonding the 'mother country' to the self-governing parts
> of the Empire . . . (Milward 2002: 271)

Primordial unionism was thus left stranded as an ideology without a purpose
once the empire had gone. Instrumental unionism became stronger on the
left than in its previous home on the right.

On the left, it came with the welfare state. Politicians came to see the
welfare state as a citizenship entitlement. This was the vision of Lloyd George
and those who joined his 'ambulance wagon' (Braithwaite 1957) in 1911. It
was filled out by the Conservative R. A. Butler and the (nominal) Liberal
William Beveridge in the Second World War coalition Government and the
socialists of the succeeding Attlee Government. The most passionate instrumental Unionist was Aneurin Bevan, the founder of the National Health
Service. Bevan viewed devolution to his native Wales as a romantic distraction
from his vision of uniform welfare entitlements funded out of progressive taxation. Entitlement should depend on need or status; tax liability on income
or wealth. Neither ought to depend on geography. The Attlee administrations
of 1945–51 were the high-water mark of instrumental unionism of the left.

On the right, it appeared first with Lord Salisbury's gloomy psephology
(1884). Salisbury believed that the coming Third Reform Act would doom
the Unionists to be out of power for ever. He toyed with proportional representation but went instead for compact and contiguous single-member districts. These he and Sir Charles Dilke (who wanted them for symmetrically
opposite reasons) forced through in the redistribution package that the
Unionists, who controlled the Lords, could demand as a condition of extending the franchise. Salisbury's idea was that, although he could not stem the
collapse of Conservatism, he could defer and mitigate it if the Unionists could
at least win rural and suburban seats, the latter dubbed the 'villa vote'.
Imperialist unionism would appeal to the villa vote, through the propaganda
quoted above. The Unionists were also saved, unexpectedly, by the Liberal
split of 1886.

Between 1964 and 1976 the leading instrumental Unionists were Harold
Wilson and Willie Ross, his Secretary of State for Scotland. Wilson and Ross
knew that the 1894 Unionist pamphlet quoted above was only too right.
Almost every radical majority, including Wilson's, was entirely due to Welsh
and Scottish votes. Thanks to population decline and Unionist-motivated
protection of their seat totals in the Commons (McLean 1995), Scotland and
Wales were significantly over-represented – and Labour held most of their
seats. The Conservatives had always been weak in Wales. In Scotland, they
had been strong in the evening of empire as late as 1955, but since then had
been in secular decline, even when they advanced in England in 1959 and

1970. Wilson's unionism required holding on to Scotland and Wales so that Labour could continue to govern the UK.

Unionism and the revival of peripheral nationalism

How then did Unionists react to the nationalist insurgency of the 1960s? In 1966, Plaid Cymru won a by-election in the Welsh-speaking constituency of Carmarthen. In 1967, the Scottish National Party (SNP) snatched Labour's safest Scottish seat, at Hamilton. The two nationalist parties did well at other by-elections and in local elections (McLean 1970). Wilson's reaction was his usual one to difficult problems: he appointed a royal commission. This one, with a leisurely remit to explore 'the Constitution', with excursions to the Channel Islands and the Isle of Man, enabled Wilson to face the electorate in 1970 and declare that something would be done about the Union but that he could not say what until the Royal Commission had reported. The Scottish Nationalists lost Hamilton (though they gained the Western Isles) and Harold Wilson lost power. However, the discovery of oil in the North Sea then changed everything. With the SNP proclaiming 'It's Scotland's Oil (so why do 50,000 people in Scotland die every year of hypothermia?)', both Unionist parties needed to do something to save the Union. The Conservatives under Edward Heath swung to devolution under their 1968 'Declaration of Perth'. Labour remained remorselessly Unionist until after the February 1974 general election, when the SNP won 7 seats and 22 per cent of the Scottish vote. The electoral system protected the Union for the time being, but Unionist politicians knew that it would flip as and when the SNP vote share rose to 33 per cent. At 22 per cent, the SNP was under-rewarded, because its vote was evenly spread around Scotland. At 33 per cent it would be drastically over-rewarded, and would win more than half of the seats in Scotland. Its October 1974 manifesto stated:

> The SNP asks for a mandate from the Scottish people for self-government. MPs thus elected will be committed to demand from the UK government the necessary legislation to set up a Scottish Parliament with full control over all the affairs of Scotland. (Times Books 1974: 343)

It (just) failed to get that mandate. In that election, it got 30 per cent of the Scottish vote (more than the Conservatives) but only 11 seats to the Conservatives' 16. The Union had been saved by the instrumental Unionist moves of both Conservative and Labour. The Conservative manifesto said that 'the Scottish people must enjoy more of the financial benefits from oil, and they must be given a far greater say over its operation in Scotland'. Labour would 'set up new development agencies in Scotland and in Wales, financed by the UK Exchequer, with extra funds to reflect the revenue from offshore oil' (Times Books 1974: 303, 320, 330). In its Scottish manifesto (only), Labour added a commitment to a legislative assembly for Scotland.

Labour won the election. In what Keating and Bleiman (1979: 167) quaintly call a 'compromise', it adopted the policy both of its Scottish anti-devolutionists – namely that Scotland must retain its seventy-one MPs and its Secretary of State – and of its Scottish devolutionists – that Scotland should get a legislative assembly. Instrumental unionism required this 'compromise'. Labour needed those seventy-one seats in order to continue to govern the UK. It extended a similar offer to Wales, where the evidence of demand for devolution was scantier. Wales was to retain its Secretary of State and its thirty-six MPs, for instrumental reasons, while gaining an elected Welsh assembly.

The 'compromise' fell apart in 1977, victim to an English backlash. The backlash originated in north-eastern England, where Labour leaders believed that they were being penalised for voting Labour and the Scots rewarded for voting SNP. By voting down a timetable (guillotine) resolution, the rebels killed the Scotland and Wales Bill. It re-emerged as two separate bills, one each for Scotland and Wales. These were enacted, but as a result of a second rebellion (this one headed by a Scots expatriate sitting for a London seat), their implementation was made subject to a referendum in which 40 per cent of the electorate (not of the votes cast) had to support devolution before it could be implemented. In Wales, devolution was thrown out by a large margin. In Scotland, it passed narrowly, but the 'Yes' vote failed to approach the 40 per cent threshold. The Government fell on a Conservative–SNP confidence motion, and the incoming Government of Margaret Thatcher immediately dropped the Conservatives' commitment to devolution.

By 1997, therefore, instrumental unionism had preserved the Union, but at a cost. Public expenditure per head in the three territories (as the Treasury calls them with careful neutrality) substantially exceeds that in England. Does that mean that Bevan's dream of equal access to services in accordance with need, not geography, has been breached? Not necessarily; the territories may be needier. An attempt to quantify territorial needs was one of the Treasury's responses to the 1977 guillotine defeat (HM Treasury 1979). It showed that, for services due to be devolved under the Scotland and Wales Bill, Scotland's spending was running ahead of 'needs', and Wales's behind. Northern Ireland's spending was also measured (although Northern Ireland was not in the Devolution Bill) and its spending was found to be marginally above assessed 'needs'.

The (now) better-known Treasury response was the Barnett formula, which is fully discussed elsewhere (McLean and McMillan 2003a; McLean 2004). The Treasury agreed with the Geordies that Scotland was getting 'too much' public expenditure. The Barnett formula was designed to do two things administratively, and one politically. The political aim was to contain the 'English backlash' to devolution. This was obscured at the time because the Barnett formula was first publicised in 1980, at a time when devolution had disappeared from the political agenda, and therefore the English backlash with it. It has become very important since the return of devolution to the UK-wide agenda in 1997. The first administrative aim was to replace programme-by-programme bargaining with a single block, so that there would be only one annual argument between the Chief Secretary to the Treasury and the territorial departments, in place of many. The second administrative aim was to bring about gradual convergence in order to reduce the Scottish spending advantage. That has not yet occurred, although the process of convergence did start seriously in 1999 (only twenty years after the formula was introduced). Barnett has turned from an acute device into a chronic headache.

Bevan's instrumental unionism is preserved on the tax side. Tax rates remain uniform throughout the UK. Only Scotland has the power to vary income tax, and that by only a trivial proportion, not so far used. On the expenditure side, instrumental unionism survives in the shape of welfare benefits which are of identical cash value anywhere in the UK. This makes them better value in poor areas, with their lower cost of living, than in the expensive, rich, south east, and therefore the tax and benefit system acts as an automatic stabiliser. However, the regional disparities in public expenditure per head on other domestic programmes do not seem to bear a close relationship to need (McLean and McMillan 2003a; 2003b).

Primordial unionism had a final baroque flourish with Enoch Powell (1912–98, see further chapter 3, this volume). His attitudes to race, parliamentary sovereignty, Englishness, Northern Ireland, and the Church of England are all of a piece. His notorious 'rivers of blood' speech in 1968 led to his dismissal from the Conservative Shadow Cabinet and his elevation for a while to the position of the most popular politician in England. The speech is an extraordinary mixture of the fastidious – 'Like the Roman, I seem to see "the river Tiber foaming with much blood"' – and the crude – 'She is becoming afraid to go out. Windows are broken. She finds excreta pushed through her letter-box. When she goes to the shops, she is followed by . . . charming, wide-grinning piccaninnies'(quoted in Heffer 1998: 453–4). The rights of Commonwealth citizens to enter the UK were destroying Englishness. Powell's attacks on West Indians echoed Victorian Unionist attacks on the Irish and Edwardian Unionist attacks on the Jews.

Powell was an ardent Diceyan. His attack on UK entry to the EC in 1972 was as bitter as his rivers of blood speech. For him, the supreme evil of the EC was that it undermined parliamentary sovereignty. Although (as his 1994, and final, book proves), he was not a Christian, he frequently told interviewers that he was an Anglican. He believed that in England 'alone . . . the identity of nation and Church survives in the symbolism of historical forms' (*ibid.*: 134). Gladstone abandoned the identity of nation and Church in about 1845 and Salisbury expected that it would not outlive him.

It is almost coherent, but empty. As with other primordial unionists, for Powell the Union is to be cherished because it exists. A UK citizen of West Indian origin might ask Powell why she should cherish it. He replied: 'The West Indian or Asian does not, by being born in England, become an Englishman. In law he becomes a United Kingdom citizen by birth; in fact he is a West Indian or an Asian still' (to Eastbourne Rotary Club, 16 November 1968, quoted in *ibid.*: 493).

Powell's unionism is *English* (not even British) unionism for English people, and fails emotionally as well as intellectually to work as United Kingdom unionism. Since Powell, eurosceptics have complained that the EU threatens both British sovereignty and the British way of life – the former through European directives and the proposed EU Constitution, the latter by allegedly encouraging a flood of migrants. Both themes featured in the 2004 campaign of the UK Independence Party (UKIP) when it won 16.1 per cent of the vote in the election to the European Parliament. Its support was highest in southern England outside London, and lowest in northern England, Wales and Scotland; it did not run in Ulster.

Nevertheless, primordial unionism lacks a potential parliamentary majority. The UKIP performance could not be repeated at a UK general election using the first-past-the-post system. Prime Minister John Major received only ridicule for his 1993 reprise of old maids biking to Holy Communion. In the 1997 Scottish Conservative manifesto, he wrote that general election day would be

> the 290th anniversary – to the exact day – of the implementation of the Act of Union which created Great Britain and from which so many benefits have derived for both Scotland and England. It would be a tragedy if the votes cast on that anniversary were to undermine and eventually destroy our Union and the stability and prosperity it guarantees. (Scottish Conservative and Unionist Party 1997: 1)

The tragedy has occurred, or, at any rate, the Scots voted for devolutionist parties. All leading Conservatives now accept Scottish and Welsh devolution as a *fait accompli*. Scottish and Welsh Conservatives are positively enthusiastic, and are joining the calls for their assemblies to be given more powers. Primordial unionism has been banished to the fringe in Ulster and the UKIP.

However, its ghost haunts the government of the UK. The ancient history analysed in this chapter shapes the governance of the UK in ways that have become more evident since devolution to Scotland, Wales and, spasmodically, Northern Ireland in 1998 (Lodge and Mitchell, and Russell and Lodge, this volume). Lodge and Mitchell show that Whitehall is still organised on a functional basis. Some departments address the whole UK; others have a mix of Great Britain, England and Wales or England-only responsibilities. Devolution has required greater territorial sensitivity, but that has not always been shown in Whitehall. An early sign of this was the English agriculture department's authorising field trials of genetically modified crops in fields that turned out to be in Wales. The trickiest problems can be expected in the largest departments. In the largest of all, the Department of Work and Pensions (DWP), as related above, the UK is still a Union in relation to tax and benefits. Therefore rates are uniform. But even here, there is potential trouble as Chancellor Gordon Brown likes to use the tax and benefit regime as an instrument of social policy, which is devolved. Thus, at this writing, local government finance in England is in a mess, which an ODPM[4]-led Balance of Funding Review Group failed to tidy. Some representations have urged the Treasury and the DWP to reform the council-tax benefit regime; others (e.g. McLean and McMillan 2003b) to introduce a system of land-value taxation. The Liberal Democrats want to introduce local income tax. But any of these changes would have complex devolution implications. For instance, local income tax could collide with the Scottish variable rate of income tax, authorised in the Scotland Act 1998 but not (yet) implemented.

In the second-biggest domestic department, health, responsibilities are reasonably clear-cut (Greer, this volume). Apart from the anomaly that policy towards abortion is reserved to the UK Government (which results from a loss of nerve in 1998 in the face of the Catholic Church in Scotland), each of the four health systems in the UK is self-contained, and each has lessons (good and bad) for the others. Education is another matter entirely. In 2003, the UK Government produced a hotly contested White Paper on higher education in England. Because education is a devolved function, this was formally an England-only matter. But any change to the funding of students in England has huge consequences for the devolved administrations, not least because students domiciled in any part of the UK may attend university in any other. Furthermore, some of the increased financial flows envisaged in the White Paper were for university research, and were themselves split between the Higher Education Funding Council for England and the Office of Science and Technology. But the former is England-only, the latter UK-wide. This problem had apparently not occurred to the authors of the White Paper in the week of its publication (McLean 2003a).[5]

In 1866, Scotland's leading public intellectual, John Stuart Blackie, called on his Oxford equivalent, Benjamin Jowett. 'I hope you in Oxford don't think we hate you', said Blackie. 'We don't think about you', replied Jowett (quoted in Harvie 1977: 121). Since the end of primordial unionism, that has been too often the attitude of English politicians to the territories. But now they have to think about them. The nationalist surge in 1974 led both UK parties to commit to devolution. From 1979 to 1997, devolution appeared dead, smothered by another bout of killing Home Rule by kindness. The Conservative (Unionist) Governments shovelled public money at Scotland and Northern Ireland, over and above the Barnett formula, in the hope of suppressing separatism and violence. But since 1997 this has all started to unravel. The grant of devolution to the territories has forced into the open a new – actually a very old, but rarely noticed – set of questions about the governance of England, the subject of this book. The fact that the formula funding of the territories, under Barnett, is apparently more generous than the formula funding of the regions of England has driven several policy changes since 1997. One is the Balance of Funding review just mentioned; another is a large study, financed by the ODPM and the Treasury and conducted by a research team headed by one of us, into the distribution of public expenditure to the regions of England (McLean *et al.* 2003). This found that some government departments, and the EU, were keeping poor or non-existent records of the regional distribution of their expenditure. The report has led to considerable improvements in data collection (HM Treasury 2004c: chapter 8, esp. at 8.2). A third is the beefing-up of English regional government (Sandford, this volume). None of this would have happened but for a chain of events in the non-English parts of the Union going back, if you will, all the way to 1707.

This story of Union since 1997 shows how English politicians, in the dominant partner, have seen (or failed to see) the Union. The Union was created essentially for reasons of defence and national security. It was an explicit treaty between England and Scotland (mostly honoured), enlarged by a later treaty between Great Britain and Ireland (now in force only in the North). Once created, the Union was held together by self-interest and imperial glory. Now that the glory has faded, the glue is cracking. The Parliament of the UK works rather badly as the Parliament of England (Russell and Lodge, this volume). The West Lothian question has reappeared and will not go away.

It is true that UK governments of both parties have now declared that they have no interest in retaining Northern Ireland in the Union against the will of its inhabitants. They have also signalled that if Scotland voted for independence it should have it (though we suspect that merely an SNP capture of more than half of the seats in Scotland would turn out to be insufficient). This could be seen as a benign or relaxed attitude to the Union. Mostly, like

Benjamin Jowett, UK politicians simply don't think about it. This relaxation has great merits. It does tend to mean, however, that devilish little policy questions suddenly creep up on the UK Government and take it by surprise – such as 'Who subsidies Scottish university students in England?' 'Who funds research support in the Scottish universities?' 'Could there be three classes of income tax in Scotland – UK, Scottish and local?' The legacies of 1707 are around us all the time. As its tercentenary approaches, British politicians will have to learn to do better than Jowett.

Notes

1 Orwell's phrase was revived by the last English Unionist, John Major, in 1993.
2 In *The English Flag* [*sic*], an 1891 poem about the Union Jack.
3 Source: http://cain.ulst.ac.uk/sutton/tables/Gender.html.
4 Office of the Deputy Prime Minister: since 2003 the title of the government department that deals with English local government and its services.
5 For non-English MPs' voting on the Higher Education Bill see Russell and Lodge, this volume.

3
The challenges to English identity

Arthur Aughey

In 1975 Enoch Powell proposed that at the heart of the devolution question was neither Scotland nor Wales nor even Northern Ireland but 'the problem of England' (Heffer 1998: 746). At the time his proposition sounded like typical Powellian contrariness; but now that Scotland, Wales and Northern Ireland have their own distinctive forms of devolution, Powell's suggestion appears less controversial. Indeed, a recent best-selling book on contemporary Englishness by the journalist Jeremy Paxman begins with the line: 'Once upon a time the English knew who they were.' Because they knew who they were, the question of national identity was a rather un-English thing with which to concern oneself. However, the conclusion to Paxman's book is that the English can no longer avoid addressing the problem that Powell had recognised a generation ago. If there is a problem it is indeed a problem of identity, of who the English are (Paxman 1998: 23). Of course, the traditional English certitude that Paxman assumes is mythological, but like all myths it reveals its political significance in the very assumption he makes. Self-understanding, he thinks, was the norm, but what if the English have suddenly realised that they have misunderstood themselves all along? This is the condition of anxiety on which the politics of identity thrives and it provides intellectual space for all sorts of historical and cultural revisions. Whereas in the past these English anxiety attacks could be attributed to high political concerns about external security, the current one, I suggest, is concerned mainly with the inner self-confidence of Englishness (or the lack of it). In short, the question of English identity today is bound up with the new complexity of British governance and with the new uncertainty of how England fits into it. Other chapters in this volume consider that new complexity and uncertainty in terms of political institutions. This chapter considers it in terms of political dispositions.

It engages with the question of English identity schematically in three related parts. The first two establish the framework within which to make sense of the third, and contemporary, part. The first part identifies an historical English narrative of integration, a narrative that reconciled Tory and Whig visions of English exceptionalism *and* its exemplary quality. This narrative was integrative in two respects. It served as a useful public doctrine of English institutionalism and it helped to integrate the other nations of the Union into the culture of that English institutionalism (see also chapter 2). This narrative survived remarkably well into the twentieth century and it can still claim adherents. One consequence of its persuasiveness was what Sir Ernest Barker once called the traditional, 'never reflective' character of political Englishness. The second part identifies a more recent British narrative of disintegration, the falling asunder of this integrative idea, understood both as a return to the particular and as the loss of the universal. This has been a very adaptable narrative, weaving together theories of decline, loss of empire, the break up of Britain and the inevitability of European integration to propose, as J. G. A. Pocock noted (2000), that constitutional *modification* in the UK must mean constitutional *disintegration*. One consequence of this narrative (and, it must be stressed, not the only consequence) is that some have been so alarmed that they are determined to ensure that political Englishness will be unreflective no longer. The third part examines varieties of contemporary engagement with the *particular* of England and Englishness through a review of some of the recent literature on national identity. Two of the many possible versions of English identity are explored (for others see chapter 8). The first is a version of the English *particular* that celebrates a civic, liberal, multi-ethnic idea of Englishness, an idea that it struggles to reconcile with native populism. This liberal vision of England is located very firmly within the *universal* of the EU. The second is a conservative version of the English 'particular' that celebrates – if not unreservedly – a more populist idea of England, an idea that it struggles to reconcile with civic, liberal and multi-ethnic values. This conservative England is sceptical of Europe and seeks to preserve its national integrity within the universal, global market.

An English narrative of integration

Dyson (1980: 195) has argued that English political theorists came from a receptive elite that was historically accessible to ideas of reform. 'Consequently, there was a remarkable continuity of assumptions among intellectuals, a relative indifference to theoretical disputes elsewhere and a tolerance for theoretical and ethical muddle'. It was a tradition that generally preferred, as Disraeli once said, government by Parliament rather than by logic; one, like Macauley, that thought little of symmetry and much of convenience; and one that could see no point in removing an anomaly simply because it *was* an anomaly. It was a tradition in which, as A. J. P. Taylor once quipped (1977), Whig plus Tory equalled eternal truth. This was a distinctive political interrelationship that Colls (2002: 28) has brilliantly explored: 'The bonding of the English with their common law could make conservatives into radicals and radicals into conservatives.' When, in the course of the nineteenth century, national identity became bound up with notions of the 'British Constitution' and 'empire', the same bonding applied for this 'was said to be a people's story'. What Colls reveals is a common framework of assumptions within which significant arguments took place about the ethnic or civic nature of English identity (Kearney 2000): whether empire was, in Seeley's terms, all 'wonder and ecstasy' or whether it was an 'excrescence' that exposed England to war and corruption (Watson 1973: 216; Rich 1989); whether, as Elton put it, 'English history most convincingly demonstrated how man should order his existence on earth' (what he called the Froude complex) or whether it served 'to demonstrate the opposite with equal coherence and conviction' (what he called the New Statesman complex). Whatever side was taken in these arguments, Elton continued, the nature of the debate testified to the belief 'that England and her history enjoyed the special privilege of providing an example to mankind' (1991: 110–11). In short, the 'English ideology', to use Watson's term, was exceptional (*particular*) but also exemplary (*universal*), and it was the positive quality of the interrelationship, this exemplary exception, from which issued a powerful liberal-conservative public doctrine. In a country of notable self-possession this is not unusual. The American sense of manifest destiny, for instance, remains simultaneously exceptional and universal, unique in the good fortune of its institutions and exemplary in the power of its attraction (Anderson 2002: 23). Where Whig and Tory met in the English case was at the intersection of the notion of being irreducibly different from others (especially continental Europeans) and of the notion of being prototypical, 'blazing trails which others followed' (Collini 1985: 41; Clark 2003: 210).

English difference was remarked upon by foreigners. Some of them found it exemplary. 'Anglophilia' derived from admiration for England's unique combination of civility, freedom and order (Buruma 1999: 16–17). Others were less impressed. In 1953, for example, Eric Voegelin commented (1953: 101; see also Shils 1972: 135–53) that Oxford political philosophers assumed that 'the principles of right political order have become historical flesh more perfectly in England than elsewhere at any time'. Happy the political philosopher, then, who finds that these principles are 'with those of his own civilisation'. Voegelin was rather contemptuous of this style of English parochialism and the continuity of its assumptions. However, this English 'ideology' did have its sophisticated and self-possessed exponents who, while drawing sympathetically on a wide philosophical inheritance, remained in no doubt about the unique value of England's tradition. Michael Oakeshott, for one, stated the case concisely. 'Reputable political behaviour', he argued, 'is not dependent on sound philosophy'. Rather 'constitutional tradition is a good substitute' and in this respect English politics was remarkably rich. He concluded that the form of parliamentary democracy which England had made 'British' was not an abstract idea.

> It is a way of living and a manner of politics which first began to emerge in the Middle Ages. In those distant times almost the whole outline of this way of life and manner of politics was adumbrated, an outline which has since been enlarged by experience and invention and defended against attack from without and treason from within. (Oakeshott 1948: 476)

It was 'not the gift of nature but the product of our own experience and inventiveness'. Left at that, Oakeshott's estimate of the British political tradition would have been unexceptional. But it was not left at that. The freedoms bequeathed by England to the UK, guaranteed by law, represented an exceptional method of social integration, 'the most civilized and the most effective method ever invented by mankind' (*ibid*.: 476; 489–90).

This method of social integration translated a specific aspect of the English political tradition – parliamentary sovereignty – into a British one in order to secure the unity of the UK (Crick 1991). This, it has been argued convincingly, made the development of a specifically English nationalism not only counter-productive but actually irrelevant. It also had the result of confusing *English* and *British* in a manner of blessed forgetfulness (Crick 1995). This usually has been interpreted as an expression of English arrogance. The opposite reading can also be made, and it is possible to interpret it as an expression of English sacrifice, for what is often ignored is the attraction of English civilisation as a method of social integration. In the mid-nineteenth century even one of the stalwarts of the proud *Edinburgh Review* was prepared to declare that 'the nearer we [the Scots] can propose to make ourselves to England the better' (quoted in Massie 2002: 13; see also Kidd 1993). Moreover, its method of social integration was also here one of multi-national integration. That was precisely Lord Roseberry's point when, according to Grainger (1986: 53–5), he proposed 'that not only did England accommodate other nations within her Ancient Constitution under skilled and patrician rule, but also, without oppressing or annoying, had the capacity to absorb them within her consciousness'. England, while remaining England, 'a concrete reference' for sure and especially for poets, in a real sense became also Britain, as its economy drew in the Irish, Scots and Welsh. As an 'absorptive *patria*', there was no need to base Englishness on blood or soil or even a flag, and 'flying the Cross of St George was a protest or a foible, usually Socialist or Anglican'. The good fortune of this social and national integration relied in large measure on the relatively stable identity that England gave to England/Britain (Stapleton 1999; 2001). The UK was a product of 'sweet ties of neighbourliness', a nationality not a nation, one that had taught 'its citizens at one and the same time to glory both in the name of Scotsmen or Welshmen or Englishmen and in the name of Britons' (Barker 1928: 17). Nevertheless, this narrative of integration was and remained decidedly anglocentric and tinged with a definite sense of universal mission, as Orwell's reflections confirmed (2001: 321–30; see also Kohn 1940).

A British narrative of disintegration

Some found this universalisation of the English exception a distinctly mixed blessing. As Oakeshott also observed (1948: 490), English experience 'became the model for peoples whose powers of social and political invention were unequal to their needs'. Unfortunately, if the rights and duties were exported, 'the genius that made them remained at home'. What 'went abroad as the concrete rights of an Englishman have returned home as the abstract Rights of Man, and they have returned to confound our politics and to corrupt our minds'. Furthermore, he feared English principles 'returning to us, disguised in a foreign dress, the outline blurred by false theory and the detail fixed with an uncharacteristic precision'. This corruption he later called rationalism in politics and for Oakeshott it was a measure of England's growing loss of self-possession. This loss has informed a recently popular narrative of the disintegration of England/Britain and has promoted a sort of inverted Podsnappian culture in which, as Johnson concluded (2000: 127), 'the majority of modern commentators on the Constitution appear to assume as a matter of course that foreigners generally do it better than we do, especially if they are our partners in the European Union'. This narrative of disintegration proved attractive because it appeared to synthesise two apparently contradictory developments: nationalism and a new global framework for politics.

This narrative located disintegration in England–Britain's loss of both uniqueness and universal significance, and this has taken a number of forms. The first was historical pessimism, the melancholy of decline summed up in Cannadine's remark that we are now 'burdened by the simple and sombre fact that the future of the British past looks bleaker today than at any time during the last forty years'. There is no longer any reason for the world to be interested, and if 'British history no longer seems a success story, then why bother to make it a story at all?' (1987: 169; 189). The second was political fatalism. The old narrative of England–Britain was exhausted, it was claimed, because it was nothing other than an imperial construct. 'You can't be an imperialist if you have no empire' (Marquand 1995: 217–18). Shorn of empire, the British could not be such a people any longer. Unfortunately, they could not be anyone else. Imperial Britain was not one of several possible Britains. 'Imperial Britain was Britain.' Thus the fatal conclusion was that empire 'was not an optional extra for the British; it was their reason for being British as opposed to English, Scots or Welsh'. What remained after the sun had set on the imperial state were separate nations on the one hand and the 'bloodless, historyless, affectless' administrative structure of the UK on the other (Marquand 1997: 200). The third was national assertiveness. Historically, the anglocentrism of the old narrative of integration promoted two anxieties within the other parts of the UK. The first anxiety was that of provincialism, in which acknowledgement by England was thought necessary to validate local cultural achievement. The second was an anxiety of influence in which such validation was thought to result in the expropriation of the local into an English cultural mainstream. The narrative of disintegration neatly reversed these anxieties. As the anglocentric narrative waned then England, formerly first among nations, was now to be pitied as the laggard of historical destiny. That was *Schadenfreude* indeed, a transition from a Celtic fringe to an Anglian fringe as England's notable self-possession collapsed. The invitation now was to pity rather than to emulate poor old England. The narrative further stressed the unnatural character of Britishness once the 'concrete reference' of England had also begun to wane. Combined with a radical critique of the monarchical constitution, it associated modernisation with the inevitable break up of Britain and the renaissance of the Celtic 'fringe'. Here Northern Ireland, the most British and so the most artificially British, seemed to demonstrate the disintegrative trend in the most dramatic way. The fourth part was European expectation. Europe was expected to provide a new model union, one in which a tolerant cosmopolitanism would complement resurgent civic nationalism in Scotland, Wales and ultimately in England.

The narrative of disintegration, then, appeared to provide a compelling explanation of British circumstances in the late twentieth century. It explained the new significance of nationalism after 1989; it related that new nationalism to the process of European integration; and it also seemed to make sense of larger global trends. For those on the left of British politics, it provided as well a narrative of resistance to the Conservatism of the 1980s. Thatcherism, in this case, was interpreted as a reassertion of the key elements of anglocentric integration. The uniqueness of parliamentary sovereignty, the distinctiveness within Europe and the universal model of market evangelism as the secret of England's greatness were promoted with an English moral fervour that others could understand only as traditional English hypocrisy (Bellamy 1989). The one writer who integrated all parts of the narrative of disintegration was Nairn (see for example 1977; 2000; 2002), and his polemical synthesis of the return to the particular (nationalism) and the loss of the universal (English institutional decay) influenced a whole generation of reflection on the question of British identities in general and on England in particular.

What is the English Question?

As Barker noted, a change had taken place in political debate by the 1990s. When it was assumed that people shared broadly similar needs, as in many ways the narrative of integration did, then politics was mainly argument about policy. When the assumption of homogeneity was challenged and when there developed a concern about power concentrating in one place, a concern provoked by Mrs Thatcher's anglocentricity, then policies 'are replaced by procedures, and radicals begin to discuss constitutional reform' (Barker 1996: 11). The devolutionary project of New Labour, then, may be interpreted as an attempt to preserve what is best in the narrative of integration, in particular the idea of British solidarity, and to prevent the worst in the narrative of disintegration, particularly the possibility of separatism. That project has been long in the making and one of its essential ingredients was thought to be the promotion of a benign form of English identity. 'We English', Crick wrote, 'must come to terms with ourselves'. It was time to stop infusing 'everything that is English into the common property of Britishness' (1991: 104). Crick later argued that the answer to the narrative of disintegration was 'not less English nationalism'. On the contrary, the English, like the Scots, the Welsh and the Irish, should develop 'a self-confident and explicit national feeling' (Crick 1995: 180). English national identity had become an urgent matter of dignity. Englishness was now defined in terms of what it *lacked* on the (questionable) assumption that everyone else does possess a dignified and proud national identity. It is important to note the tone of this argument. The pitch of English grievance rises once Scotland, Wales and Northern Ireland acquire devolved institutions after New Labour's election victory in 1997.

As the editors of *Political Quarterly* (1998: 1–3) noted, it was now time for England to engage in identity politics. The English, they argued, 'have begun to look grumpily insecure in the face of the external pressures of Europe and the internal pressures from Scotland and Wales'. Now, however, England was on the move, twitching and stirring 'as if awakening from a prolonged period of slumber'. Devolution meant that the politics and economics of territory was 'returning with a vengeance', and it was important to think through England's place within Blair's New Britain. One of those editors, Tony Wright, wrote (more grumpily) two years later that the English were the 'silent and uninvited guests at the devolutionary feast' (2000: 11). An even grumpier Kenneth Baker objected to the idea that the people of England should be treated as 'the residue of constitutional change', inverting their true significance within the UK (1998: 15). In short, one can detect a mood of English discontent that politicians were beginning tentatively to detect, express or promote. Nevertheless, one should be cautious about attributing a profound depth to that mood (see chapter 6). Cohen, for instance, has suggested that much popular sentiment revealed in the display of the Cross of St George was fake and Johnny-come-lately. For him, the underlying notion seemed to be that if 'everybody else has an identity, including some insignificant ethnic minorities, perhaps we should have one too' (2000: 578). Whatever the reasons (discussed further in the conclusion) for putting out more flags, here was a new condition of Englishness in which the politics of identity, predicated on the notion of a lack, intersected with the politics of territorial institutions, now also predicated on the notion of a lack. Together they suggested that Englishness was being denied, and even if *what* was being denied remained rather vague, the politics of denial issued in two distinctively nationalist modes of identity politics, one conservative and the other radical. What they share in common is a sense of institutional alienation and a quest for authenticity.

Conservative Englishness

The critique of English presumption by *Celtic* nationalism is a familiar one. However, it was an *English* politician speaking about *England* who best expressed the context in which a return to the particular could become politically seductive. That politician was Enoch Powell, and he revealed the unresolved tensions of conservative Englishness apparent in subsequent attempts to define it: cultural authenticity and cultural diversity; constitutional wisdom and institutional alienation; the renewal of England and the decadence of England. Ironically, like the view expressed in Salman Rushdie's *Satanic Verses*, Powell appeared to believe that because British history had happened overseas the English had lost a sense of their own selfhood. The imperial experience, rather like Oakeshott's exported principles, had confounded English politics and corrupted the minds of politicians. Only in coming home to itself, literally as well as metaphorically, could England discover that 'the continuity of her existence was unbroken when the looser connections which had linked her with distant continents and strange races fell away'. In his famous Royal Society of St George speech in 1961, Powell announced the end of this 'Greater England'. Modern England would now need to re-attune itself to an older, pre-imperial England. 'So we today at the heart of a vanished empire, amid the fragments of demolished glory, seem to find, like one of her own oak trees, standing and growing, the sap still rising from her ancient roots to meet the spring, England herself'. Home from their distant wandering the English would come to find themselves as English, a nation once again and to recognise 'the homogeneity of England', one brought about 'by the slow alchemy of centuries' (quoted in Heffer 1998: 334–40).

Here is a familiar nationalistic appeal to authenticity, a call to remember, as Kitson-Clark (1950: 13) so concisely put it, that 'the English also were English before they were British'. It is the politics of return (see Colls 2002: 144). Powell was nothing if not a complicated man. If the rediscovery of England intimated a reawakening of the national spirit it could also intimate its demise. In Powell there was that very conservative melancholy of anticipation that resembled Kipling's premonition of loss, where 'the beginning of the end is born already' and as 'men count time the end is far off; but as we, who know, reckon, it is to-day' (1898: 41–2). Moreover, as Powell was prepared to admit, faith in England–Britain as a great power – even though he knew it was not so – would not die for him 'until I, the carrier of it, am actually dead' (quoted in Brivati and Jones 1995: 15). That elegiac note was another characteristic of conservative Englishness.

Powell's idealism traced authenticity from the soil of England, to its laws, disciplines and freedoms emanating from 'a thing called "Parliament" ' that dispensed the same justice to all the people of England. But what if those institutions that had served England so well had themselves become *inauthentic*? What if they were prepared to alienate the alchemy of centuries, estrange themselves from England herself and confound the homogeneity of the country? The irony of Powell's Englishness is that in the pursuit of authenticity he discovered only alienation, internally with immigration policy and later 'multiculturalism', and externally with European policy (Rich 1988: 676). Institutional alienation presents a conundrum for conservative Englishness, and it was a conundrum that Nairn identified precisely. A modern national identity, he argued, means one thing: 'Populism is of its essence, while parliamentarianism is decidedly not.' He thought that only when Englishness became properly democratic would it become properly nationalist (Nairn 1977: 295). Nairn's formulaic and abstract notion of nationalism did not do justice to the historic distinctions of the English case (Clark 2003: 108). Undoubtedly, though, he pointed to a real tension in conservative Englishness between an idea of the constitutional people and an idea of the sovereign people. This is illustrated in the view of C. H. Sisson, who had become concerned that the contemporary trend to substitute '"democracy" for the Constitution in the minds of electors can do nothing but harm'. The English

Constitution, he believed, 'informed rather than controlled by electoral devices, is one from which we depart at our peril' (1992: 53). As this *English* Constitution changed after 1997, its alienated transformations became the very focus of discontent. As a result, conservative Englishness increasingly comes to substitute populism for old-style constitutionalism and Simon Heffer provides a good example of that robust style.

Heffer proposed that the Conservative Party should now proclaim explicitly what it had become implicitly: the party of English nationalism. It had shied away from this possibility only because English nationalism was thought to involve 'bonkers theories of racial superiority' (1999: 93). The challenge for Tories 'would be to forge a nationalism that, while respecting and advancing the aspirations of the English, does not contribute to xenophobic feelings among the inhabitants of these islands' (*ibid.*: 119). The task was indeed a democratic one, harnessing a distinctive culture to majority and not just to elitist tastes in order to subvert what Heffer believed was 'the obsessive desire by much of the political class to eradicate the notion of nationhood' in England, an obsessive desire it shared with bureaucrats in Brussels (*ibid.*: 105). He conveyed what was assumed to be a distinctively anglocentric resentment: that the English, above all, had become foreigners in their own country (Heffer 2002a: 13; see also Hague 1999). There can be no stronger expression of alienation for a conservative than this. In Heffer's view, the Blair Government was 'probably the most anti-British and certainly the most anti-English in history', and it appeared dedicated to constitutional vandalism. The ancient institutions that conservatives revered, that the English had built and that worked so well in the past had been 'wrecked in the interests of political expediency and democracy has been perverted' (Heffer 2002b: 15). So within these islands, Englishness would need to return from Britishness and from its ungrateful malcontents, especially the Scots. In his anti-Scottish polemic, Heffer was writing in the tradition of John Wilkes. What was more pronounced in the late twentieth-century version was the anxiety that England was missing out on what a devolved Scotland appeared to have in abundance – cultural self-confidence and clarity of identity. The end of the Union would provide an opportunity to strip away all those external 'relics of England as an imperial power' such as membership of the Commonwealth. This new-found independence would also have consequences for England's relations with the European Union – withdrawal was not out of the question – whose socialistic tendencies remained 'anathematical to the English spirit' (Heffer 1999: 121–4). Heffer was also explicit about wanting to foster a 'conscious atavism' in order to rescue and revive the English tradition. His newly independent England would have to think seriously about the difference between a national society that tolerated various cultures, something that was right and proper, and one that encouraged multiculturalism, something that was not right and proper (see also Lovejoy 2000: 30–76). This would no longer be 'dear old, somewhat unsure-of-itself' England-within-Britain. It would be England, *our* England in which the object of state policy would be to encourage the English 'cultural continuum'. Diversity would be acceptable only so long as it did not violate 'legitimate English sensibilities' (Heffer 1999: 42–5). The 'sometimes crude tones' of Heffer's populism jarred with many, even the *Salisbury Review* (Thompson 2001: 49). There were also those conservatives whose distaste for populism was such that the last thing they wanted was for England to arise, especially if it meant pandering to working class louts in shell suits (Worsthorne 1998).

Heffer's is one possible version of conservative England yet it is so in an unconventional way. Ian Gilmour once wrote that though the concern of English conservatism has been with the preservation of the nation's unity and its institutions, in certain circumstances there was no choice other than to be revolutionary (1977: 143). Heffer's anglocentric narrative of disintegration is quite revolutionary, albeit revolutionary in the spirit of returning to an authentic England. The actual case for English independence is not the point. Support for English independence may be limited but the book satisfies a national mood that may be called 'irritable growl syndrome'. This is a condition that cannot be cured but only satisfied, and Heffer's style is a satisfactory one, providing articulate justification for old prejudices and a reasoned explanation for present grievances. It provides an intellectualised version of 'Up yours, Delors' to which has been added a large dose of 'Up yours, McSporran', a high-brow version of Carry On England. As Adair once observed, the Carry On tradition represents an oft-repeated 'return, on the part of a substantial number of our compatriots, to the most formative and "most desirable of all caves"' (1986: 56). Heffer's political version mimics that English manner spoken of by Alan Bennett, joking but not joking, serious but not serious (quoted in Paxman 1998: 18). There is political knock-about but Heffer is not joking about a deep-seated resentment, justified or not. There are serious arguments about constitutional change but there is also the feeling that it is done slightly tongue in cheek. And this too is characteristic of the people. 'Most English people still find chauvinism a bore; yet they have noticed that, nowadays, nationalist whingeing seems to pay off.' Nevertheless, there remains an 'inescapable element of self-mockery in the current wave of nationalist fervour' (Cox 2002: 16). Intelligent Tories are aware of that too.

If Heffer can make a serious but also not so serious case for English independence, other conservatives suggest that the England he would reinvent may be no longer the England they want. This is a political version of another tradition, the literature of loss captured in Vansittart's title *In Memory of*

England (1998). In reviewing this tradition, Barker thought that the 'note is elegiac, but it is not a note of self-pity: there is little sentimentality, and if there is a feeling for the still sad music of humanity there is no indulgence in *Weltschmerz*' (1947: 558). The solid pragmatic virtue of the English did not lend itself to such soulfulness. However, Barker was writing after a titanic victory in the Second World War. Writing almost a half-century later, Light noted a very different mood, 'how prevalent was a farewell tone', and she wondered was it because we are really at the end of the sort of Englishness that liberal conservatives like Barker thought worthy of celebration. Was the very idea of English nationality, she asked, 'inevitably tinged with the elegiac?' Was it the case 'that even a history of conservatism must become an epitaph?' (1991: 19). A decade later and Roger Scruton was so certain of it that he wrote *England: An Elegy*, a book that came close to indulging in *Weltschmerz*. His is an England over which the Owl of Minerva is hovering, a civilisation 'which is now passing from the world' (Scruton 2000: vii). It is an England that has experienced disenchantment because the English have come to believe that the country is no longer theirs. This is now an alienated country and one consequence has been hostility to immigration (*ibid.*: 8). Scruton's former England consisted 'in the physiognomy, the habits, the institutions, the religion and the culture' of a very distinctive way of life. 'Almost all have died'. They depended on 'England being somewhere and a home' but that 'somewhere' and that 'home' have been dismantled. In short, 'England has been forbidden – and forbidden by the English', a development that has been orchestrated by opinion-makers. This forbidding of England from within has been complemented by its subjection from abroad, especially by Europe and 'this political disenfranchisement is also a disenchantment of their country' (*ibid.*: 244–57; for a different view of Europe but within the same tragic style see Worsthorne 1999). The unspoken preference appears to be England in the mode of Drake, a swashbuckling entity sailing the high seas of the global free market and another example of the serious (dislike for Brussels bureaucracy) but not serious (this is romance not politics).

No political enterprise necessarily follows from Scruton's elegy. 'To describe something as dead', he argued, 'is not to call for its resurrection' (2000: 244). The elegiac disposition permits a number of responses. The first is the politics of solace. This is especially the case if you believe that your future is behind you. Moreover, a diet of betrayal and loss, real or imaginary, helps to confirm a vision of the political that preserves intact one's own virtue. The second is the consolation of survival. Being able to survive in a hostile world and to manage this burden of fate can engender a form of self-esteem and a sense of nobility. In other words, this form of elegiac Englishness is as prideful in an inverted way as is the most hubristic form of nationalism. It is yet another, if disguised, version of the Froude complex. Though Scruton wrote of the disenchantment of the old England, his book is really an attempted re-enchantment, a revisiting of those qualities of Englishness that identified the country and its people as unique and special, qualities that have been celebrated and ridiculed for centuries (Langford 2000). That is the appeal of the book, and it satisfies a need since the anatomy of the 'way we were' is not only bitter-sweet but also life-confirming. Yet again the argument is both serious and not serious. It is serious when it invites the reader to consider what has been lost (even if some may think it worth losing). It is not serious when it implies that England is going to hell. Beneath the veneer of doom remains, as Grant has argued, 'profound gratitude for the existence we already have' (1998: 31). The expression of alienation is clear but its very expression in elegiac tones helps the alienated to live with reality. This is what has been called the 'idealism of nostalgia', and the idealism and the nostalgia in this case are not only conservative but also very English and enduringly popular (Berki 1981). Contemporary political events are an occasion for revisiting fondly a more beautiful Englishness rather than for turning that reverie into a nationalistic programme. That in itself is very conservative. And very English. Scruton is too intelligent not to know that the elegiac is often a means of coming to terms with the present (on such literary strategies see Nunning 2001). Conservative Englishness may celebrate the 'cultural continuum' but it needs to deal with a more complex world, and here one may suggest that its real significance is not a serious return to homogeneity but a reminder of the need for commonality. As D'Ancona suggested, the point is 'whether we have the courage to decide what we should agree upon' (2002: 12). That is a valid point and one that non-conservatives can also accept (see Colls 2002: 380;Lloyd 2002).

Radical Englishness

The vocabulary of patriotism may have come less instinctively to the lips of radicals, and the left historically may have been suspicious of nationalism because it was thought instinctively to be the preserve of the right. However, the language of patriotism could never be divorced entirely from the language of radicalism, for it also served as a 'tool of opposition, and as a means of possessing the past' (Cunningham 1981: 9). There were ambiguities aplenty in radical patriotism – see, for example, Scruton's assessment of his father's sense of Englishness (2000: 255–7). This radical tradition, of course, shared in the idea of England being not only exceptional but exemplary. E. P. Thompson's *The Making of the English Working Class* (1963) told not only a particular national story but a universal story. Thompson had been critical of those in the new left like Anderson and Nairn who thought that the only thing that distinguished the English (particular) was their failure to imitate the French (universal). For Thompson such intellectual strategies 'which thirst for a tidy platonism very soon become impatient with actual history' (1978: 47). It was the actual history of the English working class that had shaped, and continued to shape, any worthwhile radical tradition where the particular and the universal were one, now and in England. This older radical tradition claimed to embody the true spirit of Englishness against the more limited sympathies of conservative England. The neglect of this popular tradition was, moreover, the basis of Thompson's later criticism (1993: 377–82) of Colley's influential history, *Britons* (1992): hers was a top–down history that flattered 'the conservative self-image' of Britain, and while radicalism was limited by the undoubted historical strength of conservative Englishness, it was important to remember that the English were sometimes 'highly loyalist and sometimes decidedly not so' and that there were times 'when the patriot must also be a revolutionary'. Resistance to the realisation of radical Englishness lay in the centrality of a class identity that conservatives had successfully confused with national identity. If one can detect a constant in radical Englishness it has been the objective to transform England in the image of the people and to rescue it from (the wrong) class. Orwell's significance in that tradition was his ability to state that constant imaginatively. An insightful and provocative exploration of the relationship between class and Englishness is provided by Schöpflin (2000).

Schöpflin claimed that Englishness was not primarily ethnic. English identity, he argued, 'is intimately bound up with class' and whereas continental Europeans 'have ethnicity, the English have class'. For Schöpflin, the reason why attempts to change the class basis of Englishness have foundered is that class status has given the majority of English people 'a very clear and very secure identity', and this has applied as much to Thompson's working class as to Scruton's middle class. The subtle English snobberies were actually conducive to social and political stability. They also appeared to have had one important and positive effect: since England, quite unusually, has subordinated ethnicity to class 'this has helped to make the country relatively open to migrants, exiles and other foreigners'. The old conservative Englishness of class may offend the egalitarian spirit, but this analysis suggests that it could be replaced by a nationalistic offence to the spirit of tolerance. One major contemporary threat to this English identity is not internal but external – the threat of Europe. Schöpflin thought that the 'new definitions of status' deriving from membership of the EU challenged the class-based character of Englishness. Eurosceptics, therefore, 'are quite correct in their intuitions that further integration into Europe will mean the end of Englishness as it has existed for the last two centuries or more'. Ironically, self-definition against the EU *also* threatens conservative Englishness because the defensive nature of its nationalism risks ethnicising those popular attitudes often 'cognitively blanked out' by gentle, elegiac visions like Scruton's. This is a challenge to radical Englishness as well. In order to embrace modernity there needs to be the sort of popular patriotism that radicalism can deliver, but embracing it might generate an ethnic nationalism nastier than the conservative identity it seeks to replace (all quoted matter in this paragraph is from Schöpflin 2000: 298–323).

Schöpflin's argument is not entirely persuasive, but he has captured brilliantly some of the dilemmas of radical Englishness. He has captured the new importance of the ideal of the EU as an exemplar, but also the anxiety about the potential chauvinism of popular sovereignty. He has captured the frustration with the survivors of the old class-ridden culture, especially the monarchy, and the corresponding celebration of popular culture, but also the anxiety that popular Englishness may not be so respectful of 'difference' as radicals would like. He has captured the radical hostility for hierarchy that is thought to be geographical as well as social and provided one reason for the recent interest in English regionalism but also the hesitation about constituting a separate English nationalism (see chapter 6). The decline of the 'cult of the gentleman', itself a metaphor for Englishness-as-class, is not an unmixed blessing, and this has been acknowledged by the more astute of those sympathetic to a 'new Englishness' (Crick 1995: 179). These dilemmas can be found in the recent literature.

Richard Weight, for example, concluded in his survey of postwar British history that the solution to England's sense of dislocation and the solution to the democratic deficit in English political culture were one and the same: independence as a nation- state, with popular music and football as the levers of cultural transformation. Like Heffer, Weight wanted the English to take the initiative in dismantling England–Britain; like Heffer, he believed that England/Britain was becoming 'a foreign country'. Also like Heffer, he had little time for the 'Celtic elites' whose interest after devolution now appears to be that of suppressing the potential of England and of wanting English sporting teams to lose. Unlike Heffer, he wanted independence within Europe to be the foundation of modern England, a foundation that would provide the English with 'a chance to rediscover and re-imagine themselves within a progressive framework'. Weight celebrated the nationalism expressed by supporters of England's football team. The Cross of St George, he argued, was the symbol of English national inclusiveness, and that meant blacks and Asians as well as whites. He and his friends proclaimed their Englishness with the Oasis song *D'You Know What I Mean?*, the chorus of which runs 'All my people right here, right now, d'you know what I mean?' (Weight 1999:

25–7). Did Weight really know what *he* meant? Could he be sure that 'my people' would always be his (inclusive) sort of people? The progressive version of the people he favoured would automatically exclude the wrong sort of football supporter, and sociologists of British pop music have their doubts about the novelty of the 'new England' it claims to have discovered (Bennett 1997). Weight felt that the English were being betrayed by a 'self-serving political elite' and a 'myopic intellectual elite' suspicious of the people and their culture: 'England, the last stateless nation in the United Kingdom, was leaderless and adrift' (2002: 726). Conservative elegy here has become radical self-pity which, when mixed with populist self-righteousness, is the basic stuff of familiar nationalist grievance. This would confirm Colls's observation that a national story can make conservatives into radicals and radicals into conservatives. Weight gives insufficient consideration to the possibility that English people will not feel particularly aggrieved at the Britishness of England but will understand it as part both of how they imagine themselves and of how they value themselves (*ibid*.: chapter 3). Like much in contemporary conservative Englishness the focus of this type of radical literature is on what the country lacks, and what it appears to lack is what the non-English always thought it had in abundance – self-belief.

Another explorer of a radical Englishness, Billy Bragg, in word and song has gone looking for a healthy nationalism of the sort that he assumed was the norm already in Scotland, Wales and Ireland (for a more realistic view see McMillan 1999). Bragg thought that the English were stuck with 'the old sweaty sock of imperialism' and argued that it was necessary to forge an Englishness that reconciled the patriotism of the majority with the values of democracy and equality, to make 'English an inclusive identity rather than an exclusive nationality'. He was aware of the radical concern that expression of national identity was 'bound to be tainted by fears of national chauvinism and racism', but it was worth taking the risk because if radicals did not then English identity would continue to be dictated by the right (Bragg 1996: 15).

In these critiques one finds two characteristics. The first is a familiar one in the lineage of radical Englishness: faith in the basic decency of English people who, when being true to themselves, are disposed to tolerance and solidarity and 'put themselves in positions of extraordinary openness to the cultures of other peoples' (Colls 2002: 380). The other is a longing to define clear national lines to avoid becoming 'some sort of British rump' as the UK breaks down (Bragg 1996: 15). Political Englishness is experienced as a void, and it is a void that could be filled by a positive civic nationalism. The collapse of a socialistic alternative has made nationalism all the more attractive, as populism emerges from its former Labour shell (see Howe 1989). The sense of living amid the ruins of conservative Englishness appears to make the critique all the more urgent. The fear is the fear of becoming superfluous, of being left behind, of failing the test of European destiny.

Pop nationalism here intersects with pop internationalism, and the expectation is that the EU will usher in the necessary liberation from conservative Englishness. As the structures of the UK melt in the heat of the European project, 'then the constrictions imposed by the straightjacket of UKanian nationality' will dissolve and a safely civic England will finally take its place within a new EU (Haseler 1996: viii–ix). However appealing or persuasive such an outcome might appear, one cannot help thinking that there exists a subtext of mistrust of the very English identity that is being cultivated, a mistrust so unlike the affection one finds in Thompson's work or the recent work by Colls. There is something rather Germanic about the anxiety it conceals. Like the German left's support for European integration, the English version implies a revulsion against 'the "two world wars and one world cup" variety of belligerent, alcohol-fuelled nativism'(Gilroy 1999: 67). It is also one of the driving forces of postcolonial multicultural politics that intends to express and affirm a turning away 'from the morbidities of living in an old country' (*ibid.*). Perhaps that style of politics reached its height with the publication of the Parekh Report – the rather embarrassed and critical reception of which by the Labour Government has seen a certain shift of emphasis (Runnymede Trust 2000). As Alibhai-Brown has argued (2002: 47–50), multiculturalism has excluded the English as a specific group and has fostered acute resentment. The project now should be one of 'encouraging the English to be English' as part of an inclusive, progressive, multi-ethnic British identity, which 'cannot be done unless the English are brought in from the cold'. Here is an optimistic invitation to engage in the therapeutic engineering of a radical Englishness, and one cannot avoid the observation that there is something rather patronising (even paternalistic) about this.

Conclusion

In the weeks of the Euro 2004 soccer competition Boris Johnson observed that never 'in history has the flag of St George been so popular'; never 'has it been so prevalent in the decor of our streets'. He thought the ubiquity of the English flag was 'a huge political message, a statement of exuberant loyalty, and also of a certain frustration'. The loyalty was to the country and to its soccer team. The frustration was the result of a 'sense of constitutional oppression' at the consequences of devolution that had left the English without a proper forum for English laws, and he thought that this vindicated Heffer's analysis (Johnson 2004; for a discussion of this point see chapter 4 of this volume). One could also argue that it vindicated both Weight and Bragg. Actually, the pervasive presence of the English flag made it difficult to make any clear judgement of its significance. A substantial element was marketing association with the lucrative commodity of the England soccer team, something promoted and keenly sponsored by supermarkets (and this provided a new perspective on Napoleon's jibe that the English were a nation of shopkeepers). There was also an element of imitative fashion, also commercialised, with as much political significance as the recent excitement for Pokemon cards. This was, of course, a brash demonstration of nationality, but it was difficult to relate it to any popular mood of discontent, as Johnson claimed, with the absence of 'English votes for English laws' (see chapter 6, this volume). Despite the novelty of the display, it is impossible to associate it directly with a desire for English independence, an expression of euroscepticism or any political programme. What did it say about contemporary English identities?

If there was one political aspect that could not be ignored it was the autonomy of populism. For much of recent British history populism had been contained by the class system of English society. Conservative politics had contained populism within a culture of social deference. Labour politics had contained populism within a culture of working-class solidarity. The withering of social deference and the demise of working-class solidarity have permitted populism to escape the confines of traditional conservatism and radicalism; one manifestation of this phenomenon was the flag-waving of late May and early June 2004. Extracting the Cross of St George from the Union flag as a way of celebrating popular sporting emotions is a style statement rather than a proclamation of nationalist intent, a cultural projection (having a good time) rather than an exclusive identity. It is, of course, tempting to detect some turning of the tide, a confluence of those currents of national sentiment explored in this chapter. The sense of loss recounted by conservative Englishness, it argued, is actually part of a politics of confirmation. This can be in the form of an elegy, as with Scruton, in the form of a rage against the times, as with Hitchens (1999), or it can be in the form of a project of recovery, as with Heffer. These works translate specific and legitimate concerns about constitutional change into grandly metaphysical meditations on decay and possible regeneration, though the waving of flags might provide hope that popular regeneration is at hand. This chapter also proposed that the sense of frustration found in radical Englishness has been, as Pocock (2000) argued, that it wants 'the English to cease being British, but does not know whether they will or can' or, indeed, 'what they are supposed to become'. One alternative, he thought, was 'that popular, soccer-fan Republic of St George' and one could argue that it was this very alternative which demonstrated its colours before and during Euro 2004. Conservative and radical Englishness could take inspiration from that event and start rewriting the past and the present in nationalist mode. There is a possibility that things will take this self-consciously nationalist direction, but that has not happened.

For Pocock, the English can never have a past that is post- or anti-British; and their Britishness can be transformed but not terminated. England/Britain does not need the simplicity of a clear-cut identity. Rather, the English and their British partners 'need a complex history and a complex politics, if they are free to argue with themselves as well as with each other'. The English, above all, should avoid at all costs revelling in their grievances, real or imaginary, and commit themselves to sustain 'a politics in which multiple identities are both intermixed and respected' (*ibid.*: 41–52). England/Britain, albeit a modified England/Britain, would appear still to be the framework which respects that complexity. And as Vernon Bogdanor observed (2002: 15), the 'brute facts of electoral behaviour' oblige one to believe that Britain is not 'so artificial a construct or so imagined a community as many historians have suggested'. Nor, perhaps, so fragile. Indeed, if there is a common theme in the chapters of this book it is the exceptional difficulty of extracting England from Britain or, indeed, Britain from England (see chapter 4).

Paxman concluded his book (in a very English way) by stating that national identity was a good thing, but in England's case it would not be a nationalism of flags and anthems; it would be, apparently, 'modest, individualistic, ironic, solipsistic', and it could well be the 'nationalism of the future' (1998: 265–6). In other words, it would *not* be a serious nationalism at all (it would be exceptional), and, unsurprisingly, it would become *the* model for others to copy (it would be exemplary). Moreover, that was the conclusion reached by a recent academic exploration of English identity (Kumar 2003: 269–73). Even in revising their past it seems that the English are destined to confirm it. That is a discovery that may tell us a lot about the English and their sense of themselves, even when they are draped in the Cross of St George. There can even be self-possession in coping with the loss of a former self-possession and it appears that the UK continues to be the appropriate framework for its expression.

4

The government of England by Westminster[1]

Meg Russell and Guy Lodge

In debates about England since devolution in 1999, few issues have received greater attention than the country's proper governance at Westminster. While Scotland and Wales (and intermittently Northern Ireland, since 1998) received their devolved institutions, and thus changed their relationships with the UK Government, no consequent changes were made for the English. This is most visible at Westminster, where devolution has changed the roles of Scottish and Welsh MPs with respect to policy-making for their countries but the mechanisms for the governance of England remain largely untouched.

As parliamentary representation broadly reflects population distribution, the English are dominant at Westminster. Of the 646 members elected to the House of Commons in 2005, 529 (82 per cent) represented English constituencies.[2] The bulk of matters discussed at Westminster relate to England, and English MPs provide the overwhelming majority of both government ministers and members of parliamentary committees. This dominant Englishness of the UK Parliament was one of the factors that helped fuel claims for devolution and institutions where Scottish, Welsh and Northern Irish matters received dedicated attention.[3] Yet, now that devolution has happened, new claims of inequity are heard. Despite England's continued dominance, questions are asked about whether it is adequate any longer for English matters at Westminster to continue to be treated in the same way as reserved all-UK matters. In particular, interest has focused on the continued involvement of MPs representing non-English constituencies in matters which affect England alone.

This chapter seeks to explore the way England is governed by Westminster, what objections have been raised to the current arrangements and what prospects there are for reform. In order to provide a context for the current debates the chapter takes a historical perspective, comparing the current controversies with other territorial tensions at Westminster in the past. We conclude that the conundrums thrown up by devolution are not new and that there are no immediate answers. These debates do, however, lead to profound questions about the extent to which we wish to continue to be governed as a united kingdom. The 'unionist' response to the anomalies would be to accept them, as other British constitutional anomalies have come to be accepted over time. Alternatively, gradualist change might be pursued in order to accommodate English business at Westminster, as applied to Scottish and Welsh business in the past. However, we suggest that this would be likely to prove unsatisfactory in the longer term, just as had the earlier arrangements, and lead to demands for further constitutional change. Yet the two alternatives – an English parliament or 'English votes on English laws' – remain fundamentally problematical.

The government of England now

A starting point for our analysis is the way in which England is in practice governed by Westminster now, and what tensions have occurred since 1999. The first of these questions is in one sense simple to answer, as there has been almost no change. Prior to devolution, while special arrangements existed for discussion of Welsh, Scottish and Northern Irish matters in the House of Commons (through dedicated select, standing and grand committees and questions to the secretaries of state), no similar provision existed for England. Following devolution, ironically the same structures for the devolved areas still exist (and are developing new roles), while no parallel English forums have been established. The single exception is the Standing Committee on Regional Affairs, which was reconstituted in 2000, having fallen into disuse. This has, however, been of minimal impact. The committee, and the special arrangements for Scotland, Wales and Northern Ireland, are discussed in more detail later in the chapter. The only other direct response to devolution has been the agreement to reduce the number of Scottish MPs (from 72 to 59) to bring the size of Scottish constituencies into line with those in England. However, this does little to address the anomalies, and the Welsh will continue to be over-represented (McLean 1995).

The procedures that apply to the government of England remain identical to those applied by Westminster to non-devolved matters of concern to the whole of the UK. Policy is made in Whitehall, with ministers responsible to Parliament for all the policy of their departments which may apply to England only or also to other parts of the UK. In the House of Commons, accountability mechanisms include the select committees which now shadow each government department, written and oral questions to ministers, and scrutiny of government bills in the chamber and by standing committees.

As Lodge and Mitchell detail in this volume (chapter 5), the work of many Whitehall departments is now in practice largely English. As English business is not delineated, it is not possible exhaustively to document how these relationships work. But departments may be placed on a rough scale from the almost wholly English (ODPM, Department of Health), through the largely English (Department for Education and Skills) to those dealing primarily with non-devolved matters that affect the entirety of the UK (Foreign Office, Ministry of Defence). Due to the asymmetrical nature of the devolution settlement those departments that are not restricted to UK-wide matters may also deal to a greater or lesser extent with Welsh affairs. So for example the Department for Culture, Media and Sport is responsible for broadcasting policy in Wales, but not for museums and libraries (see chapter 5).

It seems natural to expect that the relationship these departments have with Westminster would reflect their territorial coverage. As all MPs represent a geographic constituency they might be expected to seek involvement only in those matters directly affecting their constituents. If this were true one result of devolution could be a reduction in the involvement of MPs from some parts of the UK (particularly Scotland) with the business of some government departments.

Tables 4.1, 4.2 and 4.3 explore this hypothesis with respect to three forms of involvement: the holding of ministerial office; membership of departmental select committees; and the tabling of (written) parliamentary questions. These figures show a more complex relationship than might immediately have been supposed.

All three tables show the situation immediately prior to devolution and in 2002–3. One of the most striking results is that this period has seen relatively little change. Certainly there are some departments which are the province mainly of the English; but this was also the case prior to devolution: the health, education and agriculture departments, for example, included no ministers from outside of England in the 1997 Government, and they were shadowed by select committees made up entirely of English MPs. The proportion of written questions put to those departments by English MPs was higher than the 80 per cent that might occur randomly, although the same could also be said for some all-UK departments. In terms of select committee membership, and the pattern of questions, there has been almost no change in the territorial representation across departments. And although there is some indication of specialisation by Scottish and Welsh members in the business of departments dealing with reserved matters (for example, the Foreign Office and the Department for International Development), any change over time has been limited at best. The biggest change over the period has been the drop in the number of Scottish ministers. At 22 per cent of the Government, Scots

Table 4.1 House of Commons ministers in UK government departments, by location of constituency

Department	May 1997				June 2003			
	Eng	Scot	Wal	NI	Eng	Scot	Wal	NI
Health	4	0	0	0	4	1	0	0
Education	4	0	2	0	6	0	0	0
Agriculture, Fisheries and Food[a]	3	0	0	0	–	–	–	–
Environment, Food and Rural Affairs[b]	–	–	–	–	3	0	1	0
Environment, Transport and the Regions[a]	7	1	0	0	–	–	–	–
Transport[b]	–	–	–	–	2	1	1	0
Deputy Prime Minister[b]	–	–	–	–	5	0	0	0
Heritage/Culture, Media and Sport	3	0	1	0	3	0	0	0
Home Office	4	0	1	0	7	0	0	0
Trade and Industry	4	1	0	0	5	1	0	0
Treasury	2	3	0	0	3	1	0	0
Cabinet Office	2	0	0	0	0	1	0	0
Foreign Office	3	1	0	0	5	0	0	0
Defence	1	2	0	0	2	1	0	0
Lord Chancellor's Department[a]	1	0	0	0	–	–	–	–
Scottish Office/Scotland Office[c]	0	5	0	0	0	1	0	0
Welsh Office/Wales Office[d]	0	0	3	0	0	0	1	0
Northern Ireland Office	1	2	1	0	4	0	1	0
Constitutional Affairs[b]	–	–	–	–	2	0	0	0
Social Security/Work and Pensions	4	0	0	0	4	1	0	0
International Development	1	1	0	0	2	0	0	0
Leader of the House	1	0	0	0	1	0	1	0
Minister Without Portfolio	1	0	0	0	1	0	0	0
Law Officers	0	0	1	0	1	1	0	0
Whips	13	2	1	0	13	2	1	0
Total	59	19	9	0	73	11	6	0
As % of total	68	22	10	0	81	12	7	0

Notes: [a] 1997 only; [b] 2003 only; [c] Scottish Office renamed Scotland Office in 1999; [d] Welsh Office renamed Wales Office in 1999.
Source: Vacher Dod (1997, 2003).

were over-represented in 1997; they now hold a more proportionate share of positions. This may, however, be due more to chance than to devolution, as the biggest shifts have occurred in departments dealing with reserved matters – such as the Treasury, the Foreign Office and the Department for International Development – as well as resulting from the slimming down of the Scottish (now Scotland) Office itself. Certain departments always were, and remain, largely English. However, devolution has focused attention on breaches of this convention. Notably there was much comment from the

Table 4.2 Membership of departmental select committees, by location of constituency

Select committee	1997–98 session				2002–3 session			
	Eng	Scot	Wal	NI	Eng	Scot	Wal	NI
Health	11	0	0	0	10	0	1	0
Education	17	0	0	0	11	0	0	0
Agriculture[a]	11	0	0	0	–	–	–	–
Environment, Food and Rural Affairs[b]	–	–	–	–	14	1	0	1
Environment, Transport and Regions[a]	15	1	0	1	–	–	–	–
Transport[b]	–	–	–	–	8	1	1	1
Office of Deputy Prime Minister[b]	–	–	–	–	11	0	0	0
Culture, Media and Sport	10	1	0	0	7	3	1	0
Home Affairs	11	0	0	0	11	0	0	0
Trade and Industry	9	2	0	0	9	2	0	0
Treasury	11	1	0	0	10	1	0	0
Public Administration	9	1	1	0	9	1	1	0
Foreign Affairs	8	2	2	0	10	0	1	0
Defence	9	2	0	0	8	2	1	0
Scottish Affairs	2	9	0	0	1	10	0	0
Welsh Affairs	2	0	9	0	2	0	9	0
Northern Ireland	9	0	0	4	5	3	1	4
Constitutional Affairs[b]	–	–	–	–	11	0	0	0
Social Security/Work and Pensions	10	1	0	0	8	3	0	0
International Development	9	1	1	0	8	2	1	0
Public Accounts	12	2	1	0	13	2	1	0
Total	165	23	14	5	166	31	18	6
As % of total	80	11	7	2	75	14	8	3

Notes: [a] 1997–98 session only; [b] 2002–3 session only.
Source: House of Commons Sessional Returns 1997–98 and 2000–3; figures apply to end of session.

opposition and the press when John Reid, an MP representing a Scottish seat, was made Secretary of State for Health in June 2003.[4] The Department of Health is not concerned wholly with English matters, as issues such as human genetics and abortion continue to be reserved. However, the Conservatives wasted no time in quoting the words of Scottish MP Robin Cook, when he was Labour's Shadow Secretary of State: 'Once we have a Scottish Parliament handling health affairs it would not be possible for me to continue as Minister of Health, administering health in England.'[5]

While there has been some controversy about the appointment of Scottish ministers to largely English departments, the main focus of attention by those who claim the English are suffering injustice has been the voting of MPs on legislation. It is here that party-political arithmetic at Westminster has

Table 4.3 Written parliamentary questions to departments, by location of constituency

Department	1998–99 session %				2002–3 session %			
	Eng	Scot	Wal	NI	Eng	Scot	Wal	NI
Health	95	2	3	0	89	6	4	1
Education	96	2	2	0	95	3	2	0
Agriculture, Fisheries and Food[a]	91	3	6	0	–	–	–	–
Environment, Food and Rural Affairs[b]	–	–	–	–	89	6	5	1
Environment, Transport and Regions[a]	94	3	3	0	–	–	–	–
Transport[b]	–	–	–	–	89	8	3	1
Deputy Prime Minister[b]	–	–	–	–	96	2	2	0
Culture, Media and Sport	95	3	2	0	89	6	3	1
Home Office	96	1	3	0	91	5	4	1
Trade and Industry	88	4	8	0	81	12	7	1
Treasury	85	6	9	1	88	7	4	1
Cabinet Office	92	4	4	0	94	5	1	0
Foreign Office	87	7	6	1	78	13	8	1
Prime Minister	84	14	2	0	78	5	14	3
Defence	87	8	5	0	84	9	6	1
Lord Chancellor's Department[a]	96	1	3	0	91	3	4	2
Scottish Office/Scotland Office[c]	35	64	1	0	51	48	1	0
Welsh Office/Wales Office[d]	33	3	64	0	60	5	35	1
Northern Ireland Office	58	4	2	35	19	2	2	77
Constitutional Affairs[b]	–	–	–	–	87	5	6	3
Social Security/Work and Pensions	90	6	4	0	84	12	3	0
International Development	88	6	5	1	76	18	5	1
Leader of the House	95	2	3	0	90	4	6	0
Law Officers	94	2	4	0	92	2	6	0
Advocate General	–	–	–	–	60	40	0	0
Total	86	6	6	1	86	6	6	1

Notes: [a] 1998–99 session only; [b] 2002–3 session only; [c] Scottish Office renamed Scotland Office in 1999; [d] Welsh Office renamed Wales Office in 1999.
Source: House of Commons Library POLIS system.

potentially the greatest impact on policy outcomes, and in close votes attention focuses on the behaviour of specific MPs. Since devolution there has been heightened interest in the behaviour of Scottish MPs, in particular, and their participation in votes where legislation directly affects only England or England and Wales. The same controversy applies potentially to Welsh MPs and their involvement in legislation that only affects England, but those cases are both less clear-cut and much less common.

This issue was raised as an objection during the devolution debates in the 1970s by the then MP for West Lothian Tam Dalyell. He asked how it could be correct that, with a Scottish Parliament in place, Scottish MPs could continue to vote on issues such as education in England when they could no longer vote on education in Scotland. This conundrum came to be known as the West Lothian Question. By raising the issue in connection with devolution Dalyell obscured the issue (discussed in the next section) that the distinct system of administration in Scotland meant that English MPs had long voted on bills that affected only Scotland, while Scottish MPs had voted on legislation that would apply only in England and Wales. His objection was thus essentially that the reciprocity of the old system was to be lost. Devolution would remove from English MPs the right to do something questionable, but would do nothing to apply the same strictures to the Scots.

When the 1997 Labour Government implemented devolution the West Lothian Question re-emerged in debates.[6] However, the anomaly created was not expected to surface seriously for some time. The real difficulty would occur if Scots' votes were to make a difference to legislative outcomes, and this appeared unlikely given the parliamentary arithmetic. Only 72 MPs represented Scottish constituencies, while Labour had a parliamentary majority of 177. As well as having won an overwhelming majority of seats in Scotland and Wales, Labour also held a comfortable majority in England (127 seats in 1997, see table 4.4). With the politics of Scotland, Wales and England aligned, tensions seemed unlikely to occur.

There have been a number of controversies at Westminster since 1997, however, which have brought the West Lothian Question to the fore. These have occurred in two sets of circumstances: first, when MPs were not subject to a party whip and instead participated in free votes; second, when there have been sizeable rebellions in Labour's ranks which could have resulted in Government defeats.

One of the first issues on which the question was raised was the Government's legislation to control hunting with dogs. The 1997 Labour manifesto had promised a parliamentary decision on the matter, which would be taken by a free vote. This was not reached until 2000, by which time responsibility for the regulation of hunting in Scotland had been devolved to the Scottish Parliament. Hence Conservative MP David Lidington asked the Home Secretary whether he would 'urge all honourable members representing Scottish constituencies at Westminster to refrain from taking part in debates and votes on the Bill?'[7] The Government was dismissive of this objection, but as the vote approached the newspapers took some interest. In the event, the House of Commons voted overwhelmingly for a total ban on hunting with dogs. Although 23 Scottish MPs took part in the division their participation made scant difference to the 373 to 158 outcome.[8]

Table 4.4 Election results 1945–2001 in UK and England

	UK						England					
Election	Con	Lab	Lib	Other	Total	Govt	Con	Lab	Lib	Other	Total	Majority[a]
1945[b]	210	393	12	35	640	Lab	167	331	5	7	510	Lab
1950	298	315	9	3	625	Lab	253	251	2	0	506	(**Con**)
1951	321	295	6	3	625	Con	271	233	2	0	506	Con
1955	345	277	6	2	630	Con	293	216	2	0	511	Con
1959	365	258	6	1	630	Con	315	193	3	0	511	Con
1964	304	317	9	0	630	Lab	262	246	3	0	511	**Con**
1966	253	364	12	1	630	Lab	219	286	6	0	511	Lab
1970	330	288	6	6	630	Con	292	217	2	0	511	Con
1974 Feb	297	301	14	23	635	Lab	268	237	9	2	516	**Con**
1974 Oct	277	319	13	26	635	Lab	253	255	8	0	516	(Lab)
1979	339	269	11	14	635	Con	306	203	7	0	516	Con
1983	397	209	23	21	650	Con	362	148	13	0	523	Con
1987	376	229	22	23	650	Con	358	155	10	0	523	Con
1992	336	271	20	24	651	Con	319	195	10	0	524	Con
1997	165	418	46	30	659	Lab	165	328	34	2	529	Lab
2001	166	412	52	29	659	Lab	165	323	40	1	529	Lab

Notes: [a] Entries in brackets denote largest party, but no overall majority. Entries in bold denote party differs from UK governing party; [b] 1945 figures for England exclude university seats.
Source: Rallings and Thrasher (2001), BBC website.

Other controversies have arisen when the Government has introduced bills which do not have the full support of its own backbenchers. On these issues the West Lothian Question, which was normally an objection raised by Conservative MPs, also gave rise to concerns among Labour members, especially those representing English constituencies. In July 2000 Labour backbencher Bob Marshall-Andrews wrote to Scottish members urging them to refrain from voting on the Criminal Justice (Mode of Trial) Bill, which sought to limit access to jury trials, as these provisions would not apply in Scotland. He and other Labour rebels hoped to defeat the Bill, which had already been rejected by the House of Lords. However, as the rebellion at third reading attracted only 27 Labour members and the Bill passed by 282 votes to 199, the 34 Scottish members who voted in favour of it were, once again, not crucial to the outcome.[9]

In the 2001 Parliament the propensity of Labour members to rebel, however, rose.[10] Although Labour's majority remained high at 165, rebellions brought the Government close to defeat on a number of occasions. In two cases these rebellions related to bills which were limited in their territorial application to England, excluding Scotland and, arguably, Wales. This gave the

West Lothian Question a new salience which had not existed in Labour's first term.

The subject of the first such rebellion was the Government's Health and Social Care (Community Health and Standards) Bill in 2003, which sought to implement proposals for foundation hospitals, that were highly controversial in Labour ranks. The changes would not apply in Scotland, where health is devolved, and although the Bill covered 'England and Wales' the specific provisions for foundation hospitals were said not to apply to Wales, and had been overtly rejected by the Welsh Assembly.[11] Former Health Secretary Frank Dobson and Chair of the Health Select Committee David Hinchchliffe led the Labour revolt. Concerned that the policy might scrape through on the votes of loyal Scottish MPs, Dobson argued that Scottish members should absent themselves from the vote on the Bill's third reading on 8 July.[12] In this claim he was supported by the Conservatives, who opposed the Bill, and by elements of the press, particularly in Scotland. At report stage an amendment tabled by David Hinchchliffe sought to remove the foundation hospital provisions from the Bill. The amendment fell, by 286 votes to 251. However, on the votes of English MPs alone it would have passed, by 218 to 217 – a fact that was widely noted. Later, when the Bill returned from the House of Lords on 19 November, the Government's majority was cut further, to just 17, with 62 Labour members voting against on the crucial amendment. On this occasion the Government would have lost by seventeen votes if only English MPs had voted.[13] As a result Tim Yeo, Conservative Shadow Secretary of State for Health and Education, declared the outcome a 'constitutional outrage'.[14]

A similar situation developed with respect to the Government's Higher Education Bill in January 2004, which sought to implement controversial student 'top-up fees'. Again the main provisions of this Bill would not apply in Scotland, which has a separate higher education system under the control of the Scottish Parliament. The bill also allowed for tuition fees to be introduced in Welsh universities but left the decision to do so to the Welsh Assembly, which had rejected the plan. At the second reading 73 Labour rebels voted against, but the Bill passed by 316 to 311. If only English and Welsh members had voted, it would have fallen by six votes.[15]

These rebellions therefore brought the issue of Scots MPs voting on non-Scottish legislation into the public eye unexpectedly early; already illustrating the likely direction of debates if a future Labour Government had a smaller majority. As the largest group, and seen as very loyal to the Government, the Scots have been the main focus of attention, although some tensions have also arisen with respect to the involvement on English-only matters of Welsh and Northern Irish MPs. At times of controversial votes the Conservative Opposition has been particularly critical of Scottish MPs' involvement and, along with the protests of some Labour rebels, this has attracted the interest of the press. For example, following the failure of the first foundation hospitals rebellion the *Scotsman* suggested that the 'English public would be outraged'.[16] Following the second vote the *Daily Mail* front-page headline suggested that the Government had been 'humiliated': 'Blair Rocked As Hospitals Bill Is Saved by Scots MPs'.[17] Such interest on the part of the press is potentially important in turning the issue into one of wider public debate.

The Conservative Party's response is to suggest a policy of 'English votes on English laws', whereby MPs from outside of England are formally barred from voting on English matters. Although this has not proved to be a high-salience issue, the proposal appears to have public support. As John Curtice reports in chapter 6 of this volume, by 2003 some 60 per cent of English people and 48 per cent of Scots believed that 'Scottish MPs should no longer be allowed to vote on English legislation'. Even higher support was found in a YouGov poll for the *Daily Telegraph* in February 2004, showing that 66 per cent of English and 78 per cent of Scottish voters favoured limitations on the voting rights of Scottish MPs.[18]

Those protests have, however, found little sympathy among most Labour MPs, and there is scant evidence of Scottish MPs changing their behaviour. Analysis of voting in the 2001–2 Parliament shows that Scottish MPs voted on average on 61.2 per cent of legislation not covering Scotland – only marginally below their turnout of 70.1 per cent on bills that did apply to Scotland.[19] A survey of MPs in 2004 found that 92.5 per cent of Conservative members believed that Scottish and Northern Irish members should be excluded from voting on legislation affecting only England and Wales; but just 8 per cent of Labour members agreed.[20] The position of the Government, which potentially has much to lose from restrictions on so loyal a body of MPs, has been resolute opposition to change. Tony Blair, speaking to the House of Commons Liaison Committee in July 2003 said: 'we have a constitutional settlement and part of that constitutional settlement is that you do not have two classes of member . . . Yes, it is true that Scottish MPs will vote on exclusively English issues but there should not be two classes of MP.'[21]

The Conservatives potentially have a strong party-political interest in establishing limits on the behaviour of Scottish (and Welsh) MPs. The party has not won a majority in Scotland since 1955, and in Wales has not done so since 1841.[22] Election results in Scotland, Wales and Northern Ireland since 1945 are shown in table 4.5. At times, however, the Conservatives have had a majority among English MPs when Labour has been in government nationally, as shown in table 4.4 – in 1964 and in February 1974 – while Labour

Table 4.5 Election results 1945–2001 in Wales, Scotland and Northern Ireland

	Wales							Scotland							Northern Ireland[a]					
Election	Con	Lab	Lib	PC	Other	Total	Maj[a]	Con	Lab	Lib	SNP	Other	Total	Maj[a]	ConU[c]	U[d]	N[e]	Other	Total	Maj[a]
1945[b]	4	25	6	0	0	35	Lab	27	37	0	0	7	71	Lab	8		2	2	12	**ConU**
1950	4	27	5	0	0	36	Lab	31	37	2	0	1	71	Lab	10		2	0	12	**ConU**
1951	6	27	3	0	0	36	**Lab**	35	35	1	0	0	71	NOC	9		2	1	12	ConU
1955	6	27	3	0	0	36	**Lab**	36	34	1	0	0	71	Con	10		2	0	12	ConU
1959	7	27	2	0	0	36	**Lab**	31	38	1	0	1	71	**Lab**	12		0	0	12	ConU
1964	6	28	2	0	0	36	Lab	24	43	4	0	0	71	Lab	12		0	0	12	**ConU**
1966	3	32	1	0	0	36	Lab	20	46	5	0	0	71	Lab	11		0	1	12	**ConU**
1970	7	27	1	0	1	36	**Lab**	23	44	3	1	0	71	**Lab**	8		0	4	12	ConU
1974 Feb	8	24	2	2	0	36	Lab	21	40	3	7	0	71	Lab		11	1	0	12	**Other**
1974 Oct	8	23	2	3	0	36	Lab	16	41	3	11	0	71	Lab		10	1	1	12	**Other**
1979	11	22	1	2	0	36	**Lab**	22	44	3	2	0	71	**Lab**		10	1	1	12	**Other**
1983	14	20	2	2	0	38	**Lab**	21	41	8	2	0	72	**Lab**		15	2	0	17	**Other**
1987	8	24	3	3	0	38	**Lab**	10	50	9	3	0	72	**Lab**		13	4	0	17	**Other**
1992	6	27	1	4	0	38	**Lab**	11	49	9	3	0	72	**Lab**		13	4	0	17	**Other**
1997	0	34	2	4	0	40	Lab	0	56	10	6	0	72	Lab		13	5	0	18	**Other**
2001	0	34	2	4	0	40	Lab	1	55	10	6	0	72	Lab		11	8	0	18	**Other**

Notes: [a] bold denotes a party that differs from UK governing party; [b] 1945 figures exclude university seats; [c] Unionist MPs returned to Westminster were formally linked to the Conservative and Unionist Party, taking the Conservative whip in Parliament prior to the 1974 election; [d] U denotes parties post 1974 defining themselves as Unionist; N denotes parties from the nationalist/republican spectrum.

Source: Rallings and Thrasher 2001; BBC website.

had no overall majority in England in October 1974. The question of who votes on legislation affecting only England would take on a new political dimension if a future Labour Government were again dependent on Scottish votes to secure all of its legislation, and controversies since 1997 have already set this issue up as a potential inter-party battleground.

In order to analyse the likely impact of such a situation, as well as how new arrangements for England at Westminster might develop, it is to historical examples that we now turn. We then return at the end of the chapter to consider what these precedents might tell us about the future.

Historical precedents

A brief look at history shows that the concerns currently troubling policy makers are far from new. Indeed with respect to the central controversy, Brigid Hadfield has commented that only 'those with short memories called this the "West Lothian Question"' (1989: 89). Such concerns can be traced back at least as far as the Home Rule debates of the late nineteenth century, while more general territorial tensions between the Scots and English at Westminster are as old as the Act of Union itself. In this section we look briefly at some of the tensions that have emerged with respect to the four different nations of the UK.

In analysing these examples it is useful to distinguish between three factors which have fuelled territorial tensions. These may also help us to better understand the anomalies that face us today. Two of these factors are strictly constitutional, while the third is political.

- First, tensions between representatives of different territories have been heightened where there have been distinct territorial bills at Westminster, which is most likely where the territories are governed by distinct bodies of law. This situation has applied in Scotland since the Union. It also applied to the whole of Ireland until 1920, and (to greater or lesser extents) to Northern Ireland thereafter. Over these periods there have been Scottish bills and Northern Irish bills, alongside bills applicable only in England and Wales, as well as others affecting the UK as a whole. This makes more transparent the involvement of some MPs in voting on matters that do not concern their constituents.
- Second, problems have arisen where there has been legislative devolution in one or other part of the UK, resulting in MPs sitting at Westminster for areas where parliament no longer controls some policy areas. Concerns about the consequences of such arrangements were raised

during the early Home Rule debates, applied during the period of the
Stormont Parliament in Northern Ireland, and have arisen again now
with respect to the Scottish Parliament, and to a lesser extent the Welsh
Assembly.

- Third, aggravation is most likely when the political balance of representation in one nation differs from that in the UK as a whole, resulting in
  that nation being subject to a Government in Westminster which does not
  reflect its political views. As tables 4.4 and 4.5 show, this applied in Wales
  during all periods of Conservative government after 1945, in Scotland
  during all periods of Conservative government after 1959, in Northern
  Ireland during all periods of Labour rule, and in England in 1964 and
  1974. The matter may come to concern the UK as a whole, rather than
  just the territory concerned, if the representatives of that territory are
  numerous enough to routinely influence the outcome of parliamentary
  votes.

Ireland

Ireland and, after 1921, Northern Ireland provide many of the closest par-
allels to the situation facing us today. Few of the anomalies currently perplex-
ing politicians were not fully aired during the Home Rule debates of
1885–1920. Ireland had been formally part of the Union since 1800, at which
time its Parliament was dissolved and Irish members took seats at Westminster.
At the 1885 election, following a widening of the franchise, 85 of the 103
Irish seats were won by nationalists who supported Irish Home Rule. This
provoked immediate territorial tensions, of the third kind suggested above,
heightened by the fact that the Irish representatives held the balance of power
in the House of Commons. Home Rule thus became a central political issue,
as the support of this group was needed to maintain a government.[23]

Throughout the Home Rule debates the issue of Irish representation at
Westminster was central. The schemes proposed would create a body in
Ireland with extensive legislative power. Thus at least 2 of the 3 criteria indicated above potentially would be met. The Irish held the balance of power in
the Commons not only in 1885 but again in 1892 and after both elections in
1910, and during those periods formed alliances with the Liberals. Hence (as
Iain McLean details in his chapter in this volume) the Conservatives were particularly exercised by the prospect of their continued presence, which would
appear indefensible if a new Irish legislature was created. The first Home Rule
Bill in 1886 thus sought to exclude Irish MPs from Westminster. But this
created new anomalies, as the Irish would continue to be taxed by London
(which would also retain control over other 'imperial' matters such as

defence) without representation. While far from the only issue of contention, this difficulty added to opposition to the Bill.

The 1893 Home Rule Bill thus sought instead to deal with the problem by implementing a compromise known as the 'in and out' solution, which Gladstone had previously rejected as unworkable. The proposal, similar to that supported by those now proposing 'English votes on English laws', would have retained Irish members but forbidden them to 'deliberate or vote on' any issue not directly affecting Ireland. This clause, however, was removed from the Bill at its committee stage (Hadfield 1989). The final version of the Bill included a different compromise, to reduce the number of Irish seats. As was pointed out to Gladstone, this could only ameliorate, rather than deal with, the problem. In 1889 he commented that 'the real problem' with Home Rule remained 'determining the particular form in which an Irish representation may have to be retained at Westminster' (quoted in Bogdanor 2001: 34). In the end the second Home Rule Bill also failed. The anomaly – at least with respect to representation of the south of Ireland – disappeared as a result of Irish independence.[24]

While the South gained its independence, however, the conundrum at Westminster continued to apply with respect to representation of the North. In 1921 a Northern Ireland legislature (commonly known as 'Stormont') with wide-ranging powers was created. At the same time, Northern Irish MPs would continue to sit at Westminster, albeit with a reduced representation of thirteen seats.[25] The situation with respect to Northern Ireland thus met the second of the key conditions identified above – the presence of a devolved institution – meaning that Northern Irish members could vote for all matters at Westminster, while many matters in Northern Ireland were devolved. This was the first time Westminster had faced such a situation. At times during this period the third condition was also met, in that the political balance of the Northern Irish seats conflicted with that of the UK Government when Labour was in power. As the number of Northern Irish seats was small this was of limited importance during the first post-war Labour Governments. However, it became more salient under the narrow majorities in the 1960s and 1970s.

In 1964 the first Wilson Government was elected with a majority of just four, and the votes of the Northern Irish MPs became a constant source of aggravation. A particular issue of dispute was the Government's plans for nationalisation of the steel industry. As Wilson recorded in his memoirs, 'the Conservatives could hold up our legislation only because they could command the votes of their twelve Ulster unionist allies, voting on steel policy in Great Britain even though the measure would not affect Northern Ireland' (1971: 178). As a result Wilson became 'adamant he would address this anomaly' (Knox 2000: 162). He therefore turned to the familiar 'in and out' solution, writing in 1966:

> We ought to make up our minds about the idea which I aired last Spring, that Northern Ireland MPs should not have the right to vote in the House of Commons on purely domestic matters affecting Great Britain, where the Stormont Parliament has exclusive jurisdiction on the same subject in relation to Northern Ireland. (Letter from Wilson to the Lord President, quoted in Knox 2000: 162)

This proposal was passed to the Attorney General, but he considered it unworkable (Knox 2000). It was also met with hostility by the Conservative Party. The then Shadow Home Secretary Peter Thorneycroft responded in remarkably similar terms to those taken by the current Government, requesting that the Wilson Government 'make it absolutely clear that that kind of nonsense does not form any part of the Government's thinking, that every Member of the House of Commons is equal with every other Member of the House of Commons, and that all of us will speak on all subjects' (quoted in Bogdanor 2001: 230).[26] Having won a greatly increased majority in the election of 1966, Wilson let the matter drop.

Northern Irish MPs were once again pivotal in the Parliaments of 1974, though by that time in changed circumstances. The Stormont Parliament was prorogued in 1972, and by May 1974 direct rule for Northern Ireland had been introduced. All matters relating to Northern Ireland were therefore now to be decided at the UK level. Certain Northern Ireland matters had never been devolved and continued to be dealt with through Northern Ireland bills at Westminster. Under the Northern Ireland Act (1974) matters that had previously been devolved were to be implemented through Orders in Council.[27] Although the second condition for territorial tension was no longer met, there were now new anomalies. While questions might be raised about Northern Irish involvement in English, Welsh and Scottish legislation, MPs from other areas continued to be involved in Northern Irish bills while much other Northern Irish business received little parliamentary scrutiny at all.

Following the election of February 1974, Conservative Prime Minister Edward Heath sought to hold on to power by forming a coalition. As well as talking to the Liberals as potential partners he approached some of the Northern Irish Unionists (who had severed their formal links to the Conservative Party due to serious policy differences). Alan Clark reports how 'Heath offered the Conservative whip . . . to seven of the Unionists, excluding the four Paisleyites' (1997: 439). However, the Unionists refused to co-operate. Had these manoeuvres succeeded, controversies would almost certainly have flared up again on the Labour side about a government in London dependent on Northern Irish votes. Instead the Conservatives did not face this problem until the latter days of the Major Government, in the 1990s, when cross-party support for peace negotiations made any Labour protests muted.

Scotland

Scotland offers a contrasting example. Here there was no separate legislative assembly until 1999. However, the two other criteria for creating territorial tensions at Westminster have long applied.

The Union of the Crowns in 1603, and then the Acts of Union in 1707, preserved Scotland's separate legal system and body of statute law. The power to legislate for Scotland passed to the Westminster Parliament, but any alterations in law started from a distinctly Scottish base. In the three centuries that followed there was a convergence, but Scotland retained many distinct traditions, including its system of courts, local government and education. Consequently distinct Scottish acts continued to be passed at Westminster, while many other acts either included separate provisions for Scotland or applied to England and Wales alone.

From the start there were territorial tensions, and in the early years of the Union both the Scots and the English were cautious about proposing Scottish legislation at Westminster, for fear that the more numerous English would impose their will. As Innes reports: 'The charge that the English were presuming to determine what was good for the Scots or the Irish was always potentially an inflammatory charge. So, for the Westminster Parliament to legislate for three kingdoms was a distinctively difficult business' (2003: 18). She shows that, more than a century after the Union, much legislation remained territorially distinct – in the period 1817–29 around 1,850 public and general acts were passed, of which only around 1,000 were UK- or Britain-wide, with around 300 applying only in England and Wales, 100 only in Scotland and the remainder only in Ireland. Within these areas 'the preponderant local view did not always prevail and this was potentially a source of tension between the nation legislated for, and Westminster' (*ibid.*: 34–5).

The inability of Scots members to control Scottish affairs through Westminster fuelled calls for devolution. Yet on the nine occasions between 1893 and 1977 when the issue of establishing a separate parliament for Scotland was voted on in the House of Commons, a majority of Scottish MPs voted in favour, only to see the proposition defeated by the votes of non-Scottish MPs (Miller 1981).

As with Northern Ireland, some territorial tensions emerged during the Wilson Governments in the 1960s. In 1969 the Conservatives opposed Labour's abolition of school fees in Scotland, despite the Government's overwhelming majority north of the border. Asked whether it was not inappropriate to use English votes in the attempt to defeat the policy, Conservative spokesman Michael Noble responded: 'I do not find it an atom embarrassing to have to ask my English colleagues to come to the House this evening and vote against the clause' (quoted in Keating 1975: 33).[28] Such tensions also applied in reverse. For example, many Scots did not refrain from voting on Leo Abse's 1966 Private Member's Bill on homosexual law reform, although it had – specifically in order to avoid their opposition – been drafted to apply only in England and Wales (Keating 1975).

Conflicting majorities between Scotland and the UK as a whole have also been frequent. Scotland voted consistently Liberal from 1832 to 1885, and has voted consistently Labour since 1959, thus bringing it into conflict with all Conservative Governments during those periods (Rallings and Thrasher 2001). On many occasions distinctly Scottish law has therefore been decided by a hostile political majority. Although this was often handled with sensitivity, hostilities reached their height under the Thatcher Governments. The most famous example relates to the piloting of the poll tax in Scotland before it was introduced in England and Wales. The Abolition of Domestic Rates (etc.) Scotland Bill was introduced into Parliament in 1986, against protests from Scotland where Labour held 41 out of 72 parliamentary seats. Donald Dewar, Shadow Scottish Secretary, derided the Conservative Government for its determination to 'lumber us with and penalise us by a scheme that is without friends or supporters in Scotland'.[29] However, Malcolm Rifkind, the Scottish Secretary, rejected the idea that the Conservative Government did not have a mandate with which to pursue its policy in Scotland. He argued that, since 'no Labour government bar one has had a majority in England since 1951 – that corresponds to the position of the Conservative Party in Scotland – the Hon. Gentleman must apply his new, curious constitutional principle throughout the spectrum of government or cease to use such arguments'.[30]

The particular legal position of Scotland always resulted in a certain separation between Scottish MPs and their colleagues south of the border. As Kellas noted (1975: 78): 'Scottish MPs are a distinct group in the House of Commons. They have their own Bills to discuss; their own committees to sit on; and their own ministers to question. These activities set them apart from other members, who do not share these duties or interests.' The Scottish Grand Committee was established in 1907 and took the second reading of uncontroversial Scottish bills.[31] In 1957 a Scottish standing committee was created (and joined by another in 1962) to take the committee stage of such bills. Finally, the Select Committee on Scottish Affairs was created in 1969 – a decade before its Welsh counterpart and the other departmental committees.

Given the extent to which Scottish business at Westminster was treated separately, the involvement of Scottish MPs in other business in the House has always been limited, and increasingly so as distinct Scottish forums have developed. Thus, while some departments have long been less involved in Scottish matters, particularly as the Scottish Office grew in influence, so Scottish members have long been almost absent from parliamentary committees dealing with the business of those departments. As already noted, such absence is not simply a result of devolution: Keating found that when the Select Committee on Agriculture was first created, in 1967, its members included no Scottish MPs. Two Scots were later added, however, 'for their interest in the formation of agricultural policy at the UK level, which involves an interplay between the MAFF and the Scottish Office' (1975: 251). Similarly Scottish MPs' representation on legislative standing committees was generally determined by whether or not there was a Scottish interest. Keating (*ibid.*) shows that of 653 bills considered by standing committees between 1945 and 1970 (excluding purely Scottish bills), 130 applied only to England and Wales and 8 to England alone. Of the 3,900 members who served on the committees considering those bills, just 55 (1.4 per cent) represented Scottish constituencies.

Wales

In Wales the situation is different again. Here there was no devolved institution until 1999 and, unlike in Scotland, the opportunity for tensions to arise from a separate legal system did not apply. England and Wales form one legal jurisdiction and Welsh bills, although not unheard of, have been rare. The main tension with respect to Wales has thus been the consistent left-wing majority (initially Liberal, latterly Labour) among Welsh MPs since 1865. This meant that Wales was frequently governed by a majority in London that did not match its own political desires, which fed support among many for devolution. In contrast, the involvement of Welsh MPs in decision-making was rarely controversial, as most bills that applied to England would also apply to Wales.

On some Wales-only issues, or issues that primarily affect Wales, controversies have occurred. The most protracted example concerned the push for the disestablishment of the Anglican Church of Wales throughout the period from 1880 to 1914. Welsh aspirations to see the removal of the 'alien church' faced prolonged opposition from English Conservatives both in the Commons and the Lords. Disestablishment was consistently supported by a majority of Welsh MPs when it was voted on in the Commons, with Welsh MPs pointing to the numerical support for nonconformity among the Welsh electorate, who consistently voted in favour of the cause.[32] Yet this did not stop the Conservative Party, which 'made clear its determination to fight the bill hard at every stage', and whose members in the Lords twice rejected the third Welsh Disestablishment Bill (Morgan 1991: 263). Morgan shows how part of the Conservative opposition rested on their claims that 'Wales had "no separate national existence" and could not therefore receive separate legislation.' (*ibid*.: 146)

Prior to establishment of the new Welsh Assembly in 1999, various concessions had been made to the desire for separate Welsh government, both in Whitehall and at Westminster. Following pressure for Welsh representation during the Home Rule debates it was agreed in 1907 that a parliamentary committee made up of Welsh members should be established to consider the committee stage of Welsh legislation. However, the committee 'had very little significance' as there were so few such bills (Jones and Wilford 1986: 6). In 1960 the Welsh Grand Committee was established to consider more general Welsh business. The Welsh Office and the post of Secretary of State for Wales were created in 1964, and responsibility for overseeing their work passed to the new Select Committee on Welsh Affairs in 1979. The Conservatives, while maintaining these arrangements, frequently had difficulties staffing them given their weakness in Welsh constituencies. As Bogdanor (2001) notes, only one Conservative Secretary of State for Wales has ever sat for a Welsh constituency.

England

Even more than Wales, England has never had a distinct legal identity at Westminster. As Keating's exhaustive study of the period 1945–70 indicates, there have been few bills relating exclusively to English business. This, combined with England's numerical dominance in the House of Commons, led to few pressures for exclusively English forums to mirror those created for Scotland, Wales and Northern Ireland. Where England's government has been decided by the balance of votes in Scotland or Northern Ireland – as in the examples above – the same has applied to Wales, with which it shared its legal system.

There have, of course, been a small number of bills that affect England alone. McLean and McMillan have drawn attention to the defeat on Celtic votes of the 1928 *Book of Common Prayer*, despite Scottish MPs' awareness that their action was controversial. This, they suggest, may have been an example of the Celts achieving 'rough justice' in revenge for the repeated blocking by the English of Welsh disestablishment (this volume, chapter 2).

Prospects for resolving the English Question

A review of historical precedents is informative for various reasons, but above all it probably teaches us two things. First, that the conundra facing us now are not new, are not a result solely of devolution and are not easily solved. Second, that interest in these questions often has been driven more by instrumental political motives than by constitutional purism alone.

We see that territorial tensions at Westminster have existed at various times in the past as a result of the UK's history as a union state and have occurred particularly when one of three conditions were met. With respect to Scotland the opportunity for tension has long existed thanks to the separate Scottish legal system and the existence of distinct Scottish bills which have long made Scottish MPs at Westminster rather different from the rest. It would be a mistake to believe that their voting on bills relating only to England or to England and Wales is new, though they have long been largely absent from committees dealing with English business. Tensions rose, however, when, from the 1959 general election onwards, Labour enjoyed a majority among Scottish MPs, which clashed with the government majority at UK level for 27 of the succeeding 38 years. This became a major driver for devolution. With respect to Ireland, solutions were sought, without success, that would solve the conundrum of MPs at Westminster representing areas for which much business was devolved. The problem disappeared with respect to the South when it gained independence, but remained in lesser measure for the North. The presence of even a small number of Northern Irish MPs with full voting rights during the Stormont period was an irritant in the 1960s (thus indicating that a reduction in numbers of Scottish MPs might ameliorate present problems, but not fundamentally resolve them). All this having been said, the current tension with respect to Scotland is new in historical context in that it now meets all three criteria which have previously presented difficulties. It has a separate legal system, leaving Westminster passing many bills relating only to England and Wales, a powerful devolved institution and a political makeup at Westminster frequently different from that across the UK. The resulting difficulties therefore may come to exceed those experienced in the past.

In terms of solutions, history teaches us that the issue of MPs from one territory being involved in policy-making for another has tended to preoccupy most those disadvantaged in a party-political sense. Thus Harold Wilson was just as aggravated by the role of Northern Irish MPs in the 1960s as are contemporary Conservative politicians about the role of the Scots today. The response that he received from the Conservative front bench was remarkably similar to that given by Labour ministers now. At that time the Conservatives supported the Unionist principle – whereas their position now arguably does the reverse. To a large extent all parties can be seen to have behaved instrumentally in deciding how to respond to territorial dilemmas at Westminster. One of the surprising counter-examples to this partisan instrumentalism is the recent behaviour of Labour rebels, who have sought to restrict the involvement of Scottish MPs when this is clearly at odds with their party's longer term interests. Even here, though, it was short-term benefit in terms of policy outcomes that underlay their ostensibly constitutional objections.[33]

We therefore face a more serious English Question at Westminster than applied previously. Moreover, there are complications. Added to the conundra of the past is the fact that the nature of the devolution settlement makes this not simply an English Question, but frequently an *English and Welsh* Question, with boundaries often being blurred. In this section we briefly review, in the light of historical evidence as well as current contingencies, the prospects for resolving this question. In particular we consider four different proposals that have been put forward: 'English votes on English laws'; an English parliament; English regional government; or gradualist procedural change at Westminster.

English votes on English laws

Since the early 1990s the Conservative Party has expressed concerns about the impact of devolution on Westminster, and particularly about the problems of the West Lothian Question. In 1994 Prime Minister John Major suggested that if a Scottish Parliament were created, it

> surely would not be possible for Scottish MPs to come to Westminster and vote on policies affecting health and education in England, Wales and Northern Ireland. To do so would destroy the natural justice that balances our Parliamentary constitution. And what would be the position if some future Labour government had a majority of 10 seats at Westminster, but a majority of 30 seats in Scotland on which their national majority rested? And then suppose those 30 MPs could not vote on some issues at Westminster. What constitutional chaos would flow from that?[34]

Once devolution had happened, however, the party began to advocate just that outcome. The proposal of 'English votes on English laws' was made first in a speech by leader William Hague in July 1999, and went on to appear in the party's 2001 manifesto.[35] The Conservative leader from 2003 Michael Howard more recently took up the proposal and expanded on how it would be enacted. Under these arrangements the Speaker would be responsible for certifying bills as not applying to Scotland, and MPs representing Scottish constituencies would be required to abstain.[36] As already indicated, public opinion polls show that such a measure has support both north and south of the border.

There are, however, a number of intractable difficulties with this approach which account for its rejection by all previous authorities that have considered it. As already noted the suggestion was dismissed by the Attorney General in the 1960s, despite the Prime Minister's support; it was also considered unworkable by the Royal Commission on the Constitution (the 'Kilbrandon Commission') in 1973. Tam Dalyell, responsible for reviving the question in the 1970s, believed that such a solution would be 'indefensible' (1977: 250). Gladstone's attempts to implement the 'in and out' solution forced him to conclude that it 'passes the wit of man' (quoted in Bogdanor (2001: 30)).

Objections to the idea can be raised at three distinct levels: the technical, the political and the constitutional. The technical barriers begin with legislative drafting: there is often no clear demarcation line between bills that do, and do not, affect particular parts of the UK. Bills may include numerous clauses, some of which have application in one area and some in another. For illustration the 'territorial extent' clause of the 2004 Higher Education Bill is produced in box 4.1. Although the main provisions of the Bill would apply only in England and Wales, it also included clauses relating to Scotland and Northern Ireland. Indeed Westminster is legislating for Scotland more than had been envisaged under the 'Sewel' procedure, by which the Scottish Parliament allows Westminster to act on its behalf.[37] This increases the number of bills which include Scottish clauses. With respect to Wales, the Higher Education Bill included provisions to allow the Welsh Assembly to introduce top-up fees if it wished, although the Assembly at the time had rejected the proposals. Under an 'in and out' solution this could leave the position of Welsh MPs ambivalent.

Box 4.1 The territorial extent of the Higher Education Bill

(1) Subject to subsections (2) to (4), this Act extends to England and Wales only.
(2) The following provisions also extend to Scotland and Northern Ireland
    (a) Part 1,
    (b) section 42,
    (c) sections 43, 44, 47 and 48, and
    (d) this section and section 50.
(3) Subsections (1), (2) and (5) of section 39 also extend to Northern Ireland.
(4) Any amendment or repeal made by this Act has the same extent within the United Kingdom as the enactment to which it relates.

Source: Part 5 of the Higher Education Bill as introduced in the House of Commons on 8 January 2004.

Although all bills traditionally include a territorial extent clause, this does not necessarily give a clear indication of a bill's territorial *application*. As England and Wales comprise one legal jurisdiction, even those bills which in practice apply to only one of them – for example the Regional Assemblies (Preparations) Bill and the Health (Wales) Bill in the 2002–3 session – have a technical extent of England and Wales. Therefore, to be clear how voting should be restricted, some new form of certification (as the Conservatives have suggested) would be required. However, even this is not a straightforward matter.

In a united kingdom there are inevitably many cross-border issues. As the Kilbrandon Commission suggested:

> Ability to vote could not depend simply on whether the matter at issue related to a reserved or transferred subject. Any issue at Westminster involving expenditure of public money is of concern to all parts of the United Kingdom since it may directly affect the level of taxation and indirectly influence the level of a region's own expenditure.[38]

This is particularly the case given that the calculation of the Scottish block grant is based on overall UK spending. In many cases there may also be overt interests, such as where an MP who represents an area near a border has constituents using services on the other side of that border. Returning to the example of the Health and Social Care Act, Part 1, Clause 1(1) stated: 'An NHS foundation trust is a public benefit corporation which is authorised under this Part to provide goods and services for the purposes of the health service in England.' However, the explanatory notes to the Act explicitly acknowledged that this may involve providing health care in Wales, and the Act thus allowed that constituencies for representation on trust boards may include areas the other side of the Welsh border. Under an 'in and out' arrangement there is thus no clear conclusion to be drawn as to whether Welsh MPs should participate in this area of policy.

In addition to these two direct effects on areas technically not covered by a bill, there may also be indirect effects through policy transfer from one part of the UK to another. For all of these reasons many Scottish MPs have argued that they have interests in English and Welsh legislation. The SNP, which has a policy of not voting on England-only legislation – the party defines it as legislation that has no 'direct or indirect legislative or financial impact on Scotland, Wales or Northern Ireland' (SNP 2003) – did however vote against the foundation hospital and higher education proposals, citing both the funding implications and a belief that these policies would have an adverse effect on the Scots. Tam Dalyell himself, having followed a self-denying ordinance on non-Scottish legislation since 1999, voted on the 2004 Higher Education Bill because of the implications for higher education in Scotland.

Robin Cook, having once ruled himself out as a future Secretary of State for Health, voted on foundation hospitals in 2003.

In addition to technical barriers there are political barriers to the 'in and out' solution. At one level, even if it proved technically possible to isolate clauses that affected one part of the UK or another, this would lead to significantly more votes, with complex whipping arrangements that would almost certainly lead to parliamentary confusion. As one Scottish MP has quipped, it would result in MPs being required to do 'legislative hokey-cokey' on different clauses of bills.[39] There are other political barriers that make this situation unlikely. While pressure for action comes from Conservatives in England, and from the right-wing Scottish press, it is Labour members in Scotland who would be required to change their behaviour. Since 2001 the Conservatives have had one MP in Scotland, Peter Duncan, and he has sought to exclude himself from votes on non-Scottish matters. In some of the closest votes this must have been difficult, as his participation could be enough to defeat the Government. The Liberal Democrats, with more Scottish members, have maintained the right to participate in all matters at Westminster. Similarly, Conservative members have voted in opposition to both Wales-only bills debated at Westminster since 2001, despite the party's total lack of MPs in Wales.[40] This suggests that behaviour is driven more by pragmatism than by principle. After an election where Labour's majority was significantly reduced and the Conservatives had won additional Scottish seats, the opposition would face a difficult choice. The instrumentalism demonstrated to date by all parties suggests that their current position of abstaining on Scottish votes might not hold in practice. Conservative complaints would be certain to go unheeded by the Government, given that a reduced majority would make Labour even more defensive about change than it already is. But Conservative votes could be crucial in bringing about defeats of the Government. Meanwhile if the Conservatives gained a UK-wide majority they would have no immediate need to legislate to limit the role of Scottish MPs. They would face a difficult debate about the state of the Union if they chose to do so.

The biggest barriers of all to the 'in and out' solution are, however, constitutional. The solution gives rise to serious questions about the role of MPs as members of the UK Parliament and about the nature of the Union itself. The Union has traditionally been built on an equality whereby all members, as members of a single parliamentary body, can vote on all matters, regardless of the territorial extent of their application. Devolution ended the reciprocity of this arrangement with respect to English and Welsh members' ability to vote on many Scottish matters. Further unravelling of the principle would have profound consequences. Taken to its logical conclusion this would require only MPs from London to have voted on the Greater London

Authority Bill, or only MPs from the North East to be entitled to vote on the Bill to create a North-East regional assembly. Such a decision (which would amount to legislative devolution to the regions) should be taken consciously as a matter of constitutional principle, rather than be made a matter of short-term political convenience.

At present the tensions between England and the remainder of the UK are limited, as numerically at Westminster England remains a strongly Labour country. The votes of Scottish and Welsh members may be used to boost the Government's majority, but on most matters they are unlikely to have a decisive influence. A return to the arithmetic of 1964 or 1974, where Labour is unable to command a majority in Parliament without the support of Scottish (or Welsh) MPs, is a more difficult prospect. The Kilbrandon Commission noted: 'A further difficulty would arise if the exclusion of some Members of Parliament from participation in certain issues were to deprive the government of the day of its majority in the House of Commons' (Royal Commission 1973: 247). An 'in and out' solution in these circumstances would result in a government that could control the Commons on reserved matters, but not on matters that had been devolved to Scotland and/or Wales. As government depends on the confidence of the Commons this would readily lead to a constitutional crisis, likely to be averted only if Labour could form a coalition with majority support in England (and/or England and Wales), probably through the support of the Liberal Democrats.[41] But this would bring about a profound change to the culture of government in England. While the electors of Scotland and Wales chose devolution, the electors of England (and Wales) were not consulted on whether they wished to accept what amounts to a parliament within a parliament, frequently under coalition control when not controlled by the Conservatives. Again, a change of this magnitude would demand serious reflection, and require a strong indication of consent from the electors of England – which is so far not apparent.

An English parliament

Changes to voting conventions would therefore create in effect separate bodies operating within Westminster, subject to distinct coalitions to secure a voting majority. In these circumstances it would be far more transparent and democratic to create an English parliament, subject to its own elections. This would allow the English an direct choice over who controlled the executive on English matters, while a separate executive, elected for the purpose, would control the UK House of Commons. A complication, of course, is that the current settlement includes many English and Welsh matters. However, an 'English and Welsh parliament' would create new 'in and out' problems with respect to the Welsh. In order to avoid West Lothian-type problems altogether, an English parliament, a Welsh parliament and, presumably, a Northern Irish parliament would need to have equivalent power to that of the Scottish Parliament – creating a strongly devolved federal state.

The idea of 'home rule all round', with powerful parliaments in all four nations of the UK, was floated during the debates at the end of the nineteenth century. However, this would be a substantial constitutional change. As John Curtice shows in chapter 6 of this volume, an English parliament is a model which wins little support among the English. Despite the fledgling CEP, in 2003 just 16 per cent of those surveyed supported such a proposal, with these figures showing no upward trend. Among English MPs the level of support is even lower, at 13 per cent in 2004.[42] There are many good reasons to be sceptical about the idea, not least the overwhelming size of the parliament in comparison to its neighbours (representing 84 per cent of the UK population) and therefore its likely clout in the federation.

While the notion of 'English votes on English laws' appears to be winning popular support there is no sign yet that the English have an appetite for its logical corollary, an English parliament. As Lloyd George said when the proposal was made in 1918, 'unless you have got a substantial majority of the English representatives in favour of it, it is idle to attempt it' (quoted in Bogdanor 2001: 46). It remains to be seen whether anger at the role of Scots MPs will be enough to drive the English towards such a solution.

English regional government

The prospects seem rather brighter for English regional government, as described by Hazell, Tomaney and Sandford, respectively, in chapters 1, 8 and 9 of this volume. However, like an Englishparliament, regionalism cannot promise an end to tensions at Westminster unless this leads to symmetrical *devolution all round*. This would answer the problem of a federation with a dominant England, but that appears even less likely. The prospect of devolved government in the regions with legislative powers equivalent to those of the Scottish Parliament is, at best, very distant. Instead the bodies currently under discussion would have significantly weaker powers than the Welsh Assembly. If symmetry with Scotland is ever to be achieved, it seems likely to be the Welsh that first achieve it, with the English regions far behind.[43]

Procedural change

An alternative to the above proposals would be to try to manage the English Question through piecemeal procedural change to existing arrangements at

Westminster. Such options were considered by the House of Commons Procedure Committee in 1999 in its report on *The Procedural Consequences of Devolution*, and by a commission established by the Conservative Party in the same year chaired of Professor the Lord Norton of Louth (Procedure Committee 1999; Conservative Party 2000).[44]

The proposals put forward by these bodies drew inspiration from the arrangements that Westminster had put in place for Scotland and Wales prior to devolution. Both reports proposed that bills should be certified by the Speaker as applying to one or other part of the UK and, where these applied to England only, or to England and Wales, they would follow a new procedure. Under the Norton proposals an English/ English–Welsh bill would have its second reading in a Grand Committee, comprising all members from the relevant area. The committee stage would then be taken by a standing committee restricted to members from the area, and the final vote on the bill would be taken in the Commons chamber, with a convention that MPs from other areas did not vote. These proposals therefore amounted to 'English votes on English laws' and effectively an English parliament operating within Westminster.

The Procedure Committee recommendations were more cautious, and would have more closely mirrored the arrangements that existed prior to devolution for Scotland and Wales. However, they would have included all of the same tensions. Here the second reading of an English bill would normally be sent to an all-English second reading committee, smaller than that proposed by the Norton Commission. As previously existed with respect to referring Scottish bills to the Scottish Grand Committee, it was proposed that this reference could be easily prevented. An objection by twenty members in the Commons chamber was to be enough to block such a referral. Consequently the second reading of controversial bills – as used to be the case for Scotland – would remain mostly in the chamber. It was then proposed that the committee stage would be taken in a standing committee on which there were at least sixteen English members. Here the normal parliamentary convention that committees must mirror the political balance of the whole House would apply – thus if the balance of English members differed from that in the chamber as a whole, this would not be reflected in the committee's membership.[45] Furthermore under the Procedure Committee's proposals the final stages of the bill would be taken in the chamber itself, with no restrictions on which members could vote. These two sets of proposals demonstrate the central dilemma of creating territorial bodies within the Westminster Parliament, even if the earlier problems of defining the territorial extent of policy were able to be resolved. Such bodies must either reflect the UK balance of parties, thus perpetuating the

West Lothian issue, or create distinct English arrangements with competing majorities which would risk perpetually clashing with the Commons chamber.

A gentler solution could be to create less powerful English-only bodies, though these (like the Scottish and Welsh Grand Committees before them) would be open to criticism as 'talking shops'. The proposal made by the Norton Commission to create an English Grand Committee was not new: similar proposals had been considered in 1911 by Lloyd George as a means of balancing Home Rule for Ireland, but were not implemented (Hadfield 2003). Similarly, a proposal for 'Grand Councils' comprising English, Scottish and Welsh MPs to consider bills affecting each area came out of the Speaker's Conference on devolution in 1919 (Bogdanor 2001). Such an arrangement had existed for Scotland since 1907 (and intermittently since 1894) and was introduced for Wales in 1960, and later for Northern Ireland. However it was never duplicated for England. The only distinctly English committee created was the Standing Committee on Regional Affairs in 1975. However, although that committee extended membership to all MPs from English seats (plus not more than five others), it focused on matters affecting specific regions (Borthwick 1978). It did not have legislative responsibilities (though in practice, of course, there was, then as now, little English legislation) and could consider only 'matters' referred to it by a minister. With this rather unsatisfactory constitution the committee rapidly fell into disuse. It was revived after devolution in 2000 in even more limited form. The new incarnation has just thirteen core members, with other English members able to attend in a non-voting capacity. With a remit similar to that of the old committee, it has attracted little interest and has met only rarely.[46] To establish an English Grand Committee in its place would be to create a huge body, with some 529 members, which would itself resemble a parliament for England if it had any meaningful powers. However, without such powers it is difficult to see how a body of this kind could succeed. This seems to be recognised by English MPs. In our survey in 2004 only 29 per cent of them (and only 15 per cent of English Labour MPs) supported the creation of an English Grand Committee.[47]

Another possibility that has been floated at times, and was given serious consideration most recently by Harold Wilson in 1966, is committees to represent the English regions (Jones and Wilford 1986). Our survey in 2004 found that 41 per cent of English MPs, and a majority of English MPs representing Labour and the Liberal Democrats, would support the introduction of such committees.[48] These would be more manageable than an unwieldy English Grand Committee. While such committees could be genuinely useful for scrutinising the impact of government policy, and even bills, on particular regions, they would not of course meet the central concern over the rights of Scottish members to vote on English and Welsh legislation.

Conclusions

This chapter has demonstrated how it is at Westminster that the English Question has achieved greatest salience, and that this interest is likely only to grow. However, the problems raised are not new, and despite the application of many great minds over more than a century, no adequate solutions have been found. In some respects little at Westminster has changed – Scottish MPs are largely absent from the detailed consideration of English matters, as they were long before devolution. The Welsh and Northern Irish at Westminster (at least when devolution is suspended in Northern Ireland) have more ambivalent relationships with English affairs. However, the presence of a powerful devolved institution in Scotland is likely to fuel future tensions, particularly over voting on legislation, to which there are no simple answers.

The 'in and out', or 'English votes on English laws', option is one which holds little promise of practical implementation. A formalised English Parliament is, however, not yet desired and has its own practical difficulties. Regionalism is even less likely to provide an adequate solution. Piecemeal procedural change at Westminster remains a possibility. However, this would create frustrations of its own of a kind which, when applied to Scotland and Wales, would simply help fuel demands for devolution outside of Parliament. The final answer to the West Lothian Question may be, as Lord Chancellor Derry Irvine once suggested, 'to stop asking it'.[49] In a constitution full of anomalies, where a party may for example win more House of Commons seats than its rival on fewer votes, but still go on to govern undisturbed, such a solution might not be out of the question.[50] However Conservative interests – instrumental as history may show them to be – seem unlikely to allow this to happen.

As Robert Hazell discusses in chapter 11 of this book, a completely different solution to the English Question at Westminster would be a change to the voting system for the House of Commons. A more proportional system would reduce the over-representation of Labour in Scottish and Welsh seats and the probability of (as has applied in the past) over-representation for the Conservative Party in England. Thus the potential tensions for the nations at Westminster would, on many occasions, be diffused. Reform of the voting system remains one element of constitutional reform, however, that Labour has proved unwilling to implement and to which the Conservatives are almost universally opposed.

Notes

1 We thank the Leverhulme Trust for its support for the research underlying this chapter, funded through the 'Devolution and Westminster' project on the Nations and Regions Programme. We wish to thank also the ESRC, whose Devolution and Constitutional Change Programme has supported Guy Lodge's quarterly monitoring reports 'Devolution and the Centre'. We are also grateful to the many colleagues (particularly Michael Keating and Arthur Aughey) who have provided material, and to Brigid Hadfield and Vernon Bogdanor for commenting on an earlier draft.

2 As representation in the House of Lords is not geographically based, this chapter relates almost exclusively to the House of Commons. However, England is also clearly dominant in the Lords. For a discussion of the impact of devolution on debates about House of Lords reform see Lodge, Russell and Gay (2004).

3 While England is numerically dominant it should be noted that Scotland and Wales have long been over-represented in terms of the number of parliamentary seats they each have in the House of Commons (McLean 1995).

4 See Lodge (2003a: 22–3).

5 Hansard reference: House of Commons Debates (HCD) 18 June 2003, col. 361. Note, however that Bogdanor (2001) makes clear that this was not the official Labour line at the time and Cook's comments were not well-received by party leader Neil Kinnock.

6 See for instance the debate on the devolution White Papers: HCD, 31 July 1997, cols 473–4.

7 *Ibid.*, 12 June 2000, col. 642.

8 *Ibid.*, 20 December 2000, cols 464–9.

9 *Ibid.*, 25 July 2000, cols 938–9.

10 See Cowley and Stuart (2004), Cowley (2005).

11 See the explanatory notes published with the House of Lords Bill 94, Health and Social Care (Community Health and Standards) Bill, 9 July 2003.

12 See his article in the *Guardian*, 8 July 2003. For a full account of the debates surrounding the first foundation hospital vote, and a full territorial breakdown, see Lodge, Russell and Gay (2004).

13 If the votes of Welsh MPs had also been included the Government would have lost by four votes; for a breakdown of this vote see Lodge (2003b).

14 Hansard reference: HCD, 19 November 2003, col. 856.

15 For a breakdown of this vote see Lodge (2004). The vote on second reading was of course about the general principles of the Bill (some of which applied to Scotland), though the focus of the rebellion was on top-up fees. At report stage on 31 March 2004 there was an opportunity to vote on a rebel amendment specifically on fees. At this point there were 55 Labour rebels, and the amendment fell by 316 to 288. If only English members had voted, the amendment would have passed by 2 votes; however, if Welsh members were included, it would have fallen by 11 votes. In total 47 Scottish MPs voted with the Government (with 2 against) and 12 Northern Irish members voted against the Government. This episode attracted far less attention than the second-reading vote.

16 *Scotsman*, 9 July 2003.

17 *Daily Mail*, 20 November 2003.

18 *Daily Telegraph*, 16 February 2004.

19 This rather crude calculation uses the 'territorial extent' clause of each bill to determine whether or not it applies to Scotland, and counts all 'Sewel motion' bills as applying to Scotland. For a discussion of the technical difficulties of such calculations see the final section of the chapter.

20 Leverhulme–ESRC-funded survey by the Constitution Unit. For the Conservatives $n = 57$, for Labour $n = 107$. The equivalent survey in 2002 found support for the proposition among 79 per cent of Conservative MPs, suggesting that attitudes are hardening.

21 Liaison Committee, Evidence Presented by the Rt Hon. Tony Blair MP, Prime Minister, on Tuesday 8 July 2003, HC 334–ii, Q281.

22 The Conservatives did win a majority in Wales in 1859 but this was dependent on the support of the Liberal Conservatives (Rallings and Thrasher 2001).

23 See Bogdanor (2001) and McLean (2001).

24 The third Home Rule Bill, which became the Government of Ireland Act (1914), proposed a total of forty-two Irish MPs at Westminster with no 'in and out' restrictions. However, the Act was suspended due to the outbreak of the First World War (Hadfield 1989).

25 This included one seat for Queen's University in Belfast, which was abolished alongside the other university seats at Westminster in 1948.

26 Hansard reference: HCD, 26 October 1965, col. 97.

27 Between 1972 and 1997, 33 Northern Irish Acts were passed but these were dwarfed by the 557 Orders in Council for Northern Ireland over the same period (Bogdanor 2001).

28 Hansard reference: HCD, 21 January 1969, col. 294.

29 *Ibid.*, 9 December 1986, col. 222.

30 *Ibid.*, 4 March 1987, col. 884.

31 Standing orders provided that if ten or more MPs objected, the second reading would instead be taken on the floor of the House.

32 For information on the numerous votes on Welsh disestablishment see Morgan (1991).

33 As McLean and McMillan suggest in this volume, even Dicey was liable to argue constitutional principle for instrumentalist motives, so it is difficult to expect politicians to behave any better.

34 Conservative Party Press Notice 823/94, 2 December 1994, quoted in Winetrobe (1995).

35 See Russell and Hazell (2000), Masterman and Hazell (2001).

36 See the House of Commons opposition day debate on this matter on 21 January 2004.

37 For a full account of the Sewel procedure see Winetrobe (2001), Page and Batey (2002).

38 Royal Commission (1973: 247); note that 'region' here is used to apply to Scotland, Wales and Northern Ireland.

39 George Foulkes, HCD, 21 January 2004, col. 1394.

40 See the second reading of the Children's Commissioner for Wales Bill on 16 January 2001 and the report stage of the Health (Wales) Bill on 9 January 2003.

41 Indeed, it potentially leads to three different government formations: one to

govern England; one England and Wales (the more commonly required); and one to govern the UK.

42 Leverhulme–ESRC-funded survey, Constitution Unit. Among English Conservatives support was 28 per cent, but among English Labour MPs support was just 3 per cent. In territorial terms the most supportive group as comprised of Scottish MPs, where 27 per cent backed the idea.

43 In March 2004 the Richard Commission recommended primary legislative powers for the Assembly, but there is no immediate prospect of this change being implemented (Richard Commission 2004).

44 For more detailed discussion of these proposals see Hazell (2000), Russell and Hazell (2000).

45 At least arrangements for England would not suffer from some of the problems previously afflicting such territorial committees. In the Scottish case the require-ment to match the balance of the whole House meant that the Scottish standing committees sometimes included non-Scottish members during periods of Conservative government. Similarly with respect to Wales the standing order requiring Wales-only bills to be committed to a standing committee comprising only Welsh members was disapplied for the Local Government (Wales) Bill 1994, as the Conservatives did not have enough Welsh members to make such a com-mittee viable (Seaward and Silk 2003). Given the number and diversity of members in England such difficulties would be unlikely to apply.

46 See Russell and Hazell 2000, Masterman and Hazell 2001, Gay 2003.

47 Leverhulme/ESRC funded Constitution Unit survey.

48 Leverhulme/ESRC funded Constitution Unit survey.

49 Hansard reference: HL Deb, 25 June 1999, col. 1201.

50 Such a situation applied at both elections in 1910, in 1929, in 1951 and February 1974 (Rallings and Thrasher 2001).

5
Whitehall and the government of England*

Guy Lodge and James Mitchell

Introduction

Until very recently, the idea that there was an *English* dimension to Whitehall would have appeared fanciful to most people. In common with the central governments of other liberal democracies across the world, Whitehall is organised largely on a functional basis with the territorial dimension taking the form of exceptions to the rule. These exceptions concerned Scotland, Wales and Northern Ireland – the Scottish Office was set up in 1885, the Welsh Office in 1964 and the Northern Ireland Office in 1972. England is the missing element. Twenty years ago, Richard Rose (1982: 29) commented: 'England is a state of mind, not a consciously organised political institution.' This was certainly true of Whitehall. England, he maintained, claimed no distinctive institutions of governance, 'though it acquires these, if only by default, when Scotland, Wales, and Northern Ireland opt out of specific policies' (*ibid.*: 31). In other words, an English dimension emerges simply because that is what is left, albeit the largest part of the State, after special provisions are made for Scotland, Wales and Northern Ireland.

Devolution to Scotland, Wales and Northern Ireland might have been expected to have provided a catalyst, increasing the perception that England is a political entity. But devolution has not altered the fundamental nature of Whitehall. England remains formally unorganised as a political institution. Even today, the English dimension can be exaggerated and there is little evidence in Whitehall that this is foremost in the minds of civil servants and ministers as they go about their daily business. Some explanation for a chapter on the subject is in order.

There are three reasons for considering this subject. The first recognises that however insignificant an English dimension in Whitehall may appear to be today, it is conceivable that at some time in the future it might become much more important. Circumstances can be imagined in which territorial conflict arises over the role played by ministers and civil servants. In an era of heightened territorial tensions, the English dimension in Whitehall could come to the fore. The second reason can best be summarised by reference to Conan Doyle's 'dog that didn't bark'. The fact that the English dimension has not become a significant issue may well tell us much about the settled state of territorial politics in the UK today. This is remarkable given the complex nature of the UK polity, its recent history and the development of devolved bodies. Third, what appears to be emerging, not in the form some expected or hoped, is an English regional dimension.

Much, perhaps too much, has been made of the asymmetrical nature of devolution, focusing on the different powers of existing devolved bodies and the absence of those in England. At least as significant, however, has been the complex nature of territorial management at the centre. Whitehall consists of departments that have responsibility for UK-wide matters only, others with British-wide responsibilities, others still with England-only, still more with England and Wales. As the Government Information Office states:

> The work of some departments (for instance, the Ministry of Defence) covers the UK as a whole. Other departments, such as the Department for Work and Pensions, cover England, Wales and Scotland, but not Northern Ireland. Others again, such as the Department for Education and Skills, are mainly concerned with affairs in England and Wales.[1]

The former Department of the Environment, Transport and the Regions (DETR) might have been seen as primarily an English department given its responsibilities for local government, though its environmental responsibilities included those which were UK-wide. Its transport responsibilities were territorially mixed. Health may be primarily an English department, but important caveats should be added to this observation. One official in the Department of Trade and Industry (DTI) remarked that the diverse territorial jurisdictions of the department did not create a problem and that for the most part 'we are speaking on behalf of the UK' (interview, 9 May 2001). Add to this the changing competences of departments and ministries, and the mergers and reconstitutions that are an ongoing feature of Whitehall, and we have jurisdictional diversity in the extreme.

From one perspective, this bewildering array of distinct territorial jurisdictions in Whitehall appears irrational, confusing and unstable. From another, notably the dominant perspective within Whitehall itself, this is seen as nothing new, creating problems, if any at all, that are surmountable. Whitehall's capacity to cope with this is no surprise. These are minor problems compared to much that it has to handle. Devolution's impact has uniformly been described across Whitehall in interviews with senior civil servants as significant but not having affected working practices to the extent, for example, that membership of the EU has done. Indeed, from Whitehall's perspective it has not required administrative reform at all. In true UK tradition, devolution's impact on Whitehall is likely to be incremental but potentially considerable.

Whitehall has always been a multi-organisation with a variety of functions; indeed, individual departments are multi-organisations, but, as McLean notes, no authoritative record of changes of function within government or movements into and out of government responsibility is kept, making difficult the tracking of the functional and territorial responsibilities of departments. What is clear is that, even prior to devolution, different territorial jurisdictions existed within as well as between departments. It is difficult to talk about departments which had an *English* or a *British* focus. Some certainly had a UK focus and the territorial departments had responsibilities limited to Scotland and Wales and Northern Ireland, but for the rest the territorial jurisdiction varied internally.

There has never been any effort to tidy up Whitehall, and the advent of devolution has not been taken as an opportunity to do so. This seems strange from one perspective. Why should Irish, Scots or Welsh MPs have the right to vote on English domestic affairs when the equivalent matters have been devolved to Home Rule bodies? When Dicey raised this matter towards the end of the nineteenth century, the State's reach was limited. Today it is extensive in domestic society and economy, and this is reflected in Whitehall. The Cabinet remains largely the same size at the start of the twenty-first century as it had been at the start of the twentieth, but ministerial responsibilities have shifted from predominantly imperial and foreign affairs to domestic matters, particularly those concerned with the welfare state, and social and economic regulation. In other words, Dicey's objections to asymmetrical Home Rule, if accepted at all, have even more relevance now than in his own day. Foreign and imperial affairs would be largely unaffected by Home Rule whereas Whitehall's policy agenda in the era of the welfare state has been affected by devolution. In other words, the Diceyian objection to devolution today has an added dimension. Not only are MPs who represent devolved parts of the UK able to vote on equivalent matters elsewhere but the scope of these matters has grown considerably since Dicey's time, and this manifests itself in Whitehall. Complicating matters further, the three devolved bodies do not have the same powers and responsibilities.

Finding England in Whitehall

Finding England in Whitehall requires finding awareness of territorial diversity within Whitehall. This awareness has long existed but is generally not seen as of high political significance. Education has long had a territorial dimension in UK government. As one official in the former Department for Education and Employment pointed out, separate treatment of Scotland is 'deep in the collective memory of those dealing with education' (interview, April 2001). However, different territorial jurisdictions existed within the former department depending on functions: employment issues are Britain-based though schools are England-based (interview, March 2001). However, in specific areas matters can be a 'little hazy' (interview, April 2001). While separate higher education funding bodies exist north and south of the border, and though Scotland has diverged from England in its policy on tuition fees, the Higher Education Funding Council for England includes representatives from Scotland and Wales and the Student Loans Company, a non-departmental public body, has representatives from Scotland and England.

In other departments something similar is to be found. This reflects the aforementioned varying territorial jurisdictions of Whitehall departments. The DETR's transport functions were mixed while local government was focused on England, and some of its environmental remit had a UK focus (interview, May 2001). Roads' policy is essentially an England-only matter while vehicle standards and emissions are UK-wide, but roadworthiness and insurance are Britain-wide. Officials dealing with these different policy areas within the same department appear relaxed, reminding us that departments are indeed multi-organisations and that we should be wary of generalised remarks about departmental cultures and modes of operation. DETR officials dealing with local government would probably have seen themselves as working primarily in an English department while officials in the environment side of the same department would have seen themselves as addressing the UK as a whole and transport officials would have seen themselves as mixed. Modes of operation and cultures differ within departments. Health is, in practical terms, primarily an English department with significant reservations. It is likely that problems arise less at the level of officials working on the details of policy than among those charged with offering departmental overviews and overall strategy. This would include ministers who are, after all, the classic amateurs in the Whitehall machine. Those who are here today and gone tomorrow are much more likely to be least conscious of departmental cultures and territorial jurisdictions. For the most part devolution has had little impact on the internal workings of Whitehall. Departments have always had to operate within complex territorial jurisdictions. Using the Adams, Robinson and Vigor typology (2003), box 5.1 breaks down Whitehall departments by territory.

The European dimension adds to the complexity. Departments such as the Ministry of Agriculture, Food and Fisheries (MAFF) had a clear UK focus

Box 5.1 Adams *et al.* Territorial breakdown of Whitehall departments

Mostly English

- Department of Health
- Department for Education and Skills
- Office of the Deputy Prime Minister

Hybrid

- Department or Culture, Media and Sport
- Department for the Environment, Food and Rural Affairs
- Home Office

Mostly UK

- Department for Trade and Industry
- HM Treasury
- Cabinet Office
- Department for Work and Pensions

International

- Ministry of Defence
- Foreign Office
- Department for International Development

Notes. A 'mostly English' department has only very modest reserved powers; a 'hybrid' department exercises functions on behalf of England (or England and Wales) that are carried out on a devolved basis in the territories, with departments covering these particular functions in Cardiff, Edinburgh and Belfast, but they also exercise significant reserved powers; a 'mostly UK' department carries out primarily reserved functions but with some English functions too. *Source*: Adams, Robinson and Vigor 2003.

in much of its European work, but while MAFF officials may have adopted a UK position when dealing with the EU and other European officials, there was a need to recognise that in much of its work it had a more restricted territorial remit. When in Brussels, officials from MAFF had a UK focus even when the department's responsibilities in the domestic arena were for England (interview, 9 May 2001).

One difference that devolution appears to have made, however, has been in Whitehall's external projection of its activities. Devolution may have led many outside Whitehall to appreciate the territorial complexities of the UK, and that has had consequences for Whitehall. When writing news releases civil servants now appear to be more conscious of the need to take greater care that the territorial jurisdiction to which a policy or initiative applies is made clear. A policy on schools, for example, coming from what is essentially that part of

Whitehall dealing with English education, is required to make this clear. As much as anything else, devolution has required greater territorial sensitivity.

Regionalisation in Whitehall

There has always been an English regional dimension to the welfare departments within Whitehall. Ayres and Pearce (2004) make a distinction between departments with limited regional involvement, those in transition and those with a strong regional dimension. The provision of welfare services required more than a department at the centre dictating policy. Implementation and policy development required a local or regional structure. Unsurprisingly, this has varied from function to function over time. The Royal Commission on the Constitution (chaired by Lord Kilbrandon) noted this in its main report (1973):

> There have been significant differences in departmental practice, both in the extent of the use made of regional staff and in the numbers and boundaries of the regions themselves. Regional organisations were set up on functional lines, and boundaries selected for very different purposes naturally did not coincide (*ibid.*: 64, para. 203).

Efforts after 1945 to standardise English regions resulted in 8 standard regions being identified, but standardisation was limited until the present pattern of 9 regions was created in 1994. Indeed, there were differences within departments as well as between Whitehall departments. The new Department of the Environment, created in 1971, for example, found itself operating thirteen separate regional organisations (*ibid.*). This is hardly surprising – the functional imperative would not lead to the same boundaries. The UK has rarely considered tidiness to be as important as is functionality.

Many English ministers see themselves still as responsible for delivering services in England. Responsibilities for Scotland, Wales and Northern Ireland may still exist in Whitehall but do so less commonly for service delivery (treasury official in interview, 22 March 2001). In many cases, that which distinguished the English aspect of Whitehall activities is that these parts have service delivery functions, with consequences for the regional dimension in Whitehall. Devolving responsibility for the delivery of policies determined in Whitehall departments differs markedly from devolving power over the strategic overview of these policies. It is likely that had elected English regional government emerged Whitehall would have seen little change in its *modus operandi*. In some cases, Whitehall may have allowed service delivery functions to be devolved to the new bodies but overall control of strategic policy-making would certainly have been retained at the centre. Indeed, it is possible that even service delivery would have continued to be seen as a matter for which Whitehall departments retained responsibility (interview, March 2001). Much education policy is centrally-driven, and even had elected regional government emerged it is doubtful whether English education ministers would have been willing to devolve reform of schools' policy. Nor indeed would it have been likely that regionalism would have brought an end to the National Curriculum (interview, March 2001). The issue of English regional government lies below the surface of debates, but there remains a belief that for many purposes England will remain the key level. In education, for example, much continues to be and will likely continue to be centrally-driven, with England treated as a whole. There has been reluctance in some parts of Whitehall to devolve matters to regional bodies within England.

Policy-making, however, does not always conform neatly with the shape of Whitehall departments. In the language currently in vogue, but in no other sense new, there is a need for 'joined-up government' as much decision-making transcends departmental boundaries. Much effort has always been spent devising mechanisms to ensure more comprehensive policy-making, and this inevitably involves bringing together departments and ministries with varying territorial jurisdictions. When this happens in England it does so *despite* rather than *because of* the structure of Whitehall. The core executive has been defined as 'all those organisations and procedures that coordinate central government, and act as final arbiters of conflict between different parts of the government machine' (Rhodes 1995: 12). These co-ordination and arbitration functions are an inevitable feature of large-scale organisations and the territorial dimension is but one aspect. The Cabinet plays a significant role in this respect, as do a number of other departments. Those departments that are important for arbitration and co-ordination for purposes of territorial politics include Number 10, the Treasury, the ODPM and the Cabinet Office. Significantly, in the early years of devolution, no department was solely responsible for devolution at Whitehall. The ODPM attempted to champion regions; but, as we will see, the regional dimension has advanced only since a more powerful champion, the Treasury, emerged.

Ministers, accountability and territorial jurisdiction

No rule ever existed, though some conventions did develop, that an MP's constituency would determine whether he or she should be excluded from any ministry. Even overtly territorial ministries were not always confined to MPs from these areas: Northern Ireland Office ministers have never come from Northern Ireland. The only convention that operated as far as the Northern Ireland Office was concerned was that one minister should be Catholic. Under the Conservatives, successive Welsh secretaries had seats outside of Wales as the party had so few Welsh MPs. But, at no stage in the history of the Scottish Office was a minister appointed who did not either hold a Scottish seat in the Commons or have some Scottish connection in the Lords. In opposition, Labour politicians in Scotland occasionally suggested that the Conservatives lacked a mandate due to the lack of Scottish Tory MPs. It is an understatement to suggest that the appointment of a Scottish Secretary who represented an English constituency in the Commons would have provoked controversy. Nonetheless, over the years various MPs from Scottish constituencies have held posts which have been responsible for predominantly English or non-Scottish matters. During the interwar period, Scottish secretaries Walter Elliot and John Gilmour went on to become ministers with responsibilities that had limited Scottish functions: Elliot at the Ministry of Health and Gilmour at the Home Office. But in the post-war period this became uncommon. An unstated convention arose that Scottish MPs would not be appointed to what were predominantly English departments. The geographical location of an MP's constituency appears to have become one qualification for appointment to certain ministerial offices. There were exceptions; but, as with appointing a member of the House of Lords to certain ministries, these were unusual if formally quite constitutional. By the end of the twentieth century, the appointment of a Scottish MP as Home Secretary or Secretary of State for Health would have provoked at least as much controversy as the appointment of a lord.

As Shadow Health Secretary, Robin Cook had stated that he did not think he could be Health Secretary following devolution (*Guardian*, 13 February 1992). Though this was not official Labour policy, there was some logic to Cook's position. The appointment of John Reid, a Scottish MP, as health minister was, therefore, paradoxical. Devolution appeared to signal that Scottish MPs would not be blocked from ministerial offices which had rarely been available to them in the past. The Burkean view[2] that has informed understanding of the role of MPs has been translated into qualification for ministerial office. If MPs are not agents of particular interests but operate collectively in the interest of the whole, then there should be no reason for appointing a minister with a seat in the Commons representing any part of the UK. Reid's appointment provoked less comment than might have been expected, largely because of Labour's overall majority among English MPs as well as the UK as a whole. Such an appointment, coming so soon after devolution had been granted to Scotland and Wales, would have been unlikely had Labour's overall Commons' majority depended on Scottish and Welsh members. But Labour's overall majority facilitated the early establishment of a precedent that in the fullness of time may prove useful, especially to the Labour Party. However, this view is not shared by the Conservatives, and electoral considerations, which have yet to become evident, may make it unlikely that MPs from devolved areas will in future take responsibility for parts of Whitehall with a predominantly English territorial remit.

Finance and spill-over

The issue of spill-over has long been an issue in UK territorial politics. The territorial departments were constrained in taking initiatives by the need to consider whether any new policy and, crucially, expenditure would be required if the policy was extended across the UK. However, the expectations that devolution should involve policy divergence has had consequences for Whitehall, especially as far as finance is concerned. As one official commented, 'things get interesting when it has to be worked out whether a certain function comes within the Scottish block grant'. This 'concentrates minds'. The £100m assistance for the road haulage industry raised this issue (interview, July 2001). Whitehall departments have had to come to terms with this following devolution. One treasury official pointed out that there was often a 'knee-jerk' response of questioning the funding implications in Whitehall (interview, May 2001). This was confirmed by another official – again referring to a 'knee-jerk' reaction – when commenting on the Scottish policy on care of the elderly. This is hardly surprising given past practice; and, combined with the financial regime, this is likely to remain the case into the future.

There appears to be less concern in Whitehall with initiatives in the devolved areas which have few or no financial implications. Controversial instances of major initiatives have each had financial implications – tuition fees, care of the elderly – while initiatives which may have symbolic significance but limited financial implications (such as the Welsh decision on prescription charges), though portrayed in the devolved polity as having significance, have proved less worrisome for Whitehall. Contact between devolved administrations and Whitehall continues, but it has changed. It has been suggested that the eagerness of devolved administrations to know what is being planned in Whitehall now has a different motive: it is less that of knowing how a Scottish or Welsh dimension to policy developments can be added on than it is of discerning whether something altogether different may be devised (interview 12 July 2001).

Whitehall and regional administration

While an all-England dimension in Whitehall lies dormant, there has always been, as already noted, an English regional dimension to the government of

England. This is hardly surprising given central government's need to implement policy and deliver public services throughout England. Reviewing regional boundaries in the 1990s, Hogwood (1996) identified the presence of around 100 distinct regional administrative structures. Given the functional imperative, however, standardisation should not necessarily have been expected. As noted above, observers of UK public administrative history can verify that tidiness has rarely been accorded the same level of importance as has functionality. Administrative logic might dictate the need for Whitehall to establish sub-national units of government at the regional level but it is clear that what was created was a fragmented regional infrastructure (Hogwood and Keating 1982). This muddle was reflected in Whitehall itself, which showed little interest in co-ordinating regional policy at the centre. Regional policy initiatives and spending programmes were driven by reference to the functional need. Moves in Whitehall to regionalise service delivery for the sake of administrative convenience should not be confused with any conversion to regional government. The overwhelming trend in British public administration has been one of centralisation. Regional institutions were creatures of Whitehall, delivery agents of the centre with limited autonomy. Indeed, as a result of the perceived failure of the regional economic planning experiment of the 1960s, the forces of centralism were bolstered (Morgan 2002). This was most apparent during the Thatcher governments, which demonstrated their enthusiasm for regionalism by abolishing the regional economic and planning councils (1979), the Greater London Council (GLC) and the metropolitan councils (1985), and slashing expenditure on regional policy (Tomaney 2003). Emphasis placed on intervention at the regional level varied from department to department, reflecting their distinctive cultures and perspectives. Given its historic involvement in regional economic policy, the DTI has a much stronger tradition of regionalism than the Department for Education (Ayres and Pearce 2004). Viewed as a whole, however, by the end of the 1980s regionalism had failed to embed itself into Whitehall's culture. England was governed predominantly by Whitehall, in a top–down 'command and control' model.

Regionalism, Whitehall and the Major Government

Having been largely ignored under Margaret Thatcher, the regional agenda was brought in from the cold by John Major. Prompted by fresh concerns to integrate disparate strands of central government activity in the regions, the Major Government established ten GOs in 1994. Initially, the GOs encompassed the policy programmes and corresponding funding streams of four

Whitehall departments: industry, the environment, transport and employment. No new powers were devolved to the GOs, instead they absorbed the functions already performed by the regional offices of the four parent departments. Reflecting their departmental make-up the GOs were primarily concerned with implementing economic development and regeneration programmes.

However, the GOs did not prove particularly successful in their efforts to co-ordinate central government activity in the regions (Mawson and Spencer 1997). They lacked the autonomy needed to develop a strong integrative capacity and were further weakened by the blurred lines of accountability within which they operated. The regional directors who headed up the GOs were responsible, following traditional lines of ministerial accountability, to the minister and department from which programmes and budgets emanated. This created a complex environment for the GOs, especially when policies from one department contradicted those of another. They were powerless in the face of tensions that arose from inter- and intra-departmental disputes and deprived of any cross-departmental champion in Whitehall (Constitution Unit 1996). The parent departments continued to work through functional needs while the mechanisms designed to provide some central oversight of GO activities lacked the political teeth to be effective (Tomaney 2000a).[3] The Trade and Industry Select Committee was critical of the fact that Whitehall lacked a minister responsible for co-ordinating the work of GOs across central government (Trade and Industry Select Committee 1995).

The GOs represent an example of the top–down administrative devolution favoured by Whitehall. Control over functions, resources and powers remained in the hands of the sponsoring departments. The GOs were intended to be the 'eyes and ears' of Whitehall in the regions, rather than to act as regional advocates in Whitehall. The perennial issue of non-coterminous boundaries remained for those departments with regional structures which did not participate. However, though the birth of GOs was problematical, they represented an attempt by central government to bring some coherence to the regional tier. As we will see, the GOs were subsequently built on as Whitehall began to pay more attention to its regional architecture.

New Labour and regionalism

It was not until the election of Labour in 1997 that the potential for transforming the profile of regionalism within Whitehall became possible. To understand this we need to explore developments within the Labour Party in opposition. Expectations had been raised mainly because of Labour's constitutional commitment to some form of elected regional government for England. Jack Straw MP, as Shadow Home Secretary, argued, despite his doubts about regional government for England, that some form of democratic oversight was needed to correct the democratic deficit that existed across England's regional administrative tier. Labour's 1997 manifesto committed the party to establishing indirectly elected 'regional chambers',[4] and promised to introduce elected regional government in those regions that wanted them, which would be established by holding referendums in each region. Elected regional government would not be imposed but instead would be demand-driven.

If the democratic imperative was one motive for Labour's regional policy, the other, indeed the most significant, was economic (Morgan 2002). In opposition, Labour had become troubled by the widening regional economic disparities within England. The 'North–South' divide formed the sub-text to countless policy debates, and had been at the forefront of the mind of Labour's chief regional advocate, John Prescott. Prescott established the Regional Policy Commission, under the chairmanship of Bruce Millan, the former EU regional policy commissioner, with the task of drafting Labour's regional policy in opposition. In 1996, Millan recommended the creation of an RDA in each of England's regions to tackle the regional economic malaise. English regional government also had the attraction of offering, at least in theory, a response to the West Lothian Question.

However, on coming to power, the regional agenda quickly fell down the list of Labour's priorities. The regional advocates in the government soon felt resistance from ministers and officials. There was no urgency within government to move forward with elected regional government, especially when compared to the energy invested in establishing devolution for Scotland, Wales, Northern Ireland and London. Ministers reiterated the position that regional government would only be considered in those regions that wanted it and there was little evidence of support for it within the regions and no consensus on what form English devolution should take. The Prime Minister was believed to be unconvinced and promoted the idea of elected-mayors, 'city–regions' and local government reform as an alternative way of rejuvenating sub-national democracy within England.

In its first term, Labour's main regional achievement was the establishment of the RDAs in 1999. The policy was the responsibility of the newly formed DETR. Under the guidance of Secretary of State John Prescott and his deputy Richard Caborn, the other key regional champion in the government, the DETR became the hub of regional policy. However, Prescott and Caborn's enthusiasm for regionalism was not shared by their colleagues, something demonstrated by the inter-departmental disputes that overshadowed the creation of the RDAs. The DTI and the Department for Education and Employment (DfEE) resisted devolving powers which meant that the RDAs began life weaker than Millan had envisaged, with powers narrowly drawn from the DETR. As Tomaney shows, one consequence was that the RDAs were deprived of the necessary functions to perform the central task demanded of them – raising the regional economic performance of England's regions (Tomaney 2000a: 124). Instead the RDAs primarily focused on regeneration issues. Determined not to lose competencies to the RDAs, the DTI rejected the idea of handing over control of Regional Selective Assistance (RSA). Further, the RDAs lacked powers over skills and training while RDA budgets for promoting local area regeneration dwarfed those devolved to tackle regional competitiveness (Robinson 2000).

At the outset, the RDAs were responsible for spending less that 1 per cent of total government expenditure in the regions (Groom 1999). But it was not just the size of the budgets which proved problematic. RDAs were funded through eleven separate funding streams which were often 'ring-fenced' for specific national programmes. The problems afflicting RDAs provoked a reaction from the RDA boards, which criticised Whitehall's approach, demanded greater resources and responsibilities, and more financial flexibility enabling them to 'vire' funds between spending programmes. Their concerns were echoed by parliamentary select committees (Tomaney 2000). The 2000 Spending Review committed the government to increasing the total RDA budgets from £1.2 billion in 2000–1 to £1.7 billion in 2003–4, and committed the Government to establishing a 'single pot' of RDA funding by April 2002. RDAs had previously required permission whenever they wanted to transfer money between their 11 funding streams. However, additional resources came at the price of having to meet 'challenging outcome targets' prescribed by the centre (HM Treasury 2000a, quoted in Tomaney 2002).

The 2000 Spending Review offered some degree of financial flexibility for the RDAs in the form of a 'single cross departmental funding framework'. This was not enough, however, to satisfy RDA chairs who issued a joint statement in January 2001 to the Government suggesting that RDAs represented a 'counter-cultural' challenge to Whitehall's traditional way of doing things:

> The concept of the 'single pot' is so counter-cultural (to the civil service) and the accountability mechanisms, the command and control nature of Whitehall, that it makes it a quite difficult thing to get through . . . they find it incredibly difficult to deal with things across more than one department. (Quoted in Tomaney 2002)

With RDAs largely confined to working within DETR parameters, the opportunity to develop a more joined-up regional policy was missed. To some, RDAs reflected Whitehall's inability to build integrated regional infrastructure. It was unclear how the RDAs and the GOs would relate to each other

(Environment, Transport and Regional Affairs Select Committee 1999). Moreover, the RDAs had little influence over other tiers of regional government, which further frustrated efforts to deliver on the ground (Morgan 2002). An example concerns the establishment of the Learning and Skills Council (LSC). Eager to raise the level of post-16 skills, the government set up a national LSC along with 47 local LSCs. Despite the importance of skills in raising regional economic performance, DfEE deprived the RDAs of any regional control of LSCs while the absence of coterminosity between LSC and RDA boundaries fragmented central government activity.

The story of regionalism in Labour's first term took on a familiar shape. Regional policy was department-led and lacked much cross-departmental coherence. Traditional lines of accountability ensured fragmentation as did the absence of standardised regional and sub-regional boundaries. The lack of regional champions needed to overcome Whitehall's reticence also impeded progress. John Prescott was left isolated after Richard Caborn was moved from the DETR to the DTI and replaced by Hilary Armstrong. The DETR proved far too unwieldy to promote and 'mainstream' the regional agenda across Whitehall. Regionalism played only a walk-on part in the theatre of Whitehall.

New Labour's mission to modernise public services involved a centralist approach characterised by 'national' policy-making and the proliferation of centrally set targets and inspection regimes, which had implications for the regional agenda. An example was the literacy and numeracy targets pursued by the DfEE. These were driven from the centre using Whitehall's 'command and control' model, bypassing administrative structures at the intermediary tier, straight into schools themselves. As one civil servant remarked, 'I would be very surprised if a minister were to come into this department and say, "We must create a regional tier of bureaucracy that stands in the way of allowing teachers to teach"' (Interview, April 2001).

The return of the regional dimension

However, Labour's experience of government led to a revival of interest in the regional dimension. As the first term progressed, government ministers became increasingly frustrated by the pace of public service reform and the capability of government to 'deliver'. The complex administrative machine was deemed part of the problem. The *Modernising Government* White Paper identified two issues of concern. First, it was felt that Whitehall's organisation into traditional 'chimney-stack' functional departments prevented government from dealing with cross-cutting departmental problems. Secondly, it was thought that policy-making had become too centralised and that policy design had become separated from implementation impeding successful delivery. It recommended that delivery, when appropriate, should be decentralised to the most relevant level (Cabinet Office 1999). *Modernising Government* also highlighted the problem of non-coterminous administrative boundaries. To address this it recommended:

> Wherever possible, boundaries should coincide with local authority boundaries at local level, and with Government Office regions' boundaries at the regional level. The Government will work from a presumption that geographical boundaries should be aligned in this way whenever public bodies next review their administrative, managerial or delivery arrangements and structures. (*Ibid.*: 33).

The publication in 2000 of the Cabinet Office report *Reaching Out: The Role of Central Government at the Regional and Local Level* provided the most significant catalyst for change in Whitehall vis-à-vis regionalism. The report was highly critical of the fractured state of English regional governance and the impact this was having on policy outcomes, emphasising the need to join up government policy and delivery mechanisms, both horizontally and vertically. It endorsed increasing local and regional input in the heavily centralised policy process and recommended that GOs be strengthened in order to act as the main vehicle for joining up government activities in the regions. In Whitehall, the report called for the creation of a regional unit that would be responsible for coordinating departmental initiatives with a regional dimension and would act as a single point of contact for GOs in Whitehall. In response, the Government established the regional co-ordination unit (RCU) in April 2001 located within the DETR. Whitehall now had a central apparatus specifically designed to manage and coordinate the disparate strands of central government regional activity (table 5.1). The RCU was also expected to promote and mainstream regionalism across Whitehall (Ayres and Pearce 2004). Equipped with a relatively small staff of fifty, this task was always likely to prove challenging.

The Cabinet Office report strengthened the GOs by increasing the scope of Whitehall's representation in them (Tomaney 2002). The Home Office, MAFF and the Department for Culture, Media and Sport (DCMS) had all located staff in the GOs to assist their regional policy-making capacity by September 2001. The report also envisaged a stronger role for the GOs in policy development, feeding specialist regional knowledge into policy design. At one level this involved greater involvement of the GOs in negotiating and meeting targets. The evolving role of the GOs continued throughout the second Labour term. The 2002 White Paper *Your Region, Your Choice* advocated a stronger role for them, as Whitehall's 'eyes and ears' in the regions by encouraging the GOs to build partnerships with and co-ordinate the activities

Table 5.1 Whitehall's 'regional' turn

Year	Regional turn	Department
1999	Regional Development Agencies established	DETR
1999	*Modernising Government* White Paper published	Cabinet Office
2000	*Reaching Out: The Role of Central Government at the Regional and Local Level* published	Cabinet Office–Performance and Innovation Unit
2000	Spending Review 2000 (RDA funds increased)	HM Treasury
2000	White paper on 'enterprise, skills and innovation'	DTI
2000	Ed Balls and John Healey publish pamphlet on the 'new regional policy'	HM Treasury[a]
2001	*Productivity in the UK: The Regional Dimension*	HM Treasury–DTI
2001	Government publishes green paper on *Planning: Delivering a Fundamental Change*	DTLR
2002	Spending Review (Single Pot established; reducing regional economic disparities PSA)	HM Treasury
2002	*Your Region, Your Choice* White Paper published	DTLR–Cabinet Office
2003	*Our Fire and Rescue Service* White Paper	Home Office
2003	McLean Review: *Investigating the Flow of Domestic and European Expenditure into the English Regions*	ODPM–DTI–HM Treasury
2003	The Haskins Report	DEFRA
2003	The Lambert Review of Business–University Collaboration	HM Treasury
2003	Regional emphasis documents	HM Treasury
2003	*Building Safer Communities* White Paper	Home Office
2004	Spending Review and *Meeting Regional Priorities: Response to the Regional Emphasis Documents*	HM Treasury
2004	Barker Review of Housing Supply	HM Treasury
2004	The Allsopp Review	
2004	*Devolved Decision Making: Meeting the Regional Economic Challenge*	HM Treasury–DTI–ODPM
2004	The Lyons Report (Independent Review of Public Sector Relocation)	HM Treasury
2004	Spending Review	HM Treasury

Note: [a] The pamphlet was not an official Treasury publication, though Balls was chief economic adviser to HM Treasury and John Healey was a minister there at the time of publication.

of other departmental agencies and non-departmental bodies (Cabinet Office–DTLR 2002). By 2003 ten Whitehall departments were represented in the GOs, administering programme budgets of around £9 billion per annum (HM Treasury–DTI–ODPM 2004; see box 5.2) though most of this money was tied to specific expenditure programmes set by the parent departments in Whitehall.

Box 5.2 Whitehall departments represented in the government offices for the regions as of 2002

- Office of the Deputy Prime Minister
- Department for Transport
- Department for the Environment, Food and Rural Affairs
- Department for Trade and Industry
- Department for Education and Skills
- Department for Work and Pensions
- Home Office
- Department for Health
- Department for Culture, Media and Sport
- Cabinet Office

A series of changes to the machinery of government with implications for the regional agenda within Whitehall were instituted during Labour's second term. At first regional policy appeared fractured as musical chairs were played across Whitehall after the 2001 election. The struggling DETR was abolished and replaced with the new leaner Department for Transport, Local Government and the Regions (DTLR). The environment remit was hived off and merged with agriculture, forming the new Department for the Environment, Food and Rural Affairs (DEFRA). The DTLR was to share responsibility for the elected regional government agenda with John Prescott's newly created ODPM, which resided in the Cabinet Office. A central task was to produce the regional government white paper. Responsibility for the RCU and the GOs did not stay in DTLR but were moved to the Cabinet Office with Prescott. The other major development for regionalism came when responsibility for the RDAs was transferred to the DTI bringing together the necessary policy instruments for tackling regional economic disparities. Regional policy, therefore, lay across three departments: the DTLR, the DTI and the Cabinet Office. This potentially damaging division was, however, rectified in 2002, when following the resignation of Stephen Byers from DTLR, a further change took place, which saw the creation of a free-standing ODPM, which merged the DTLR and the Cabinet Office's regional policy, placing them under one roof. The ODPM did not absorb the transport remit as a new Department for Transport was also created.

The machinery of government changes were accompanied by reforms to the Cabinet committee structure, which had further implications for regional policy. In 2001 a new Cabinet Committee of the Nations and the Regions (CNR) was established, chaired by John Prescott. Its remit was 'to consider policy and other issues arising from the Government's policies for devolution to Scotland, Wales, Northern Ireland and the regions of England'. The creation of the CNR signalled the new lease of life which had been granted to the *democratic regional* agenda in Labour's second term by aligning Celtic devolution with English regional devolution. Indeed, Prescott and the ODPM also led on the Government's wider devolution and inter-governmental relations policy. However, this constitutional fusion was severed in June 2003 following another machinery of government change. The new Department for Constitutional Affairs (DCA) took over responsibility for overseeing the Scottish and Welsh devolution settlements from the ODPM, which retained its control of English regional policy. At the Cabinet committee level, the CNR was replaced by two separate committees: Devolution Policy, chaired by the Secretary of State for Constitutional Affairs, with a remit to 'consider policy and other issues arising from devolution to Scotland, Wales and Northern Ireland'; and English Regional Policy, chaired by Prescott with a remit 'to develop policy on the English regions'.[5]

John Prescott published his long-awaited white paper on elected regional government in May 2002 but it was undermined by a series of Whitehall turf wars, not dissimilar to those that had afflicted the creation of the RDAs, and with a similar result in that fewer powers than initially intended were earmarked for the proposed new elected regional bodies. Tomaney describes how departments, especially the DTI and the DCMS, fought to retain control over functions proposed for the assemblies (Tomaney 2003). Whitehall's revolt stripped Prescott's plans of powers and functions, resulting in a very cautious set of proposals (Sandford 2002a). The democratic regionalist agenda culminated in the referendum in the north east in November 2004, in which the overwhelming 'No' vote killed off the idea of elected regional government for the foreseeable future. But delivery, which had become the rallying cry of Labour's second term, assured an accelerated pace of administrative regionalism within Whitehall, as departments revisited their regional infrastructure with a view to achieving their desired policy outcomes through them.

The most important development in this process was the growing involvement of the Treasury. Disappointed by the failure of economic policy to increase productivity and growth rates, and to reduce economic disparities between England's regions which had increased since Labour came to power (Adams, Robinson and Vigor 2003), Treasury thinking changed. In short, the Treasury woke up to the potential of tackling the productivity and growth challenges besetting the UK economy through regional policy instruments. The Treasury's interest in regional policy was driven from the top. In 2000, Ed Balls, chief economic adviser to the Treasury and the Chancellor's closest adviser, argued for a 'new regional policy' in an influential pamphlet:

> Our new regional policy is based on two principles – it aims to strengthen the essential building blocks of growth – innovation, skills the development of enterprise – by exploiting the indigenous strengths in each region and city. And it is bottom-up not top-down, with national government enabling powerful regional and local initiatives to work by providing the necessary flexibility and resources. National government does not have all the answers – it never could. (Balls 2000: 12–13)

This was echoed by the Chancellor in a speech in January 2001 in which he distinguished the new regional policy from its predecessors. The first generation of 'ambulance work' had provided relief to the poorest regions and the second sought to incentivise business and industry to locate in poorly performing regions (Brown 2001). Brown's 'third generation' regional policy focused on the need to build capacity in the regions themselves. This would involve bolstering the architecture of English regional government. At official level, the Chancellor's thinking culminated in the Treasury–DTI (2001) White Paper *Productivity in the UK 3: The Regional Dimension*. This identified and measured the core drivers of productivity – skills, investment, enterprise and competition – by region, and advocated a more significant role for the RDAs as the main vehicle for delivering the Treasury's new regional policy.

Given its privileged position in the core executive, including its control of the purse strings and, especially under Brown, its dominance of much domestic policy, the Treasury has been able to push its regional policy with much more success than Prescott and the ODPM has managed to push democratic regionalism. The Treasury rapidly became, in the words of one senior official, 'the champions of regionalism' (interview, May 2004). In particular it forged an alliance with the DTI, which had started to re-evaluate the importance of the regional dimension and the potential of the RDAs. In March 2001, the DTI took the first tentative steps towards reconciling its industrial policy with broader regional concerns in its plans for industry 'clusters' (DTI 2001). Having acquired responsibility for the RDAs in 2001, the DTI set about rejuvenating their economic development functions.

From 2000 onwards, and especially from 2002, Treasury-led administrative regionalism began to embed itself across Whitehall. In April 2002, the

RDAs moved to 'single pot' funding, ending funding by department. Another major turning point came in the 2002 Spending Review when a dedicated chapter on the English regions described the RDAs as 'key strategic drivers of economic development and regeneration in the regions' (HM Treasury 2002). The Spending Review increased the RDAs' budgets and devolved new powers and responsibilities to them (table 5.2). At the Treasury's behest, RDAs were given powers over housing and planning and were given new responsibilities in relation to tourism and transport (HM Treasury–DTI–ODPM 2004; see box 5.3).

Table 5.2 Central government spending (£ millions) on regional development agencies

	2004–5	*2005–6*	*2006–7*	*2007–8*
DTI	234	463	476	483
ODPM	1,511	1,568	1,633	1,676
DEFRA	46	72	73	74
DES	42	43	44	45
UK Trade International	13	13	13	13
Department for Culture, Media and Sport	2	6	6	6
Total	1,847	2,163	2,244	2,297

Source: HM Treasury (2004a).

Box 5.3 Regionalism in Whitehall departments

Departments with limited regional involvement

- Department of Health
- Department for Education and Skills

Departments in transition

- Department for Transport
- Home Office
- Department for Environment, Food and Rural Affairs
- Department for Work and Pensions

Departments with a strong regional dimension

- Department for Trade and Industry
- Office of Deputy Prime Minister
- HM Treasury
- Department for Culture, Media and Sport

Source: Adapted from Ayres and Pearce 2004.

Most significantly, the 2002 Spending Review saw the Treasury refine and re-focus its central regional policy objectives. In 2000 the Treasury had established a joint public service agreement (PSA) target with the DETR and the DTI to 'improve the economic performance of all regions, measured by the trend in growth of each region's GDP' (HM Treasury 2000a). This was heavily criticised for failing to take account of the disparities among regional growth rates. Recognising the problems of 'treating unequals equally' (ODPM Select Committee 2003), the Treasury replaced this PSA in 2002 with a new target to 'make sustainable improvements in the economic performance of all English regions and over the long term [to] reduce the persistent gap in growth rates between the regions' (HM Treasury 2002). A further requirement imposed was that of 'defining measures to improve performance and reporting progress against these measures by 2006' (*ibid.*). The new PSA target, with its emphasis on reducing growth-rate disparities between regions, formed the bedrock of the new regional policy. By sharing responsibility for the PSA target with the ODPM and the DTI, the Treasury ensured co-ordination of regional policy across these key departments. Institutionally, this target was serviced by a joint secretariat comprised of staff from the three sponsor departments. The need to make progress on the PSA encouraged further developments which drove the economic regional agenda in Whitehall. In 2003, the three departments published the Green Paper, *A Modern Regional Policy for the UK*, making the case for 'renationalising' EU structural funds back to member states in response to concerns that the UK's regions would receive less funds following the EU's enlargement to the east (HM Treasury–DTI–ODPM 2003).

Having focused minds in Whitehall, the PSA prompted fresh concerns about the quality of departmental regional expenditure data. The Treasury recognised that poor data impeded analysis of regional policy. As such, the ODPM and the Treasury commissioned the McLean review to review the quality of regional data. The scale of the problem was identified in the McLean report published in 2003:

> We have found that the quality of data on the flows of domestic and European public expenditure into the English regions is highly variable. Departments that feel they have a mission related to regional policy have tended to keep data of high quality; departments whose mission has not involved a regional component have tended not to. (McLean 2003b: 187)

Other evidence of rising acknowledgement of the need for regional data was found in the Allsopp review of national statistics. The Barker review on housing, the Lyons review of public sector relocation and the Lambert review on business–university development each had a regional dimension. Notably, the Treasury was the driving force behind this development in Whitehall. Not only was the Treasury a key part of the core executive with influence through-out Whitehall but traditionally it had been unsympathetic to calls for more regional data. However, government data had now assumed a far more sig-nificant regional dimension. While John Prescott at the ODPM has struggled to influence other departments, the Treasury has been more successful in ensuring that a regional dimension is taken seriously. An example came when the Treasury argued that the LSCs should be organised to correspond with the RDAs. This was resisted by the Department for Education and Skills (DfES) and, according to a Treasury official, the introduction of regional skills partnerships came about 'under Treasury influence' (interview, May 2004).

Conclusion

The functional organisation of Whitehall has long been and continues to be the norm (see also chapter 10). The territorial dimension that most obviously manifested itself was found in special institutions to deal with Scotland, Wales and Northern Ireland with England existing only as the great residual. The regional dimension of England has struggled to emerge and different views of how to deal with it existed. The 'No' vote in the referendum in the North East of England killed off, at least from some time, the idea of elected regional assemblies. Part of the problem was the absence, certainly as compared with Scotland, Wales and Northern Ireland, of a clear historically based official rec-ognition of English regions. At the regional level, Whitehall has required regional offices but these have been functional with regions defined differ-ently depending on function. The regional dimension for regeneration that was deemed relevant for education was not deemed relevant for health and, indeed, Whitehall has for many purposes, most notably those associated with the economy, been regionally blind.

Devolution to Scotland, Wales and Northern Ireland was the result of demands for greater democracy and accountability in these parts of the UK. Similar pressures existed in the English regions but these were faint by com-parison. Any regionalist development would require a different basis. This has come from an unusual source, unusual at least when viewed historically. The regional dimension that has emerged has emerged separately from the debate on devolution elsewhere and has come from within Whitehall as much as from the regions themselves, significantly, after gaining a powerful champion in the Treasury. The motives behind this regionalism have been more technocratic than democratic and this is reflected in the shape it has taken. Regionalism has developed incrementally and *unevenly* across Whitehall. Those departments with a tradition and culture of regionalism – the DTI and the ODPM – have embraced regionalism much more keenly than say the Department of Health or the DfES. Elected regional assemblies are not the answer, but a greater awareness within central government of the need to accommodate regional disparities and differences has been growing. Its shape, therefore, is more evident in the growth of data and an appreciation of the need to understand regional diversity. It is also taking shape, though as yet less strongly, in formal institutional structures. In time, if these structures become rooted, it is conceivable that regional awareness will develop among elites in the regions as well as throughout Whitehall. That would involve a significant shift. However, much else besides may occur and it is worth noting that it took 114 years from the establishment of the Scottish Office, Whitehall's acceptance of the need for a Scottish institution in the heart of Whitehall, before a Parliament was established to provide a democratic veneer.

Notes

The authors would like to thank the ESRC for funding the 'Devolution and the Centre' project.

1   Cited on Britannia.com at: www.britannia.com/gov/gov6.html.
2   See Judge (2004) for a discussion of the question 'whatever happened to parliamentary democracy in the UK?' Burke's famous statement on representation is: 'Parliament is not a congress of ambassadors from different and hostile interests, which interests each must maintain, as an agent and advocate, against other agents and advocates; but Parliament is a deliberative assembly of one nation, with one interest, that of the whole – where not local prejudices ought to guide, but the general good, resulting from the general reason of the whole' (quoted in *ibid.*: 684).
3   Central government co-ordination was provided by the Government Office Management Board, the Government Office Central Unit and an Inter-departmental Support Unit.
4   See the Sandford chapter for a detailed analysis of regional chambers.
5   Available online at: www.cabinetoffice.gov.uk/cabsec/2003cab.com.

6
What the people say – if anything

John Curtice

Since 1999 the government of Scotland and Wales has no longer simply lain in the hands of the UK central government. Power there is shared with independently elected bodies that have substantial discretionary authority. But with the partial exception of the Greater London Authority (GLA) there has been no equivalent change in England. Each government region has acquired a regional chamber/assembly and an RDA but neither of these bodies has an independent electoral mandate.

Armed with an acute knowledge of the inconsistencies of this constitutional settlement, many a commentator has doubted whether people in England would be willing to tolerate their lack of regional government and devolution (Paxman 1998; McLean and McMillan 2003a). If Scotland and Wales enjoy devolution, would not England eventually want to do so as well? After all, the current settlement gives MPs in Scotland the right to vote on laws that would apply only in England, while denying MPs from England a similar right with respect to laws that will apply only in Scotland (Dalyell 1977). Backed by a favourable public expenditure settlement, both Scotland and Wales have greater latitude to take supply-side measures to boost their economies than do the new RDAs in England. In any event, do not some of the factors that helped fuel the demand for devolution in Scotland and Wales, such as the London-centric character of the UK Government and the relatively poor economic performance of the northern half of the country, apply with equal force in many of England's regions too? In short, there seems little logical reason to believe that the devolution ball will stop rolling at Hadrian's Wall and Offa's Dyke.

Yet when, in November 2004, people in the North East of England were given the chance to vote for an elected regional assembly, they overwhelmingly declined to do so. It would appear that whatever might have happened in Scotland or Wales, people in England are happy to be governed as they are now. Yet that might be to jump to too rapid a conclusion. After all, the assembly would have had relatively limited powers (Cabinet Office–DLGTR 2002), so perhaps people did not think they were being offered enough devolution, a view that would certainly be endorsed by the Liberal Democratic Party (2004). In any event, we should bear in mind that regional devolution is not the only possible answer to the apparent anomalies created by the current devolution settlement. One other possibility would be to create an English parliament with a range of functions similar to that available to the Scottish Parliament in Edinburgh, an idea with which William Hague toyed in his early months as Conservative Party leader, but which currently is not supported by any of the major political parties. Meanwhile, a different option would be not to create any new institutions but rather to reform Westminster by banning Scottish and perhaps Welsh MPs from voting on English legislation, a position that has been adopted in recent years by the opposition Conservative Party (2001). To assess whether people in England really are happy with the status quo we need to consider their views, too, about these possibilities.

In this chapter, then, we examine the extent and character of public support for a change to how England is governed now that Scotland and Wales have had several years' experience of a devolved form of government. Does England want what Scotland and Wales enjoy? Has support for some form of change increased in the wake of Scottish and Welsh devolution? And, if so, why have these developments occurred? Our principal source of evidence is the British Social Attitudes survey (hereafter, BSA), which has tracked attitudes towards devolution in England on a regular basis between 1999 and 2003 (Curtice and Heath 2000; Curtice and Seyd 2001; Heath, Rothon and Jarvis 2002; Park *et al* 2003). In so doing it has been able to administer many of its questions to relatively large samples, comprising in the 2003 survey in particular over 3,700 respondents. This makes it possible to look at attitudes not only across England as a whole but in each of the individual government regions, and thereby to ascertain whether the demand for devolution is greater in some parts of the country than others.

This analysis proceeds in two stages. First we examine the level of support for the three possible ways of changing how England is governed, looking at the evidence of other surveys as well as the BSA survey.[1] Having ascertained the level of support for the various proposals we attempt in the second half of the chapter to identify what it is that influences people's attitudes towards the English Question and thus to account for the level of support for the three options. The focus is in particular on two possible sets of influences – identity and instrumentality. People may support a change to the way they are governed because they believe alternative arrangements would better symbolise their sense of identity. Or they might want change because they believe that a new form of government would be more effective and efficient than the status quo. The demand for devolution in Scotland certainly appears to have been stimulated by both these potential influences, albeit that there has been some dispute about their relative importance (Brown *et al* 1999; Curtice 1999; Surridge and McCrone 1999). They would thus seem obvious areas on which to focus the attempt to understand the character of support for constitutional change in England.

Does England want change?

Throughout the period 1999–2003, the BSA survey presented people with a set of alternative ways in which England might be governed in future, and invited them to indicate which would be best, given 'all the changes going on in the way different parts of Great Britain are run'. These options were, in essence:

- an English parliament with powers similar to those of the current Scottish Parliament;
- assemblies in each of the regions of England with powers similar to those of the National Assembly for Wales; and
- the status quo whereby England is run by the UK Government.

As can be seen from table 6.1, faced with these options a majority of people in England have consistently rejected devolution and opted for the status quo. True, there is some suggestion that the advent of the Scottish Parliament and the Welsh Assembly has created a little more enthusiasm for devolution – as indicated by an eight point fall between 1999 and 2000 in the proportion opting for the status quo – but this drop was still too little to generate majority interest in some form of change.

Still, there is some suggestion that support for regional devolution, as opposed to an English Parliament, has increased somewhat since 1999, with nearly 25 per cent now backing that option. Moreover, our question does

Table 6.1 Attitudes (as %) towards how England should be governed

	1999	2000	2001	2002	2003
England to be governed as it is now, with laws made by the UK Parliament	62	54	57	56	55
Each region of England to have its own assembly that runs services like health	5	18	23	20	24
England as a whole to have its own new parliament with law-making powers	18	19	16	17	16

not refer to the rather weaker form of regional devolution that the UK Government was hoping to introduce; nor does it make it clear that a regional assembly might be elected – perhaps there is rather greater support for this proposal than that reported for regional devolution in table 6.1, though there is no more than the weakest of evidence. In the 2003 survey just 25 per cent of respondents were asked the question outlined in table 6.1; the remainder were asked a new question on which the middle option was described as: 'each region of England to have its own elected assembly that makes decisions about the region's economy, planning and housing'. Just 3 per cent more people opted for regional devolution when this version of the question was administered – indeed at the same time 3 per cent more people opted for an English parliament, too, even though the wording of that option was unchanged! It seems that however it is described, the idea of regional devolution all round does not evince a great deal of enthusiasm.

Perhaps we are still underestimating the demand for devolution. While around half may not want it, the other half might back it, but simply have different preferences about what form it should take. After all, on the alternatively worded question introduced on the 2003 survey, the 48 per cent who said they favoured the status quo was almost matched by the 46 per cent who backed either regional devolution or an English parliament. And there does indeed appear to be some truth to this perspective. Table 6.2 shows the answers obtained when people have been asked an alternative question designed to tap their attitudes towards regional devolution alone, and which, for good measure, also reminds respondents more explicitly that Scotland and Wales already have some form of devolution. As can be seen, the proportion favouring regional devolution almost matches the proportion that is actively opposed. Even so, that still means that no more than 30 per cent support regional devolution, while 25 per cent say they neither agree nor disagree with our proposition and another 10 per cent say they are unable to provide an answer at all. In short, it appears that regional devolution is not a subject on which many have firm views one way or the other.

Much the same might be said about the idea of excluding Scottish MPs

Table 6.2 Attitudes (as %) towards regional government

Now that Scotland has its own parliament and Wales its own assembly, every region of England should have its own assembly too

	2001	2002	2003
Agree	29	27	30
Neither	25	23	25
Disagree	33	37	33

Table 6.3 Attitudes (as %) towards Scottish MPs

Now that Scotland has its own Parliament, Scottish MPs should no longer be allowed to vote in the House of Commons on laws that only affect England

	2000	2001	2003
Strongly agree	18	19	22
Agree	46	38	38
Neither agree nor disagree	19	18	18
Disagree	8	12	10
Strongly disagree	1	2	1

from voting on English legislation. As table 6.3 shows, nearly 20 per cent say they neither agree nor disagree with this proposition, while another 10 per cent or so say they are undecided. But here at least there does seem to be a broad sentiment in favour. Even so, it is far from clear that this sentiment is a strong one, with nearly twice as many people saying they simply agree as there are saying they strongly agree. It appears that people in England are quite happy to continue to have many of their affairs determined at Westminster. If anything needs to change, it is simply that now that Scots can determine much of their domestic business for themselves, their representatives at Westminster might be expected to keep their noses out of England's affairs.

However, perhaps we have been making a mistake so far in looking at attitudes across England as a whole. After all, why should we expect people in London and the South East to be as keen on devolution as those living elsewhere? They have little reason to complain if indeed the government in London listens to the rest of the country through Cockney-attuned ears. So table 6.4 looks separately at the answers given in each region in the 2003 BSA survey to the first of our two questions about devolution. (As the distributions of answers to the two alternative versions of that question were similar, we have combined the two sets of responses in the figures that follow.)

Table 6.4 Regional variation in attitudes (as %) towards how England should be governed

	NE	NW	YH	EM	WM	SW	E	GL	SE
As now	48	50	48	49	47	49	55	52	50
Regional assembly	33	27	30	26	29	27	21	24	21
English parliament	19	18	16	20	20	18	19	15	21

Notes: NE: North East; NW: North West; YH: Yorkshire & The Humber; EM: East Midlands; WM: West Midlands; SW: South West; E: Eastern; GL: Greater London; SE: South East.

Table 6.4 exhibits only limited regional variation: as many people in the North West support the status quo as do in the South East. Even so, support for regional devolution does appear to be highest in the region most distant from London, the North East, and lowest in the two regions that are closest, the South East and the Eastern region. It is also relatively low in the capital itself even though it has an elected regional body already. Moreover, although they may be small, the differences in table 6.4 were largely present in the 2001 and 2002 BSA surveys (both of which interviewed nearly 3,000 people in England) as well. Support for regional devolution does, then, appear to be highest in the North East and relatively low in three regions in the south-eastern corner of the country. This is confirmed by the evidence in table 6.5, which looks at regional variation in the responses to the questions that focused specifically on regional devolution.

Table 6.5 Regional variation (as %) in attitudes towards regional government

Now that Scotland has its own Parliament and Wales its own Assembly, every region of England should have its own assembly too

	NE[a]	NW	YH	EM	WM	SW	E	GL	SE
Agree	39	30	34	29	28	38	29	25	27
Neither	22	27	23	34	22	20	28	24	25
Disagree	28	31	33	31	39	32	36	30	35

So despite the results of the referendum, we can probably conclude that there is somewhat greater support for the creation of an elected regional assembly in the North East than elsewhere. This is after all the region of England where concern about the potential impact of Scottish devolution has been greatest, and where elite demands for some form of regional government have probably been loudest (Benneworth and Tomaney 2002). It may indeed also be relatively high in the other two northern regions, the North West and Yorkshire & The Humber, where the Government originally had intended to hold referendums at the same time as in the North East, though these hardly stand apart in their attitudes from a number of other regions. However, even in the North East support for regional devolution is no more than lukewarm, and certainly not strong enough to withstand what, in the event, proved to be an effective 'No' campaign.

Interestingly, the pattern of responses to the two questions on devolution appear to be very different from the answers obtained by a number of other surveys that have attempted to ascertain the attitudes of those living across England towards regional devolution. A poll conducted by ICM in January

2003 for the County Councils' Network found that 41 per cent said that in a referendum they would vote in favour of creating a regional assembly while only 21 per cent would vote against. Equally, a poll conducted by MORI the following month found that 44 per cent supported 'your [named] region having its own elected assembly', while just 27 per cent were opposed. Even more strikingly, a poll conducted by ORB for the BBC in March of the previous year reported 63 per cent in favour of the creation of a regional assembly for their region and just 22 per cent opposed. It would seem that our analysis so far has seriously underestimated the level if support for regional government in England.

There are in fact three important observations we can make about the difference between the results obtained by the BSA survey and those obtained by these three polls. First we should note that while the balance of opinion in the polls is more favourable to regional government, two of them still only find just over two in five in favour not least because relatively large numbers of their respondents emerge as having no strong views. In MORI's poll 27 per cent said either that they neither supported nor opposed having a regional assembly, or that they did not know. In ICM's case as many as 35 per cent either said that they did not know how they would vote or that they definitely would not vote. Such figures suggest not so much that people are opposed to regional government as simply uninterested in what it might offer.[2]

But what of the ORB figure of 63 per cent in favour? Here it is important to understand that this poll did not explicitly offer a middle option, such as neither support nor oppose, an option that all other surveys find to be relatively popular. Forced to choose, most of those who might otherwise have opted for such a response, it appears, indicated weak approval of regional devolution. Certainly, no less than 44 per cent of ORB's respondents said that they were 'somewhat in favour' of regional government rather than 'strongly in favour'.

Indeed the need to take proper account of indifference towards regional devolution was evident in the very first piece of major research undertaken on the subject, by the Kilbrandon Commission on the Constitution in 1970 (Commission on the Constitution 1973). Details of the key question asked on the survey commissioned by Kilbrandon are given in table 6.6. As can be seen, nearly 25 per cent backed a middle option that effectively allowed people to sit on the fence. Meanwhile, if that group were left to one side those who clearly favoured some form of devolution for their region were almost exactly counterbalanced by those who were clearly opposed.

The third and final observation to be made about the difference between the results of the BSA survey and those of other recent surveys is to note that

Table 6.6 Attitudes towards English devolution in 1970

For running [name of region] as a whole, which of these would you prefer?	%
Leave things as they are at present	14
Keep things much as they are now, but make sure that the needs of the region are better understood by the Government	24
Keep the present system, but allow more decisions to be made in the region	24
Have a new system of governing the region so that as many decisions as possible are made in the area	21
Let the region take over complete responsibility for running regional affairs	15

Source: Survey on attitudes towards devolution conducted for the Commission on the Constitution.

the three other surveys all addressed a subtly different issue than the BSA survey. The latter asked people about the merits of creating a system of regional assemblies throughout England; the former, in contrast, asked their respondents whether they supported or opposed the creation of a regional assembly in *their* particular region. The latter at least leaves open the possibility that a respondent's own region would acquire a regional assembly while other regions would not. While asking this question might be a way of ascertaining how people would vote in a referendum on the subject in their region, it is unsatisfactory if the interest lies, as here, in the level of public support for a systematic answer to the English Question that could be applied to the country as a whole.

Again, previous research confirms that the distinction matters. In both 1991 and 1995 the State of the Nation survey series asked, 'would you support or oppose giving greater powers of government to other regions of Britain, such as the West Country, the North West, East Anglia etc.'; on both occasions around 60 per cent said that they would oppose such a move while only around 25 per cent were in favour. Indeed it was the only constitutional reform covered by the survey where a majority were clearly opposed (Dunleavy, Weir and Subrahmanyam 1995). When the researchers returned to the field in 2000, and again in 2004, they asked: (*'Thinking now about England, which of the following options do you think is the best way of deciding how to generate new jobs, develop major road and public transport, and other similar issues?'*

- *Government ministers in Whitehall should decide, taking into account the needs of the country as a whole.*
- *An elected assembly for this region should decide.*
- *Government officials meeting at regional level should decide.*

- *Appointed business and local government representatives from this region should decide.)*

They found just 12–14 per cent in favour of no form of regional devolution at all (Dunleavy *et al.* 2001a; Joseph Rowntree Reform Trust 2004). Even so, at the same time only around one-third supported the idea of an elected regional assembly. Between 24 per cent (in 2004) and 29 per cent (in 2000) actually backed the fourth option of an appointed body not dissimilar to the existing regional chambers, while another 15–16 per cent were happy to leave matters in the hands of government officials in the manner of the existing GOs. So even with this question the survey still tapped considerable support for the status quo.

There is in fact one further piece of evidence testifying to the relatively limited character of public support for regional devolution in England that can be gleaned from the 2003 BSA survey. Respondents were asked which body ought to have most influence over the way that England is run in the event that elected regional assemblies were to be created across the country. Just 28 per cent said that regional assemblies should have most influence whereas no less than 43 per cent indicated that the UK Government should have that role. Very different answers were obtained by parallel surveys in Scotland (the 2003 Scottish Social Attitudes survey) and Wales (the 2003 Welsh Life and Times survey). In Scotland no less than 66 per cent believe that the Scottish Parliament should have most influence on affairs north of the border while in Wales 54 per cent give a similar response in respect of the National Assembly. Evidently, despite the examples set by Scotland and Wales, most people in England cannot envisage anything other than central government continuing to have most influence over their country's affairs.

So it appears that the English themselves are far from convinced that the creation of devolved institutions in Scotland and Wales means that they, too, need to have similar institutions. True, there is not so much opposition to some form of devolution as there is indifference. And there is somewhat greater support for regional devolution in those regions furthest from London than there is elsewhere. But there is certainly not the same kind of wish as there evidently is in both Scotland and Wales for the locus of power to be shifted significantly away from central government in London. Rather it appears that people in England still expect their affairs to be run largely by central government. In so far as they recognise that any change is required, in order to answer the English Question their response would be to bar MPs from outside England from voting on English laws, though even here the demand looks as though it will not be a strong one. Why there is apparently so little enthusiasm for change is the matter to which we now turn.

Why so little enthusiasm?

As we indicated earlier, two main reasons as to why people might want the way they are governed changed envisage may be envisaged. First, they may regard different institutional arrangements a more satisfactory expression of their sense of identity. As a political creed nationalism has long argued that those who share the same sense of national identity should have that identity recognised by distinctive state institutions (Gellner 1983). So we might look to see the extent to which people in England have come to develop a distinctive *English* (rather than *British*) identity that they now wish to see expressed either in the creation of an English parliament or in having only English MPs voting on English laws. Meanwhile, so far as regional devolution is concerned we might look at the degree to which people have a sense of regional pride which they would like to see reflected in the way that they are governed.

Alternatively, however, people may wish to see a change in the way that they are governed because they regard the existing structure as in some way inefficient or ineffective. They may believe that more locally based institutions would make decisions that are better attuned to the particular needs and concerns of their part of the country. Or people may feel that if decisions are made closer to home they are more likely to have some influence over them. In contrast the existing structure may be considered both remote and London-centric.

There is of course nothing new about these possibilities. They could be expected to generate a demand for new institutions at any time. But one reason why these forces may be thought to have become more influential in recent years is the example set by Scotland and Wales. If devolution there were thought to have made a difference then there might be good reason for England, too, to want to adopt it. Perhaps devolution is thought to have brought valuable benefits that England now wishes to enjoy. Or perhaps people in England have come to the view that asymmetric devolution is indeed unacceptable and wish to put something in place in England in order to militate against its effects.

Yet there is little sign of either reaction. The BSA survey has been regularly monitoring the reaction of people in England to devolution in Scotland and Wales. On the one hand it has ascertained what contribution people in England feel that the creation of the Scottish Parliament and the Welsh Assembly has made to the way that Britain as a whole is governed. As table 6.7 shows, the dominant reaction has simply been that it has not made any difference (while around another one in six simply say they do not know whether it has made any difference). Moreover, far from this becoming less true as devolution has had more time to prove itself, the opposite has been the case. For example, there has been a ten-point increase in 2003 in the pro-

Table 6.7 Perceived impact (as %) of devolution on how Britain is governed

	2000	2001	2002	2003
Scotland				
Improved	18	18	19	12
No difference	54	54	54	64
Made worse	13	13	10	6
Wales[a]				
Improved	15	11	–	8
No difference	57	65	–	66
Made worse	12	7	–	6

Note: [a] No consultation in 2002.

portion thinking that having a Scottish Parliament has not made any differ-ence to how well Britain is governed. True, among those who do think that devolution has made some difference those who think that it has improved matters outnumber those who think it has made things worse, but there is nothing in these figures to suggest that devolution in Scotland and Wales has been regarded as so successful that it has helped put devolution on England's political agenda.

Yet despite the perceived lack of impact, in practice people in England appear to be sympathetic to Scotland and Wales having their own institu-tions while at the same time remaining part of the UK. As table 6.8 shows, 60 per cent now support the existence of a devolved Scottish Parliament, with most backing the idea that it should be a body with taxation powers. A similar proportion favours devolution for Wales, with nearly two-thirds of pro-devolutionists saying that the devolved institutions in the principality should in fact have powers on a par with those of the Scottish Parliament. Moreover, such opposition as there was in England towards separate insti-tutions in Scotland and Wales appears to have dropped permanently by ten points or so once the new institutions were in place, and just one in seven or so are opposed to any kind of Scottish Parliament or Welsh Assembly.

It would be wrong, of course, to infer from such evidence that there is necessarily strongly felt support for Scottish and Welsh devolution among people in England. Doubtless many respondents had not considered the matter much at all before being quizzed by an interviewer. But such evidence does contradict the idea that people in England feel any antagonism towards Scotland and Wales as a result of devolution. True, immediately after devolu-tion was introduced there was a 7–10-point rise in the proportion of people saying that Scotland and Wales should be independent, a response that could be considered evidence of a wish to be rid of England's Celtic neighbours,

Table 6.8 English attitudes (as %) towards devolution in Scotland and Wales

	1997	1999	2000	2001	2003
Scotland should . . .					
. . . be independent, separate from the UK and the EU, or separate from the UK but part of the EU	14	24	20	19	17
. . . remain part of the UK with its own elected parliament which has some taxation powers	38	44	44	53	51
. . . remain part of the UK with its own elected parliament which has no taxation powers	17	10	8	7	9
. . . remain part of the UK without an elected parliament	23	13	17	11	13
Wales should . . .					
. . . be independent, separate from the UK and the EU, or separate from the UK but part of the EU	13	20	17	17	16
. . . remain part of the UK, with its own elected parliament which has law-making and taxation powers	37	34	35	39	37
. . . remain part of the UK, with its own elected assembly which has limited law-making powers only	18	22	17	19	20
. . . remain part of the UK without an elected assembly	25	15	20	14	15

Source: 1997: British Election Study

but even this modest increase appears largely to have been reversed more recently.[3] Meanwhile, there is no sign at all of people in England becoming antagonistic towards the higher levels of public expenditure being enjoyed elsewhere in the UK. In 2003 only 22 per cent said that Scotland received more than its fair share of government spending, little different from the 20 per cent who gave that response in 2000.

In short it appears that devolution in Scotland and Wales is thought neither to have been so successful that it demands to be emulated nor to have done so much harm that the damage needs to be repaired. To that extent there is little reason to believe that any of the potential sources of demand for change should have been unleashed in recent years. But let us see what appears to lie behind such support for constitutional change as does exist in England.

I look, first of all, at why people might support the creation of an English parliament or wish to have only English MPs voting on English laws. Is such support an expression of a growing sense of *English* rather than *British* national identity? Certainly there is some evidence, as table 6.9 shows, that if people in England are asked to choose a single national identity that best describes the way in which they think of themselves, rather more now choose *English* and rather less *British* than was the case a decade ago. Moreover, this increased sense of an English identity appears to date from the establishment of devolution in Scotland and Wales in 1999. There is, however, no evidence that this growth in a sense of Englishness has continued thereafter – rather, if anything, the opposite has been true. And in any event, still around only 40 per cent of people say that they are best described as 'English', fewer than the 50 or so per cent who say they are 'British'.

Table 6.9 Trends (as %) in forced-choice national identity

	1992	1997	1999	2000	2001	2002	2003
English	31	34	44	41	43	37	39
British	63	59	44	47	44	51	48

Source: 1992 and 1997: British Election Study.

In any event, most people in England do not feel English *or* British rather than English *and* British. In table 6.10, which reports the answers obtained in England to the so-called 'Moreno question' (Moreno 1988), only just over a quarter say that they are English and not British or vice-versa. Nearly two-thirds claim to be some mixture of both. But intriguingly there does appear to have been a decline in the proportion who regard themselves as *equally* English and British, while the proportion claiming to be either exclusively English or else more English than British reached an all-time high of 36 per cent in 2003. So there is perhaps some evidence here of an increasing awareness that being English may not be entirely synonymous with being British.

Table 6.10 Trends (as %) in Moreno national identity

	1997	1999	2000	2001	2003
English not British	7	17	19	17	17
More English than British	17	15	14	13	19
Equally English and British	45	37	34	42	31
More British than English	14	11	14	9	13
British not English	9	14	12	11	10
Other	5	3	6	7	6

Source: 1997: British Election Study.

But if such increase in English national identity as has occurred is to have any relevance to the debate about the English question, then we should be able to demonstrate that those who feel English rather than British are more likely to support the creation of an English parliament and/or having only English MPs voting on English laws. As table 6.11 shows, they are, but hardly spectacularly so. Those who say that they are best described as English are just 7 points more likely to favour an English parliament than are those who say they are best described as British and only 12 points more likely to feel that Scottish MPs should not have a vote on English laws. It appears that having an English parliament is not regarded as an essential expression of a distinctively English national identity, while support for having only English MPs vote on English laws is far from being the preserve of those who would consider themselves as primarily English.

Table 6.11 Attitudes (as %) towards how England should be governed, by forced-choice national identity

	British	*English*
As now	52	49
Regional assembly	28	24
English parliament	16	23
Scottish MPs should no longer be allowed to vote in the House of Commons on laws that only affect England		
Strongly agree	17	29
Agree	41	38
Neither agree nor disagree	19	15
Disagree	10	6
Strongly disagree	2	1

So far as support for an English parliament is concerned, this conclusion is supported by the evidence produced by further questions that also tried to tap people's affective orientations towards different geographical entities, among which were both 'England as a whole' and 'Britain as a whole'. Most people (76 per cent) in fact gave the same answer to both these questions, but a sizeable minority of 17 per cent indicated that they felt closer to England than they did to Britain (while just 7 per cent felt closer to Britain than England). Yet the former were just 3 points more likely to favour an English parliament than were those who said they felt equally close to both, and only 5 points more likely than those who said they felt closer to Britain. When it comes to barring Scottish MPs from voting on English laws, however, feeling closer to England than to Britain makes somewhat more of a difference.

Those who feel closer to England are 10 points more likely to favour barring Scottish MPs than are those who feel equally close to Britain and England, who in turn are 10 points more likely to favour that step than the small minority who feel closer to Britain than to England. Nevertheless, even among the latter group nearly half are still in favour, confirming that support for barring Scottish MPs from voting on English laws is far from being the preserve of those with a strong sense of Englishness.

There is little sign either that perceptions of how the current system of government is working provide much impetus for people in England to demand a parliament of their own. As table 6.12 shows, even when reminded that 'the United Kingdom Government at Westminster has responsibility for England, Scotland, Wales and Northern Ireland', over half say that they trust the UK Government to work in the best long-term interests of England either 'just about always' or 'most of the time', while less than 10 per cent say they trust the Government almost never. In contrast, in both Scotland and Wales little more than 20 per cent trust the UK Government to work in the long term interest of their country. It appears that people in England are simply much less concerned than are those in Scotland and Wales about losing out if decisions are made by the UK Government. In any event even among those who are less trustful of the UK Government's ability to work in England's long-term interests, support for an English parliament is only nine points higher than it is among the relatively trusting, while this perception makes no difference to people's views on whether Scottish MPs should be barred from voting on English laws.

Table 6.12 Trust (as %) in the UK Government

How much do you trust the UK Government to work in the best long-term interest of England/Scotland/Wales?

	England	*Scotland*	*Wales*
Just about always	7	2	2
Most of the time	46	19	20
Only some of the time	35	58	58
Almost never	9	20	19

Sources: Scotland: Scottish Social Attitudes survey (2003); Wales: Wales Life and Times survey (2003).

So while a sense of English national identity is somewhat stronger now than it was prior to the advent of devolution, this sense of national identity is not strongly associated with a wish for distinctively English political institutions, not least perhaps because for many people England's interests are served adequately by existing constitutional arrangements. Much the same can also be said for sympathy with the idea of having only English MPs voting on English legislation. But this conclusion need not necessarily apply to support for regional devolution. Even if England as a whole is not thought to be losing out to the rest of the UK, it still might be thought that a system of regional government could improve the governance of England. And having such regional governments might also be regarded as an expression of a distinctive identity or an affinity with their own particular corner of England.

Let us consider, first of all, the degree to which people do feel some affective bond with their part of England. The 2003 BSA survey asked people how much pride they had in 'being someone who lives in' their named region of England. As table 6.13 indicates, nearly half say they feel 'very' or 'somewhat' proud to live in their region of England. However, they are matched by an equal number who say they do not feel that way at all. In contrast, no less than 79 per cent say they feel 'very' or 'somewhat' proud of being British, with a very similar proportion, 76 per cent, saying the same about being English. While far from being absent, pride in one's region is evidently a far less widespread phenomenon than is pride in one's country.

Table 6.13 Regional variation in regional pride (as %)

	NE	NW	YH	EM	WM	SW	E	GL	SE	All
Very proud	50	33	37	10	17	27	11	21	10	22
Somewhat	27	30	27	20	25	29	20	29	19	25
Not very	4	5	5	3	4	1	4	9	3	4
Not at all	1	1	2	1	2	0	0	2	2	1
Don't think that way	19	31	30	65	53	44	63	40	67	48

Note: For details of regions see notes to table 6.4.

Still, we should note that pride in one's region does vary substantially from one part of England to another. It is far more prevalent in the north of England, and especially the North East, than it is elsewhere. Moreover, this also appears to be a consistent feature of the English landscape as exactly the same was true when this question was asked on the 2001 BSA survey. However, a sense of regional pride does not, it seems, automatically translate into support for regional devolution; for, as table 6.14 shows, those who feel very proud to live in their region are only nine points more likely to agree that every region of England should have its own assembly than are those who say they do not think of themselves in that way at all. Indeed, even among the people who feel proud of their region, those who agree with regional devolution all round only slightly outnumber those who disagree.

Table 6.14 Attitudes (as %) towards regional government by regional pride

Now that Scotland has its own Parliament and Wales its own Assembly, every region of England, should have its own assembly too

	Very Proud	Somewhat proud	Not very/at all proud	Don't think that way
Agree	36	32	32	27
Neither	18	29	22	27
Disagree	34	29	38	34

Much the same conclusion is reached if we look at how close people feel to their region. Fewer people feel close to their region than they do to England or, indeed, even Britain as a whole, the North East being the one clear exception. And those who say they feel closer to their region than they do England as a whole are only nine points more likely to favour regional devolution all round than are those who feel closer to England than to their region. So it seems that with the possible exception of the North East (and to a lesser extent the rest of the north of England), people in England lack a strong sense of regional identity or affiliation. Moreover, even if they do, this seems to make no more than a marginal difference to their likelihood of supporting regional devolution. In short, support for regional devolution in England is not clearly rooted in identity. But what of perceptions of the efficiency and effectiveness of government? Might these account for such support as there is for regional devolution?

Certainly, there is one feature of the way that government works at present that does appear to give rise to criticism: people may not feel that England as a whole is losing out to the rest of the UK, but apparently they do reckon that some parts of England are advantaged over others. Asked whether the Government 'looks after the interests of all parts of England more or less equally' or whether 'it looks after some parts of England more than others', no less than 76 per cent opted for the latter response and only 17 per cent for the former. And there seems to be widespread agreement as to the advantaged parts: no less than 36 per cent (of the whole sample) named the south of England as a whole, while another 31 per cent named London in particular; only 5 per cent thought it was the Midlands and the north of England that were advantaged.

It would seem that jealousy of what London and the south of England are able to secure is potentially a far more potent force for regional devolution than is envy of what Scotland and Wales are enjoying. But this depends, of course, on those who believe that their region is losing out translating that feeling into a demand for regional government. Yet, to date at least, this for the most part seems not to have happened. Table 6.15 divides the social attitudes sample into those who feel that the Government looks after its own part of the country (20 per cent of respondents), those who believe it looks after a region or regions other than its own (who constitute no less than 61 per cent) and, finally, those who believe that the Government looks after all regions equally. It can be seen that the level of support for regional devolution is only seven points higher among those who believe that their region is currently disadvantaged than it is among those who feel that the Government looks after all regions equally. Indeed, support for regional devolution among this group proves to be no higher than it is among those who believe that the Government actually advantages their region.

Table 6.15 Attitudes (as %) to English regional government by perceptions of government bias

Now that Scotland has its own Parliament and Wales its own Assembly, every region of England, should have its own assembly too

	Government looks after the interests of		
	Own region	*All regions equally*	*Other regions*
Agree	33	23	30
Neither	22	21	28
Disagree	32	37	31

In any event, discontent with the current system of government is likely to translate into a demand for change only if the alternative is thought likely to improve matters. And it appears that, to date at least, people's experience of the regional devolution that is already in place has not convinced them that it would. As table 6.16 shows, a majority of people believe that having a regional chamber or assembly will make no difference either to how much say ordinary people have in government or to the prospects for their region's economy, while around another 15 per cent said they did not know.[4] Even in London, where an elected Assembly has been in place since 2000, the majority impression is that devolution is not making any difference. In fact it appears that it is the unelected regional chamber in the North East of England, which according to 32 per cent is giving ordinary people more say and according to 33 per cent will help improve the region's economy, that has so far made the most favourable impact on its citizenry; otherwise the differences between the various regions are relatively small.

This lack of perceived impact is important. Thinking that having a regional chamber or assembly can make a difference appears to be vital if people are to be convinced of the merits of regional devolution. For, as table 6.17 indicates, those who believe that their regional assembly is giving ordinary people more say are no less than 18 points more likely to support regional devolution, while those who say their assembly is making the prospects for the economy better

Table 6.16 Perceptions (as %) of the impact of regional chambers/assemblies

From what you have seen or heard so far do you think that having a regional chamber or assembly for [region] will give (2003: is giving) ordinary people. . . in how [region] is governed?

	All England			London			
	2001	*2002*	*2003*	*2000*	*2001*	*2002*	*2003*
More say	32	25	19	45	38	35	26
No difference	55	59	62	45	51	51	53
Less say	2	3	4	6	2	3	8

Will the region's economy become better, worse or will it make no difference?

Better	29	21	23		34	24	27
No difference	55	60	58		50	54	52
Worse	3	4	4		3	7	6

Source: London 2000: London Mayoral; Election Study.

Table 6.17 Attitudes (as %) towards regional government by perceptions of impact of regional chambers/assemblies

Now that Scotland has its own Parliament and Wales its own Assembly, every region of England, should have its own assembly too

	Perceived impact of regional chamber on giving ordinary people a say:		
	More say	*No difference*	*Less say*
Agree	45	27	27
Neither	24	25	18
Disagree	24	37	44

	Perceived impact of regional chamber on regions economic prospects:		
	More say	*No difference*	*Less say*
Agree	42	28	18
Neither	25	25	12
Disagree	26	37	62

are 14 points more likely to favour regional government. Indeed if we undertake a step-wise regression analysis of support for regional devolution, giving an opportunity for all those measures that we have considered in this chapter to enter the equation, we find that only our measure of whether their regional assembly is giving people more say (which itself is strongly intercorrelated with perceptions of its impact on the region's economy) proves to be significantly associated with attitudes towards devolution.

We should of course exercise some caution here. Doubtless some people's views on the impact of their regional chamber/assembly is a consequence of their views about regional devolution rather than vice-versa. Even so, it seems reasonable to conclude that one of the reasons why regional devolution has not been embraced with greater enthusiasm is that it is not thought likely to make much difference. In the absence of any clear symbolic link in people's minds between their affective feelings towards their region and regional governmental institutions, little such enthusiasm can ever be expected until people have been convinced that regional government would be better than the status quo.

Conclusion

England has yet to embrace with much enthusiasm any form of change to the way that it is governed. Whatever the constitutional anomalies and difficulties it might have created, the establishment of devolved bodies in Scotland and Wales is not thought to have made much impact on how Britain is governed, and thus has not provided a compelling reason why England should follow a similar path. Devolution to Scotland and Wales is something to be tolerated rather than resented or imitated, though the logic that, following devolution, Scottish MPs should not be voting on English laws attracts widespread sympathy if not necessarily deep-rooted support. Meanwhile, people in England still have neither a distinctive sense of national identity nor a strong sense of regional pride, and even those who do are not particularly inclined to feel this should be reflected in their country's constitutional structure. Although many apparently feel that the Government is focused on the south of England, given the failure of the current regional assemblies to provide a positive role model, it does not appear that many people have been persuaded that a system of regional government would provide an effective remedy to this ill.

Indeed, in one respect at least the impetus for devolution looks weaker now than it did when the Kilbrandon Commission first investigated the subject thirty years ago. Governments have become increasingly concerned about differences in the scope and effectiveness of public-service provision in such areas as health and education. Thus, the rest are encouraged to emulate the best through such mechanisms as the publication of hospital and school league tables. Such moves clearly encourage the view that public services should be of the same standard across the country as a whole rather than vary in accordance with differing regional or national priorities. Indeed, as table 6.18 shows, people in England are markedly more inclined now than they were in 1970 to say that the standard of public services should be the same in every part of Britain.

Table 6.18 Attitudes (as %) towards public service standards

Thinking about things like the health service, schools, the roads, the police, and so on, in general do you think it better that the standards for such services be . . .

	1970	2003
. . . the same in every part of Britain	53	66
. . . or each region should be allowed to set its own standards?	44	33

Source: 1970: Survey on attitudes towards devolution conducted for the Commission on the Constitution.

None of this means that it was inevitable that people in the North East of England would vote against having an elected regional assembly. Yet even there, with its relatively strong sense of regional pride and a perception that the unelected regional chamber might have achieved something, the evidence indicates insufficient enthusiasm for regional devolution to win the argument. Now that the argument has been lost, it can be expected that, for the time being at least, the rest of England will be happy to acquiesce in the idea being quietly buried.

Notes

The research reported in this paper has been supported financially by the Leverhulme Trust under its Nations and Regions programme, by the Economic and Social Research Council under its Devolution and Constitution Change programme, and the O DPM. I am grateful to the UK Data Archive at the University of Essex for providing the data set of the survey conducted for the Commission on the Constitution and that of the first of the State of the Nation surveys. While these organisations should take the credit for making this research possible, they are not responsible for the interpretation of the data provided in this paper, for which responsibility lies solely with the author.

1 All figures quoted in this chapter are taken from the BSA Survey unless otherwise stated.
2 Indeed, another poll conducted by MORI for *The Economist* in 1999 still found only 50 per cent in favour of giving 'greater powers of government to regions in England' despite failing, like ORB, to offer a middle option at all and explicitly reminding respondents that elections were just about to take place to the Scottish Parliament and the Welsh Assembly. No less than 23 per cent said that they did not know whether they supported or opposed the proposition, while 27 per cent said they were opposed. See www.mori.com/polls/1999/ec990308.shtml and the *Economist*, 26 March 1999.
3 And in the case of Scotland is little different from the 15 per cent recorded by the State of the Nation poll in 1995, on a somewhat differently worded question, and

well down on the 34 per cent registered by that poll in 1991 (Dunleavy *et al.* 2001b).
4 We might note, too, that these figures are well below the equivalent statistics for Scotland and Wales, in both of which 35–40 per cent feel that having a parliament/assembly is giving ordinary people more say and will help improve their economy.

Part II
The governance of England

7
From functional to political regionalism: England in comparative perspective

Michael Keating

The English Question

It is a premiss of this collection that there is an English Question within the UK constitution, but there is less agreement on just what this question is and what the objectives and forms of English constitutional reform might be. In this chapter, I put England in a European comparative perspective, in an effort to clarify the issue and explore future possibilities. There are two broad objectives that might be set for constitutional reform in England: first, to rebalance the State and the Constitution following devolution to the smaller nations; second, to improve the government of England in its own right. It may be that these two are inconsistent.

The first objective implies a need to find forms of government in the centre similar to those in the periphery – nothing else will answer the West Lothian and related questions. In Spain, this approach has largely been followed since the 1980s, with the central state resisting concessions to the nations and then, when it has to concede, seeking to generalise them to all autonomous communities in a tactic known as *café para todos* (coffee all round). Canada, similarly, has tended to match concessions to Quebec with the same treatment for the other provinces. This strategy might be criticised for giving the periphery too little and the centre too much, and for a tendency to ever more decentralisation, not in response to genuine demands, but as an inbuilt logic of the system. It may be that the refusal to recognise special or differentiated status, far from stabilising the system, destabilises it, giving the nationalities less than they want and the non-national regions more (Herrero de Miñon 1998). Other countries have sought to limit the impact of devolution by conceding special status to particular territories, so avoiding the need to disturb the centre. This has been done with the five Italian special status regions, Corsica, the Åland islands, Greenland, the Azores and Madeira.[1] This has not stopped governments from treating the remainder of the State as a 'unitary state'.

This is the route that British governments also have adopted since 1997. It is made easier by the fact that the UK has always been a differentiated state, a political union rather than a nation state on the French model (Mitchell 1996). Such unions, with differentiated provisions for the various territories, were common in Europe prior to the nineteenth century, but were swept away in the wave of nation- and state-building after the French Revolution. Uniformity of constitutional status, centralisation and a lack of entrenched intermediary bodies were the hallmarks of the French *jacobin* concept of democracy, imitated widely across Europe. The German conception was more federalist, resting on a limitation of central power and the need for intermediaries, but this too evolved into a uniform regime, in which each part of the State had the same relationship with the centre. Once political legitimacy came to rest on the principle of popular sovereignty, it was assumed that there must be an undifferentiated populace or demos on which it could rest. The British constitution has been criticised by reformers for over 100 years for its unmodern features, its untidiness and the lack of a principle of popular sovereignty. Yet these archaic features might give it a distinct advantage over other European polities in the transition to a new era of differentiated and complex government, in which nations are embedded in different ways in states, which in turn are embedded in a broader European political order, since it has few jacobin prejudices to overcome. Indeed, one might argue that the UK has achieved the remarkable feat of making the transition from an *ancien*, or pre-modern, *regime* to a post-modern constitution, without having passed through the phase of modernity. The time for an overarching UK Constitution, with everything in its place and a symmetrical distribution of power, came and went in the nineteenth and twentieth centuries, and it is futile to try to recapture that moment. It is this continuing union tradition, among other things, that explains why the English appear so relaxed about Scottish devolution and that the debate on English constitutional reform has been divorced from the issue of Home Rule for the peripheral nations. Thinking about democracy in a plurinational state, indeed, needs to start from these premises, rather than from assumptions rooted in the unitary tradition (Keating 2001).

This leaves the second question, that of the need for constitutional reform in England, freed from any equivalence or parallelism with the other nations of the UK. England (although not actually a state) has a unitary state tradition and its experience needs to be considered alongside that of other decentralising unitary states. Here we need to make a fundamental distinction between functional regionalism and a broader political regionalism. Functional regionalism refers to institutions designed around specific policies and tasks. These institutions and tasks will tend to draw in groups and interests related to those tasks, which together with government will constitute policy communities, including some actors and excluding others. Political regionalism on the other hand refers to general mechanisms of representation and policy-making, with a broad functional remit, and based on communities of identity and principles of self-government. The broader their responsibilities and the more representative their mode of selection, the more interests and groups they will draw into the policy process. Of course, these are ideal types and any given regional reform will have a bit of both, but it is important to keep them separate conceptually, so as to understand what are the stakes in the arguments. British local government reform has tended to be based on shifting functional requirements, hence the regular re-organisations, but there is an accompanying rhetoric about empowering communities and deepening democracy. It has proved impossible, on the other hand, to reform French local government on functional lines, so deeply embedded is it in the political system, hence reforms have built around it. Other countries have combined functional with political regionalism and, as argued below, there is a tendency for the former to lead to the latter.

Functional regionalism in Europe

The first initiatives in functional regionalism in post-war Europe came in the 1960s in connection with national planning and economic development. They were linked to national spatial development policies whose aim was to integrate regions into national economies, which in turn were to be inserted into the expanding European economic space. Machinery was rather technocratic in inspiration, with mechanisms for the co-ordination of central policies in the regions linked to consultative devices to incorporate local economic and social interests. In this way, the more dynamic social and economic forces within the regions (what the French called the *forces vives*) were to be co-opted into an agreed development strategy. The general assumption was that development policy is a non-zero-sum matter from which all can gain and therefore not a matter for political contestation. At the same time, there was a political strategy to bypass the traditional local elites and notables who were both rooted in existing local government systems and committed to more distributive politics.

In France, this took the form of the CAR (*conférence administrative régionale*) for the civil servants, which was linked to the CODER (*commission de développement économique régionale*) in turn comprising regional actors, including business leaders, farmers, trade unions, academics and independents (Grémion 1976). Similar arrangements were established in Italy and in Belgium. In 1964, the British Labour Government followed suit with the regional economic planning boards (REPBs) and regional economic planning councils (REPCs). Spain under Franco was experiencing some pressure from the rising technocrats in the regime to establish something similar, but the very idea of regionalism was anathema to the governing elite and the idea made no progress (García Barbancho 1979). In Germany, similar arrangements had to be inserted into an existing federal system of government, through the Joint Task Framework for Regional Economic Development (*Gemeinschaftsaufgabe Verbesserung der regionalen Wirtschafts-struktur*) (Anderson 1992).

These experiments all suffered from an ambivalence in their aims and political objectives: they were expected at the same time to carry out central government policies for restructuring the regions in accordance with national priorities, and to engage local and regional actors in taking responsibility for their own development. They were part of an essentially technical, depoliticised policy frame, based on the assumption of shared interests in development, but at the same time they had representative elements, bringing in different ideas on what type of development there should be. In France, this quickly led to disillusionment, especially when Gaullist Party interests began to take over the development networks. A similar fate befell an earlier innovation, the *Cassa per il Mezzogiorno*, established in 1951 to undertake 'extraordinary interventions' in the Italian south. While it was rather successful in its early years, it was gradually absorbed into the clientelist networks of the Christian Democratic Party and its allies. In England, the members of the REPCs rapidly became disillusioned with their lack of influence, especially after the collapse of the National Plan in 1967 removed their frame of reference and confirmed the old pattern of subordinating long-term growth plans to short-term Treasury thinking. Yet, while the regional planning machinery and its representative elements may have failed, they did serve in many cases to identify the region as a relevant level for public policy and political mobilisation. They also undermined the position of old territorial intermediaries, helping to break down systems of territorial management and open the way for regionalist movements, bringing with them opposing priorities in development (Keating 1988). Centralised regional policies also provoked a politics of territorial defence, seeking to protect sectors threatened by modernisation schemes. So the policy field rapidly politicised and regionalised.

Responses were varied. In Italy, functional regionalism made way rapidly for elected regional government, already provided for in the 1948 Constitution, although the regions were set up only in 1970 and given their powers in 1976. It was many years more before they made their mark politically. In France, de Gaulle's referendum of 1969 on regions and the Senate was intended further to undermine the old notables rooted in the politics of the Third and Fourth Republics, and strengthen the Gaullist hegemony. After its

failure and de Gaulle's resignation, his successor Georges Pompidou effectively handed over the regional level to the notables in the form of indirectly
elected councils chosen by the local governments. It was only in 1981 that the
new Socialist Government moved to elected regional government, and even
then the elections were postponed until 1986. In Belgium, developments were
caught up in the progressive reforms of the Belgian State, which intended to
deal with the issues of functional economic regionalism and of language politics separately, by having different institutions for each. Over time this led to
the federalisation of the State, with the regional governments in the dominant
position. In England, on the other hand, the regional development machinery was abolished by the incoming Conservative Government in 1979 and the
focus moved to selective urban regeneration initiatives. Not until the 1990s
did central government return to a regional perspective, with the GOs.

Political regionalism

Regionalism has also been introduced for more overtly political reasons, as a
measure of democratisation and pluralism, and to satisfy demands from below.
After 1945 the German State was rebuilt from the bottom, culminating in the
Basic Law of 1949 which rested on already constituted *Länd* governments.
Italy's 1948 Constitution realised an ambition of reformers since the 1860s
by stipulating that there should be regional governments. Apart from the five
special-status regions, these were not set up, however, until the 1970s. In the
1990s, bottom–up pressures, including the emergence of the *Lega Nord*, put
the issue back on the agenda, and a series of measures was taken to strengthen
local and regional levels. In 2001 and 2003, further laws were passed to transfer powers to the regions. The Spanish Constitution of 1978 prescribes an
Estado de las autonomías as an essential element in democratisation. Here
there was also the need to accommodate Catalan and Basque nationalism, and
the other regionalist movements that had been inspired by them. From the
1970s, Belgium gradually transformed itself into a federal state of regions and
language communities, responding to both economic and cultural pressures.

An important force in putting regional government on the agenda has
been a change in attitude on the part of the social democratic parties, traditionally committed to a strong central state to engage in economic intervention and social redistribution. In some cases this meant rediscovering older
traditions from the nineteenth and early twentieth centuries, prior to the
adoption of economic planning and nationalisation. The French socialists
were converted to regionalism during their long period in opposition, when
they engaged in a 'march through the institutions' before gaining the presi-

dency and a parliamentary majority in 1981. In Italy the post-Communist *Democratici di Sinistra* (DS) also had a jacobin past, although it was prepared to use localism and regionalism as an instrument against the ruling Christian Democrats. They, too, built up their electoral base from the bottom, and used their control of several prominent cities and regions as a show-case for their capacity to govern. Spanish socialists also rediscovered decentralist traditions, accepting the *Estado de las autonomías* in the 1980s. Of course, the British Labour Party went through the same experience. Yet social democrats have remained ambivalent about regionalism, retaining strong centralist impulses. They also have a strong municipal base, which tends to be wary of experiments in regionalism that might undermine their own power. So in France and Italy, as in England, support for regional government is accompanied by protection of local government and of its direct links to the centre. In the French case, this produced a rather confusing outcome, in which all three levels of local government (region, department, commune) were strengthened simultaneously. Given the strength of existing notables in the big cities and the departments, these were the levels that did best.

There are both centralist and decentralist traditions on the centre-right as well. Indeed in the nineteenth and early twentieth centuries, regionalism in France, Belgium, Italy and some parts of Spain was often a defensive measure by conservative social forces, against the modernising secular and centralising state. Christian democratic parties have inherited some of this, linking it to doctrines of subsidiarity and the limits of the central state. The principal minority nationalist parties in Catalonia and the Basque Country are Christian democrat in inspiration, while Flemish Christian democrats are strongly regionalist. In France, Gaullism for most of the post-war period was thoroughly centralising, but in recent years the centre-right (including the present Government) has adopted a line of rather moderate and limited regional reform. We see some echo of this in traditional British Conservative thinking, although this has contributed little to English regionalism, as opposed to local government and the Union State. Neo-liberals, on the other hand, have shown little interest in regionalism of any sort.

Party change has also favoured the rise of regions, as the collapse of dominant parties with their capacity to manage territorial interests and integrate them into national politics has allowed the emergence of more autonomous regional formations. This happened in Italy in the 1990s, breathing life into regional institutions as politicians used them to construct their own power bases. The transition in Spain offered an opportunity for territorial politics, while in Belgium the national elites used the recurrent crises in the national system of consociational accommodation to build their own regional power bases and press for the federalisation of the State.

Business interests have varied in their attitude to regionalism. In the 1960s and 1970s there was support for the experiments in functional regionalism from large business groups, with an interest in infrastructure development and coherent planning. Some regions also produced new and modernising business elites, keen on economic transformation and on breaking old power structures and attitudes. Many small businesses, operating in local protected markets, were less enthusiastic, preferring to rely on traditional mechanisms of political patronage. Business, however, has tended to be suspicious of political regionalism, which complicates the agenda and allows in potentially hostile forces, as I discuss further below. Since the 1980s, trade unions have become more regionalist, having been involved in local conflicts over closures and restructurings which, starting off as sectoral issues, have often become territorialised and have brought in a wider range of actors. New social movements and parties, including environmentalists, have tended to favour political regionalism, since the region is often a space potentially open to new influences and not colonised by existing interests. This points to support for political regionalism, as opposed to the forms of closed or quasi-corporatist regionalism practised in the 1960s.

The new regionalism

Since the 1990s there has been a debate about the emergence in Europe of a new regionalism (Keating 1998). This might be seen as a synthesis of old themes of functional and political regionalism with some new ones, and in a context marked by the transformation of the traditional nation-state and by European integration. Regions have emerged in various senses, and in some places these coincide while in others they do not. This provides another series of factors by which to assess the English regional debate.

Perhaps the most important theme is the new salience of regions for economic change and development (Storper 1997; Cooke and Morgan 1998; Scott 1998). Whereas in the past *place* was important merely in the sense of location, notably distance from raw materials and markets, in the new interpretation place becomes important in its own right as a nexus of economic and social relationships. Drawing on theories in economic sociology, the new approaches explain the success of some regions and the failure of others, not by reference to traditional factor endowments, but as the result of social networks and cultural traditions, and an ability to combine market competition with social co-operation. There is a wide range of variations on this theme, some interpretations emphasising the importance of proximity for reducing transaction costs, others stressing less tangible social and cultural norms

(Keating, Loughlin and Deschouwer 2003). Regions are presented not merely as locations of production, but as production systems, with their own internal logic. Once thus conceptualised, they are then portrayed as engaged in competition with each other in an international division of labour characterised by competitive (or absolute) advantage. This is not the place to review these theories, which have indeed been challenged (Lovering 1999). What is clear, however, is that they have shaped political strategies and behaviour, adding a strong economic argument to the case for autonomist or political regionalism. They have also altered the dynamics of regionalism, since regions are now presented not as complementary pieces in a national division of labour but as competitive actors in an international and European market. Regional policy, hitherto conceptualised as essentially a central task, has thus been progressively devolved to the regions themselves.

It is less clear whether regions are becoming important spaces for social solidarity, although there is evidence that in some cases they might be, especially where there is a strong cultural or national identity. In most cases, however, solidarity is located at the national or local level, so that, like Europe, regionalism may tend to separate out the productive from the redistributive functions of government, a point to which I return below.

Culture has also undergone a process of deterritorialisation, partially delinking it from the nation state, and a reterritorialisation, being rooted in local and regional communities. In spite of the advent of instant communication, it appears that territorial proximity is important for cultural production and reproduction, including the maintenance of minority languages. So we see a territorialisation of language policies in places like Flanders, Catalonia or Quebec, and a broader regionalisation of cultural policies.

More generally, *culture* has emerged as a key element defining the new regionalism. Of course, culture is a vague term that encompasses a great deal. On the one hand, there are specific and easily identifiable cultural practices like language, music and folklore, which are generally seen as specific to stateless nations or cultural regions. There are hegemonic cultures, as in the territorial 'sub-cultures' of many parts of Europe, providing a dominant representation of the region and a mechanism of socialisation around shared themes and interests. Such local and regional cultures have often been linked to *statis* and a lack of social and economic dynamism. A more modern understanding of culture, however, is as a set of themes and images through which a society can examine itself and debate its future. Such a culture is never hegemonic and is constantly being contested. Its power lies less in the answers it gives to questions about who we are and what we believe than in sustaining a continued and unending debate about these matters. This is the type of political culture that we find in places like Scotland and Catalonia, places which are being reinvented as historic nations (the paradox is deliberate) replacing the old certainties with a continuing debate. It may also be found in less historic regions where the very fact that people are debating intensely about whether they have a culture and what it is, constitutes evidence that they have one. The same can be said about history. Its power depends less on what history actually was, as the path-dependency theorists would have it, but rather on the way it is invoked, interpreted and reinterpreted. The idea of Putnam (1993), that regions are trapped in their past, can thus be shown to be profoundly misguided. This, again, is very familiar in places like Ireland, Scotland, Wales, Catalonia or the Basque Country, but may equally be true in the regions of England (Tomaney 1999).

We are also seeing, to differing extents, a territorialisation of interest representation. This has two dimensions. One concerns the rise of a 'regional interest' in which the territory itself is seen as having a shared interest uniting its inhabitants and pitching it against others. This arises from new regionalist theories in which regions are seen as competing against each other for absolute advantage and, particularly, from the way in which politicians have adopted these themes in order to build broad support bases in the face of declining class and other attachments. It is remarkable to note the prevalence of themes of competitive economic development in political appeals made at the regional level across Europe and the use of neo-mercantilist arguments which simplify and vulgarise the new economic theories. The second dimension is the use of the regional territory as a framework for the appreciation of sectoral change and for the articulation of sectoral, class or other demands. The evidence here is more mixed. Regional and local bourgeoisies declined all across Europe in the twentieth century, although they remained stronger in parts of Germany. More recently, there has been a certain revival, especially in the small and medium-sized enterprise sector, for example in Flanders, although a region like Catalonia, previously known for the strength of its indigenous business class, finds itself polarised between large multi-national firms and very small and local businesses. Business organisations at the regional level have arisen, often as a result of functional change and the need for interlocutors with regionalised agencies for development. Trade unions have also adopted a regional perspective, to a greater or lesser degree, as have social and environmental activists. Party politics has been regionalised, partly through the emergence of territorial parties and partly through the efforts of state-wide parties to accommodate territorial interests (Jeffery, Hough and Keating 2003).

Regions have been institutionalised across the major countries of Europe as an intermediate, or meso, level of government (Sharpe 1993). This covers a range of types. At one pole there is the entrenched federalism in Germany, in which the *Länder* have general and broad competences for the government of their territories. At the other, there is the French model, in which regions remain functionally limited, serving a specific role in the management of state policies and the programming of investments. Other cases lie in between. It has proved difficult to insert regions where there is already a crowded institutional space, as in France, where the communes and departments are well entrenched and defended by powerful politicians, or in Italy of the 1970s. Competing with both central and municipal governments, regions in these countries found themselves marginalised, or reduced to narrow functional roles and relays in the national political–administrative system. Spain at the time of the transition and Belgium from the 1980s offered more powerful examples of regions that were less constrained by the existence of strong municipalities, although even here they have had to make some accommodation with them. Another key factor is the strength of vertical or horizontal bureaucratic ties. Decentralisation reforms in France have consistently sought to strengthen the horizontal level, in the form both of elected governments and of deconcentrated and integrated arms of the central government (notably the regional prefects), but the vertical connections within departments always seem to re-establish themselves. In Italy and Spain, the emphasis has been on reducing the role of the prefects and civil governors in favour of the regions but, once again, sectoral departmental interests constantly reassert themselves.

So we can see regions as functional spaces, as cultural spaces, as political spaces and as institutions, providing a series of variables to assess the degree of regionalisation in any case. French regions are functional spaces and institutions, but it is difficult to see them as political spaces. Italian regions were at one time portrayed as 'regions without regionalism' since they did not correspond to the functional systems emerging in the spatial economy or the patterns of interest articulation (Pastori 1980; Bagnasco and Oberti 1997). Scotland prior to 1999 was a political space but lacked elected and autonomous institutions. Putting these factors together in a dynamic analysis creates the possibility that the region will emerge as a level of interest aggregation, intermediation and compromise; or political actors may operate primarily in sectoral and state-wide networks, with little interaction at the territorial level. It is through examining this dynamic process that we should approach the much-debated question of regional identity. The interesting thing is not whether individuals will own, in a survey, to a regional identity, whether or not nested within other territorial identities, but the extent to which these identities are instrumentalised by political and social actors in pursuit of sectoral, class and other interests. To the extent to which they are, regionalism is socially rooted, providing a general framework for politics. Formal institutions, in state and civil society, take on meaning. This in turn permits the emergence of distinctive models of regional development, conditioned by cultural values, institutions and the prevailing mode of social and political mobilisation (Keating, Loughlin and Deschouwer 2003). Evidence on regional identities and their meanings is patchy and different questions are asked in different national surveys. There are, however, some grounds for distinguishing between old regionalists, who tend to be localist, defensive and rooted in traditional political networks, including those of dependence and clientelism, and new regionalists, who tend to be upwardly mobile, modernising in their outlook and pro-European (Keating 1998). This is not surprising, as the region is an *imagined community* at a rather abstract level, and one which is open to penetration by new social interests opposed to traditional territorial power structures. Yet this also means that the new territorial level is always contested.

This is a feature that escaped much new regionalist writing, which is often rather determinist or reductionist. One strand of thinking emphasises new forms of social regulation, sometimes characterised as a move from government, marked by hierarchical control, to governance, in which policy is negotiated within networks. Such analyses would suggest that functional networks, with actors interacting informally and repeatedly, may be the pattern of the future, in which case regional government is the wrong answer. Another strand is somewhat normative, arguing that at the regional level we are seeing a new social equilibrium, a form of regulation that is both economically more efficient and socially more integrative than what is found in national politics (Cooke and Morgan 1998). This in turn is explained by the concept of 'social capital', an attribute of local societies that facilitates collective action and has benign consequences in both the economic and social dimensions (Putnam 1993). Other scholars dismiss this as wishful thinking or mere propaganda (Lovering 1999). Another form of determinism is Ohmae's 1995 neo-liberal version, which sees the region as a competitive space, dedicated to market values and unencumbered by social considerations.

In fact, while changing the spatial scale may serve to reshape the political arena, it does not predetermine political, economic or social outcomes. The European cases show in the longer run that it is difficult to insulate the functional concern of economic development from wider political, cultural and social issues. Indeed, the new regionalist theories place so much emphasis on norms, values and social networks (often captured by the popular but perhaps misleading term 'social capital') that an economic development strategy which confines itself to narrowly economic concerns is almost a contradiction in terms. European experience also suggests that functional regionalism will, to a greater or lesser extent, become politicised and that appointed, indirectly elected or corporatist bodies at the regional level will suffer from severe tensions in reconciling the diverse strands of policy, leading the central state either to reassert control or to hand over the management of territory to elected regional bodies, which can undertake the integrative function.

The case of England

In England, the predominant mode of regionalism has been functional. There has been a big expansion of functional regionalisation since 1997, covering planning, economic development, housing, health and social services, the arts and sport (Tomaney and Humphrey 2002). The main focus, however, remains economic development. The institutions put in place after 1997 bear some family resemblance to those of 1964, and build on developments in the later years of the Conservative Government. The RDAs are defined by the needs of development, and there is a provision for business domination of their boards, although the role of the technical bureaucracy, as in other countries, is of critical importance. Regional assemblies[2] are not directly elected, but are chosen to reflect a wide range of social and economic interests and those of local government. They are not in charge of the RDAs although they do scrutinise them. They have a greater or lesser role in strategic planning and guidance, depending on the case. The experience of other countries, as well as of England in the past, suggests that this is a way of framing conflicts without providing a clear way of resolving them and that functional regionalism will pave the way for demands for political regionalism.

The new institutions and the emphasis on regional development have certainly helped to reshape politics and the articulation of interests, although not in a consistent manner. Business is now strongly committed to the notion of the region as an appropriate framework for economic development, and to the need for strategic planning and investment in infrastructure. Business groups have strengthened their regional level of organisation in relation to the national and local levels, so as to constitute themselves as interlocutors with government and the new institutions. Enthusiasm for the regional approach varies among organisations and, indeed, individuals and firms within them, and the CBI remains London-oriented. On the other hand, the rise of the regional chambers of commerce represents a new and regionally oriented focus for business lobbying, as do regional business forums and regionalised sectoral bodies. There is some business support for moving to the next stage, that of elected regional government, albeit with some provision for guaranteed business representation. There is some evidence that business leaders have a stronger regional identity in the sense identified above, using the region as a frame of reference to appreciate policy issues.

In general, however, the business community is overwhelmingly hostile to regional government. This is not always expressed bluntly, especially in public declarations, as business likes to maintain a non-political stance and is wary of getting on the wrong side of the debate should regional government come about; the same thing happened in Scotland (Lynch 1998). So it will tend to say either that regional government may be acceptable, as long as it is accompanied by stringent restrictions or guarantees for business, or that it is unacceptable unless these conditions are met. While one might accentuate the positive and the other the negative, they come to much the same conclusion, that the functionalist model and a corporate mode of representation must be preserved. One reason for this is the absence in many regions of a local business class, although regional business leaders are now more identifiable than in the recent past. Another is the long tradition of British capitalism, committed to the market and non-intervention and unused to having to negotiate with social partners. After a break in the 1960s and 1970s, this tradition was reinforced in the 1980s and 1990s. It contrasts both with Germany, where capitalism is more socially embedded, and with France, where local chambers of commerce with compulsory membership have long had a role in managing local infrastructure in partnership with the State. Another reason is the fear of introducing to the development project competing social interests, particularly those committed to environmentalist goals or social redistribution. They are also highly suspicious of local government and fear that regional government could be much the same on a larger scale.

The trade unions share much of this logic of functional regionalism. They, too, have organised at a regional level and are committed to regional development as a complement to national economic strategies. With the decline of traditional class confrontation, they are more inclined to co-operate with business in pursuit of shared regional interests. On the other hand, they want to press further, towards elected regional government. This is a change from the 1970s, when they tended to prefer regional corporatism, giving them guaranteed representation (Keating 1982). The shift is part of the general trend identified above, but may also reflect the decline of the power of trade unions and their need to bolster it through political institutions in which Labour interests would be important. It may also be connected with the shift in the weight of trade unionism from the private sector to the public sector, and their interests in getting more sympathetic interlocutors in public sector institutions.

Environmental interests and campaigners for social redistribution have tended to favour regional government, seeing it as a forum more open to their concerns and less dominated by productivist interests than the RDAs. The voluntary sector tends to be fragmented and to operate at a very local level; but here, too, we see some signs of a stronger regional presence and a growing interest in the regional government debate. Local governments are divided. There is much less hostility than there was in the 1970s, when regions were clearly seen as rivals. Now they are seen by many in the Labour Party as a way of rebuilding territorial power structures that have been seriously weakened over the last twenty years, although a great deal of suspicion remains.

Right across the spectrum, the regional level of interest-group organisation co-exists with a stronger national one, so that horizontal links must compete with vertical sectoral links. Regional politics has thus taken on distinct contours from national and local politics. It is not so marked by traditional right–left divisions or the conflict between capital and labour. Often, it pitches productivist interests in business and the unions against environmental and redistributive interests as represented by social movements and local governments. Shared regional interests are being constructed around the common theme of growth and competition with other regions, as is the case across Europe, but these co-exist with divergent interests within the region.

As in other regionalising countries, there have been efforts to strengthen the regional cohesion of central government itself, notably through the GOs, but the line departments have consistently reasserted themselves (Bennett and Payne 2000). The lack of an elected element at the regional level has encouraged this fragmentation, as one would expect from experience elsewhere.

As elsewhere in Europe, there has been a search for cultural traits that can serve as a unifying theme, can draw in disparate interests and bridge political divisions. In England as elsewhere, these sometimes verge on the comical. Visitors to County Durham are welcomed to the land of the prince–bishops, taking them back to a pre-industrial age of social integration,[3] and skipping the conflicts of industrialism and mining. Arriving in Hartlepool one can visit the Historic Quay, a brand new old building in which we can share our horror of the slave trade (actually a west-coast activity), while again not being troubled with more recent social conflicts. On the other hand, north-east England hosts an artistic genre strongly rooted in the representation of a mining and industrial past, and rehearsing themes last played out in the streets in the miners' strike of twenty years ago. Memories and suspicions persist of the hyper-modernism of the era of T. Dan Smith with its promises of the Brasilia of the north, with urban highways and Le Corbusier housing. There is as yet no motif for the new post-industrial economy, no rooting in a rediscovered past; but the fact that the absence of a distinct regional *culture* is being debated is, as elsewhere, a sign that something by way of a common narrative does indeed exist.

These pressures are pushing some English regions beyond functional regionalism into a more political phase. The debate, however, is still phrased largely in functional terms, about the need for effective regional policy-making, adding to this the need for more accountability and participation. There is a widespread assumption that regionalism should be a matter of consensus, based on partnership and shared interests. If power is involved, it is *power to* in the form of the capacity to address policy issues, rather than *power over*, in the form of domination of one social interest by another. There is little appreciation of politics as a means of managing conflicts or mediating different social interests; or that reformed institutions will produce a new pattern of winners and losers. Yet experience elsewhere shows that regions must find their own synthesis of growth and social solidarity, or of sustainable development. They are slowly emerging as a level of interest intermediation and social compromise, something that has yet to happen in England. The presence of 'new regionalists' promoting a new imagined community above local divisions is also uneven, visible in the north east and perhaps the north west, but much less so elsewhere.

What are the implications for institutional reform? One option is to retain a system of *governance*, with networks of actors engaged in problem-solving on the basis of shared assumptions. This, however, seems too depoliticised to last in the longer run, without more authoritative institutions based on the ultimate legitimating factor of universal suffrage. Business and other interests may resist, but evidence from other devolved systems in Europe and the experience of the UK thus far indicates that, if meso-level institutions are set up, then groups will adapt. Strong regional government with universal suffrage draws in a broader range of social interests and politicises the issues, creating a more difficult political agenda. On the other hand, it makes it difficult for any groups, including the business community, to opt out or to by-pass the regional level by going directly to central departments. This in turn provides strong incentives for compromise, dialogue and the search for positive-sum solutions for policy questions.

There is a final thought from European experience, including that of Scotland: functional regionalism does, indeed, provoke a mobilisation of interests around the new issue agenda. These may, and often do, press for the move to regional government, recognising the politicisation of the issues. When meso-level governments are established, however, the management of change reverts to the professional politicians and there is a sharp social demobilisation. This causes serious disillusionment in the short turn, although interest networks do gradually reconstitute themselves around the new institutions. A related problem is that much of the discontent that feeds into the demand for regionalism is part of a more diffuse disillusionment with conventional electoral politics, with parties and politicians. A response which gives them more of the same thing may not therefore answer this. If regional government is established in England, therefore, this will be the beginning only of a process of institutional renewal.

Conclusion

Regional government in England must be seen as part of the experience of European unitary states, which have seen the need for an intermediary, or meso, level rather than as part of the restructuring of multi-national states. This suggests that functional requirements can be specified and institutionalised, but that politicisation eventually develops, pointing to elected solutions. Development agencies, consultative machinery and mechanisms based on social partnership can deliver specific policies related to economic development in the narrow sense, but not a broader social and economic project. 'Governance', a notoriously loose concept, is often used to hide these critical questions about the balance of power, the representation of interests and the direction of policy. However conceptualised, governance is not a substitute for government. Elected regional government in England thus represents a significant constitutional change as well as a measure of institutional modernisation. It does not, however, rebalance the multi-national Constitution directly, since the questions raised for the UK Constitution by Scottish, Welsh and Northern Irish devolution do not find their answer in the English regions. In another sense, however, it can respond, by tailoring the English solution, not to demands that have their origin in Scotland, but to the condition of England and its regions themselves.

Notes

1 The fact that these are mostly islands does not seem in itself to be germane.
2 Also commonly known as regional chambers.
3 This was of course a very violent age, marked by civil and political strife, and border warfare, but this slogan is not about factual history.

8

The idea of English regionalism

John Tomaney

Introduction

In its report on the Constitution, the House of Lords Select Committee on the Constitution (2003) was keen to emphasise 'that devolution has been a long-standing source of political debate' which 'did not materialise in 1998 out of the ether':

> We have been conscious in carrying out this inquiry that . . . Gladstone and Chamberlain discussed implementing [devolution] across Great Britain in the late nineteenth century. It was a major concern for Asquith's Liberal Government in the early years of the twentieth century during the debates on Irish home rule, and was the subject of the Speaker's Conference in 1919. The development of devolved administration through both the Scottish and Welsh Offices was an answer to calls made for devolution at different points during the twentieth century and created a basis for the present arrangements for devolution. It was most notably recommended by a majority of the Royal Commission on the Constitution chaired by Lord Kilbrandon in 1973. (*Ibid.*: 9)

This larger history is well known, but parallel to the debate identified by the Lords is another, in a lower key, that has taken place in England about the case for regional institutions. The history of this debate is obscure to a large measure because it took place at the extreme periphery of England, although periodically it gained national attention. The purpose of this chapter is to excavate the intellectual history of regionalism in England. The archaeology is primarily to be found in north-east England, a region that has played a disproportionate role in the debate about English regionalism. Throughout the twentieth century, elite-level discussion in (and about) the region has made claims about the efficacy of regional institutions. The intellectual lineage of this debate can be traced back to the Home Rule debates of the First World War. The reasons why the north east appears to have played such a large role in the debates are several and complex, but they include:

- the relative isolation of the region and its proximity to Scotland;
- its role as the pre-eminent Labour heartland in the twentieth century;
- the enduring nature of the region's economic underperformance; and
- the sense of the region's historical identity, which was deeply felt by many of the protagonists of regionalism.

While this debate about English regionalism has been at the margins of discussion about devolution in the UK, it has proved to be surprisingly enduring in the north east, although it seeped out of the region to the rest of England only sporadically until the last part of the twentieth century (see, chapter 9, this volume).

The themes of the debate were surprisingly consistent throughout the twentieth century. On the one hand, they comprised political and democratic arguments about ensuring a strong regional voice and a belief that centralised government disadvantaged peripheral regions and was inherently inefficient. On the other hand, they included arguments that stronger regional institutions would assist economic regeneration. The relative weight attached to those arguments shifted over time, but in the north east of England, in particular, the debate was always underpinned by claims that the region possessed a special identity to which some political expression should be given.

English regionalism is an idea at least a century old, but it is one which has evolved. As a solution to both economic and constitutional problems the notion of English regionalism has been advocated by figures on both the left and the right. A common theme in the evolution of both academic and political writing about English regionalism has been the prominence of voices from the English periphery, especially the north east. They included academic and political actors, although differences existed between such writers in their definitions, diagnoses, remedies and practices. Among the main academic contributions were those from C. B. Fawcett, Henry Daysh and John House – all with connections to north-east England. During the interwar period it was principally Conservative politicians who raised the case for regional devolution, although thinkers such as G. D. H. Cole were prominent advocates of regional government. From the 1960s onwards, the idea of English regional government began to be debated more widely inside the Labour movement, especially in the north east by T. Dan Smith and his allies. The first explicit thinking about regions can be found in W. S. Sanders's Fabian tract *Municipalisation by Provinces* (1905), as part of the New Heptarchy series. But it is C. B. Fawcett's *Provinces of England* that has the best claim to be the foundation text of English regionalism.

Provinces of England

C. B. Fawcett is rightly regarded one of the founders of modern British academic geography (Freeman 1982). A student of Herbertsen and Mackinder at Oxford, he published his *Provinces of England* in 1919.[1] This work emerged from the fertile, if complex and contradictory, intellectual milieu that surrounded Patrick Geddes – the widely acknowledged founder of modern urban and regional planning – and others in the period immediately before and just after the First World War. This group placed great hope in the emerging possibilities of planning and saw 'the region' as the key focus of these possibilities. At the heart of Geddes's approach was the 'regional survey' – an attempt to view the region as an organism incorporating the natural and human worlds – which provided the foundation of modern town planning (Evans 1986; Meller 1990). Geddes's ideas and those of his followers were outlined in a series of books and pamphlets under the general title 'Making the Future'. Fawcett's study was a contribution to the series and was influenced by Geddes's reading of the French social scientist Frederic Le Play. Although not overtly political, this group of writers is understood best, perhaps, as contributing to the new technocratic vision of social change favoured by the Fabians.

More immediately, though, Fawcett's essay was a distinctive English contribution to the debate about 'home rule all round'. Bogdanor (2001) has noted that the original Home Rule debate raised all the questions that dominated the discussion of devolution in the last quarter of the twentieth century. With this in mind, the twenty-first-century reader of Fawcett's book is struck by its farsightedness and the degree to which it raises issues that had begun finally to be grappled with at the close of the twentieth century.

Fawcett began by quickly rejecting the idea of an English parliament, which was proposed as a solution at the Speaker's Conference on Devolution in 1919, opining that such an institution would dominate the federation in the manner that Prussia had dominated the German empire prior to 1914. Moreover, an English parliament would not speak to the desire for local autonomy and would replicate the failures of the existing British Parliament, which even in 1919 was 'overburdened by its manifest duties' (Fawcett 1961: 27).

Fawcett also addressed what he regarded as the inadequacies of existing local government, especially the shires. By 1919, existing local authority boundaries were not fit for the purposes for which they had been designed originally – reflecting their origins in the pre-industrial age: 'The present planning authorities are the County Councils, but there is hardly any aspect of land use of development plans which does not immediately involve areas beyond the County boundary' (*ibid.*: 31). Planning, in Fawcett's view, was best done at the regional level, as demonstrated by the design of the civil defence regions from 1918, which represented, broadly, the foundations for later regional boundaries. While some claimed that counties were the ancient and untouchable units of English governance, Fawcett shows that this argument is specious by reference to the hundreds of changes to existing local boundaries in the inter-census period of 1901–11 alone, concluding: 'Evidently there is nothing sacrosanct in the boundaries of the administrative sub-divisions of England' (*ibid.*: 50).

Fawcett outlined a set of principles for the creation of provinces from which he produced a map of the provinces of England. In doing so he adapted Geddes's 'regional survey' method which sought to link 'natural' geography with population distribution and questions of regional identity. But while acknowledging the importance of 'natural' divisions, such as watersheds, Fawcett stipulated that regional boundaries should 'pay regard to local patriotism and to tradition' (*ibid.*: 62). Fawcett's outlook was heavily influenced by his strongly northern roots, seeing the north east of England as having a clear and historically determined identity (see Tomaney 2003 for a longer discussion of this).

The opportunities for political regionalism were fleeting at the end of the First World War. On the one hand, the debate about devolution evaporated, following partition and the creation of the Irish Free State, while the interwar period was characterised by a grave economic crisis in regions such as the north east, which required urgent action. However, although the political conditions for devolution had disappeared, the geographically uneven character of the interwar crisis meant that the north east, in particular, became the focus of a new debate about regional policy.

Regionalism and economic crisis

Regionalism in the interwar period rapidly became associated with a response to the collapse of the traditional industries, principally coal-mining, steel-making and ship-building and engineering. Despite the fact that the Tyne, the Wear and the Tees together had produced 25 per cent of the global output of shipping in the first decade of the twentieth century, the underlying weaknesses of the region's industry had been masked by the exigencies of wartime production. The heavy concentration of employment in a small number of industries, all of which were closely interlinked in terms of supply chains, meant that employment loss was concentrated and severe. The coal industry, in particular, faced a severe drop in demand following the end of hostilities. The regional character of the unemployment problem during the interwar period required action on the part of government. The idea of the north east as a region with special claims was reinforced by a new series of 'regional surveys' in the interwar and the immediate post-Second World War periods, which sought to quantify and explain the character of the region's economic crisis (e.g. Pepler and MacFarlane 1949; Armstrong College 1931, 1936; see also Mess 1928). Such studies formed part of the background to the designation of the north east as a 'special area' under the terms of the Special Areas Acts of 1934 and 1937.

Throughout the interwar period successive governments, notably in the form of the Treasury and the Bank of England, especially under the tenure of Montagu Norman, held fast to the orthodoxies of *laissez-faire* economics. Politically, however, the region was changing, exemplified by the Labour Party's capture of Durham County Council in 1919. As the regional problem intensified, and as solutions to it were more keenly sought, a body of academic work began to emerge that sought to define and analyse regional problems. In the initial phases though, responses to the regional problem were shaped by Conservative interests in the region. Much of the early work was designed to justify state intervention, albeit on a modest scale, to regenerate regional economies. For, instance a key figure in the study of the north east and the promotion of its interests, before and after the Second World War, was Henry Daysh, a geographer at Armstrong College in Newcastle (which in 1937 became King's College, University of Durham, and then in 1967 the University of Newcastle upon Tyne). Daysh ended his career as Deputy Vice-Chancellor of Newcastle University, but made his name as the author of Armstrong College's influential studies of the region's economic conditions in the late 1920s and early 1930s. The north east studies were part of a set undertaken for the Board of Trade by universities in the regions: a Lancashire area study was undertaken by the University of Manchester, a Merseyside study by the University of Liverpool, a Scottish study by the University of Glasgow and a south Wales study by the University College of South Wales and Monmouthshire.

Henry Daysh, although rooted in the concerns of the north east, was well connected into national debates. His career included a spell during the Second World War as director of the research division in the Ministry of Town and Country Planning, during which he served as the ministry's representative on the inter-departmental committee on regional policy which contributed to the White Paper on employment policy (Edwards 1966; Forster 1966). In 1938 Daysh had presented evidence to the Royal Commission into the Geographical Distribution on Industrial Population (the 'Barlow Commission').

In addition to undertaking influential research on the north east, Daysh promoted action to address the regional problem. With the Teesside industrialist S. A. Sadler Forster, he was the moving force behind the establishment

Figure 8.1 Schematic history of regional bodies in north-east England

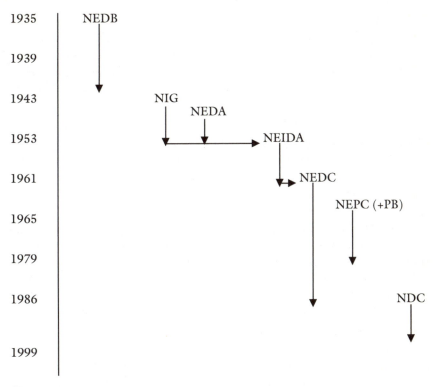

Key:
NEDB North-East Development Board
NIG   Northern Industrial Group
NEDA North-East Development Association
NEIDA North-East Industrial Development Association
NEDC North-East Development Council
NEPC Northern Economic Planning Council
PB   Planning Board
NDC   Northern Development Company

of the North-East Development Board (NEDB), building on earlier local efforts to promote economic revival (see Edwards 1966; Forster 1966; see also Hudson 1989). The NEDB proved to be the first in a series of organisations that sought to promote the region as a location for investment and as requiring special assistance from government. The NEDB folded with the outbreak of the Second World War, though Daysh was influential in setting up a successor body, the North-East Development Association (NEDA), in 1943 (see figure 8.1).[2] While such bodies focused primarily on economic development, they sought also to promote regional identity. For instance, the North-East Industrial Development Association (NIEDA), which replaced

NEDA in 1953, sponsored a regional history textbook for schoolchildren (Bowling, Coombes and Walker 1958).

Daysh, although originally from Hampshire, was involved heavily in regional politics. According to a colleague he was 'essentially a businessman' and 'an active Conservative – what we would nowadays call a "one-nation" Tory'. His experience in the north east and in wartime planning meant he eschewed *laissez-faire* policies and, instead, was 'much in favour of government support to the depressed areas and of an element of regional devolution and planning'.[3] Although Daysh saw the north east as being characterised by a 'regionalism of discontent' (quoted in House 1970: 11), he did not himself support political devolution. According to the same colleague, in Daysh's view, '[r]egional development was best achieved through the co-operation of influential individuals from industry and government, applying information supplied by geographers, economists and statisticians as they saw fit'.[4]

The idea that regional problems could be tackled best by regional bodies dominated by regional elites was established as the *modus operandi* of regionalism in England in the interwar period and continued after the Second World War, but was very much associated with the capitalist interest (Cousins *et al.* 1974; Benwell CDP 1979). The character of the regional economy as a form of 'carboniferous capitalism' meant that coalfield-owners and others had large amounts of wealth tied up in fixed assets in the region; consequently the early regional organisations were dominated by figures, Lord Ridley for example, from such families. Ironically it was the nationalisation of coal and railways in 1947 that liquidised those assets and led both to a switch from productive to rentier investments and to the flight of capital from the region, as well as signifying the beginning of the end of the leading role of such families in regional politics (*ibid.*).

At the same time, though, some influential voices in the north east made the case for political devolution. A key figure was a diplomat, Conservative politician and bearer of a great Northumbrian name, Lord Eustace Percy. Percy raised the notion of devolution explicitly to the region in a language not dissimilar to that of Fawcett, but linked it also to the failure to deal with the interwar crisis. In the Introduction to a series of essays by the northern antiquarian and Conservative MP Sir Cuthbert Headlam, he argued:

> English government is at bottom provincial government. To-day, when we are beginning to realise that our existing units of local administration can no longer meet all our local needs, it is good to be reminded once again that there are larger units, marked out by geography and by history, which deserve some share of the local patriotism which we have hitherto devoted to county and municipality . . . The time may come when this Northern Province will find in a regional council the solution of some of those social problems which have baffled our statesmanship during recent years. (Percy 1939: xi–xiii)

Percy was minister for health in 1923–24 and then resident of the Board of Education until 1929. However, he wanted Baldwin to give him a different office. According to a contemporary: 'He had wanted to become Minister for his economically depressed native North East; Neville Chamberlain, the Chancellor of the Exchequer, was determined to retain any Government action in the regions in his own hands' (Loebl 2001: 232).[5]

Percy's attitudes appear to have been conditioned by a number of factors:

- First, the Dukes of Northumberland remained important land and coal owners prior to nationalisation and, like other coal owners, had significant sunk costs in the region.
- Second, Percy had a deep sense of Northumbrian history and the role of the Percys in it, especially during the Middle Ages when they were effectively the rulers of the region – the notion of regional autonomy was not without historical precedent.
- Finally, Percy's interventionist instincts as far as the region was concerned were in tune with his broader attitudes to economic policy. For instance, he was the chairman of the Special Committee on Higher Technological Education, appointed by R. A. Butler in January 1944, where he fought for a technologically oriented system of higher education (see Barnett 2001). Percy could be seen as an early advocate of the 'developmental state', and his attraction to regional planning and governance fitted well within that rubric.

Despite interest in regionalism, economic intervention remained firmly in the hands of central government. The central authorities' limited forms of intervention in the region to promote rationalisation of industry – notably by the Bank of England and the Treasury – were concerned with precluding more radical demands than with industrial rationalisation. The governor of the Bank of England, Montagu Norman, appreciated the scale of the problem in regions like the north east, but sanctioned intervention only so long as it was 'limited, temporary and exceptional'. It involved modest efforts to promote mergers in the traditional industries, but only on a voluntary basis, and generally neglected issues of technological change and productivity. These efforts were far from enough to offset the bank's commitment to financial orthodoxy, which eroded further the competitiveness of the region's export base (Heim 1986).

The Government did eventually act during this period to address the regional unemployment problem, albeit in a modest way. The intervention came in the form of the Special Areas Acts of 1934 and 1937. Four 'special areas' were designated, of which one was in the north east. These Acts provided loans and aid to firms willing to invest in the designated areas and for the construction of publicly funded 'trading estates'. The first of these in the country was the Team Valley Trading Estate at Gateshead, which aimed to attract the new type of consumer industries that were growing quickly in the midlands and the south. Although operating on a tiny scale when compared to the scale of the problem, this approach set the pattern for regional policy in subsequent decades. In particular, it defined the regional problem as one of over-reliance on 'old' industries, such as coal-mining, and defined the solution as 'diversification' of the industrial bases (i.e. the creation of 'new' plants in 'new' sectors).

The special area commissioner for Durham and Tyneside, the Conservative MP Captain D. Euan Wallace who reported on conditions in the region in 1934, argued that reform of local government was necessary to tackle the region's enduring economic problems. He maintained that existing local government was too small to organise effective industrial assistance and called for the creation of a royal commission to investigate the way forward (Special Areas Commissioners 1934). The Royal Commission on Local Government in the Tyneside Area was appointed in 1935, which investigated conditions in Northumberland, Tyneside and Durham. It concluded that the existing system of local government did not allow for services to be administered efficiently and called for amalgamations. Moreover, it concluded that a regional council should be established to administer the 'national services' which required control over large areas, while the remaining services should be administered by smaller units (Royal Commission 1937). This thinking was lost in the run-up to war, but it rehearsed arguments that had been aired first by Fawcett.

The Labour Party in the north east continued its long march through the region's political institutions during the interwar period. This was a period of intense social conflict exemplified by the General Strike and the Miners' Lockout of 1926 and the Jarrow March of 1936. The attitude of the Labour Party to the regional question was by no means settled. It contained strongly oppositional and anti-capitalist strands. Ellen Wilkinson, MP for Jarrow, for instance, wrote a polemical account of the background to the Jarrow crusade, *The Town that Was Murdered* (1939), and proposed to 'rouse the people' (Pimlott 1985: 236) as the solution to the unemployment crisis.

Within the Labour Party the regional-policy question was taken up most thoroughly by Hugh Dalton, who was elected MP for Bishop Auckland in 1929, a town which, according to Pimlott, 'had strong local and regional loyalties based on the pits' (1985: 175). The scale of the town's unemployment made an impact on Dalton, who was convinced that active state intervention was required to address the problems of the 'distressed areas'. Dalton became the political and intellectual driving force behind the development of regional policy inside the Labour Party and later in the wartime coalition, and his 'achievement as the architect of regional policy [was] based on direct experience as County Durham MP' (Pimlott 1985: 176). He lost his seat in 1931 as Labour's voted collapsed following the formation of the National Government, but Dalton continued to promote solutions to the regional problem until his re-election in 1935. Specifically, Dalton chaired the Labour Party's investigations into the problem of the 'distressed areas'. Dalton's committee proposed a 'location of industry' policy of the type which was implemented after the Second World War and also called for defence expenditures to be made in the distressed areas. (Indeed, it was it was the run-up to war, rather than regional policy, which in the end boosted the north east's traditional industries.)

As president of the Board of Trade in the wartime Coalition Government, Dalton found himself in a position to implement his ideas on regional policy – they were largely reinforced by the conclusion of the Royal Commission on the Distribution of Population (Barlow Report) – which also called for a policy of control and relocation of industrial activity to the distressed areas. Dalton ensured that a commitment to a 'balanced distribution of employment' was included in the 1944 White Paper on employment policy, created regional structures within the Board of Trade and instituted the Distribution of Industry Act. In all this Dalton paid particular attention to the north east, appointing Sadler Forster as the first regional controller of the Board of Trade there. Dalton's approach, which drew on his larger, Keynesian inspired, 'democratic socialist' vision, focused on the role of *national* government in addressing regional problems. Indeed the Miners' Unions in the north east – as well as elsewhere, including Scotland and Wales during this period – were calling for the nationalisation of the industry. This top–down regionalism was to set the framework for the post-war period.

Regionalism in the era of nationalisation

Regionalism had a good war. Regional planning had been integral to the war effort and appeared replete with possibility when peace returned, and its attractions were acknowledged across the political spectrum. In a contribution to Sir Ernest Barker's famous effort to find the 'spirit of England' immediately after the Second World War, the Conservative historian G. M. Young opined: 'We may not have a demand for Home Rule in Northumbria or the East Midlands. We may very likely hear a claim for Regional Rights; for a legal delimitation of the powers of Parliament and the regional assembly; for an infusion of Federalism into the constitution' (Young 1947: 111).

On the left, for the Fabians, 'Regionaliter', acknowledging the contribution of Fawcett, proposed that, building on the experience of wartime
regional commissioners, directly elected 'regional councils' be created with
the purpose of improving regional planning and to secure 'intelligent coordinated action' among the various government departments operating at the
regional level (Fabian Society 1942). G. D. H. Cole (1947) published a call
for the creation of regional government, which acknowledged its debt to
Fawcett.

The economic and political conditions immediately after the war did not
lend themselves to the regionalist argument in England, any more than they
did to nationalism in Wales and Scotland. The Labour Party consolidated its
hold over local government in regions like the north east, but the basic industries, notably coalmining, were *nationalised*, eventually leaving the north east,
for instance, a 'state managed region' (Hudson 1989). Although the White
Paper on employment policy drew attention to the need for a 'balanced distribution of industry and employment' and an apparatus of regional policy
was established, the basic industries during this period were working to full
capacity, reflecting the exigencies of post-war reconstruction and the demands
of the Korean War. After 1951, the Conservative Government reduced
regional policy, although strong voices within the north east (now designated
a 'Development Area') – and even some in Whitehall – acknowledged that the
staple industries were still characterised by major structural weaknesses. For
instance, in 1951 Board of Trade officials prepared a note for the incoming
(Conservative) minister Peter Thorneycroft giving a pessimistic view of the
economic outlook in the 'development areas'. Thorneycroft ignored this
warning. The Treasury, in particular, saw no economic case for regional policy
and was sanguine about prospects for staple industries. Voices in the north
east, however, were raised to complain about the ineffectiveness of the government's approach. The chairman of North-East Trading Estates, Sadler
Forster, complained to the House of Commons Select Committee on
Estimates in 1962 that the inconsistency and short-termism of government's
approach hindered development of a long-term strategy in the north east
(Scott 1996). Such prognostications were borne out when recession at the
end of the 1950s led to a sharp rise in unemployment in the region.

The Conservative Government's response was to appoint Lord Hailsham
as 'minister for the north east'. Hailsham, famously sporting a workers' flat
cap, visited the region to assess its problems. The outcome was the 'Hailsham
plan' of 1963, which was published as a government White Paper, although
it was largely produced by officials from within the region. While the stimu-
lus to its preparation had been a rise in unemployment, the focus for the plan
was the promotion of economic growth rather than the direct alleviation of

unemployment. Accordingly, new development was to be focused on 'growth points', including 'new towns', rather than existing mining communities. The plan advocated an integrated programme of infrastructure development, advance factories and grants to firms (Board of Trade 1963). According to one later commentator, though, Hailsham's 'contribution is to be measured not in terms of millions of pounds invested in motorways but rather as a crucial step forward in regional thinking on the broadest possible front' (Smith 1970: 79). According to this view, the significance of the Hailsham plan lay in the extent to which it led to a wide acceptance of the need for active regional planning in order to promote economic restructuring.

Hailsham's approach was endorsed by the incoming Labour Government of 1964, which, as part of its more interventionist approach to the 'under-performance' of UK industry, massively expanded expenditure on regional policy to levels which were more or less maintained by governments of both main parties until the late 1970s. An important innovation of the Labour Government was the introduction of REPCs, which brought together government, business and trade unions to advise ministers about regional investment priorities. REPCs were established in all regions of England, but had no executive powers. Moreover, central government activity in the regions remained split between many different departments, the activities of which were determined by national priorities. The notion that governance of the English regions was both too centralised and too fragmented to be effective, especially in poorly performing regions like the north east, was to become an important theme of the debate about regional development.[6]

Despite its handicaps, the Northern Economic Planning Council (NEPC), however, developed a relatively high profile under the charismatic (and controversial) leadership of the local Labour politician T. Dan Smith. Smith had ambitions for a more active role for the NEPC, for instance, in developing a policy on science for the region. These ambitions, however, went far beyond what the Government had in mind and, given the dominance of central government in the framing of regional policy, little came of them (see Smith 1970). The arrival of T. Dan Smith on the regional stage marked a transition from the old *bourgeois* regionalism to a new *Labourist* regionalism. Smith was its flag-bearer. His entrance was a reflection of the hegemony of Labour in the local state, on the one hand, and, on the other, the political decline of the coalfield-owners and landed families of previous eras.

Smith claimed that it was following discussion with the Labour Party in the north that the Wilson Government created the REPCs. In Smith's view, however, the growth of economic regionalism should be used to fuel a more overt political regionalism. Smith advocated a unified Tyneside (and Teesside) as the appropriate local government arrangements to accompany a devolved government, drawing on a debate that stretched back to the interwar period (see Mess 1928; Royal Commission, 1937) and sought to secure the role of 'regional capital' for Newcastle. He wrote: 'Enough seats had been put in the new [Newcastle] Civic Centre to act as a regional parliament. No one asked us why 124 seats had been installed, but my thinking had been that this was just about right for a regional parliament' (Smith 1970: 87).

Smith's voice was not the only one in the Labour Party calling for devolution. For instance the Tyneside Fabian Society (1966) made the case for a 'regional government for North East England', which emphasised how there had been a rapid growth in 'regional administration' following the Second World War, but that this tier of regional administration was poorly co-ordinated and lacked accountability, again prefiguring the arguments that would be used in the White Paper *Your Region, Your Choice* in 2002. Political regionalism, though, remained a minority taste inside the Labour Party during this period, notwithstanding the support of some MPs, such as the former minister Arthur Blenkinsop (Guthrie and McLean 1978).

The possibility of regional government remained a largely elite level discussion, but it had an impact on national debates about constitutional change. The Wearside industrialist Sir James Steel was appointed to the Kilbrandon Commission on the Constitution. Steel along with Lord Foot were the only 2 members of the Commission (out of the 11 who contributed to the main report) who supported a scheme of executive devolution in England. Kilbrandon proposed the devolution of executive powers to Scottish and Welsh assemblies. Foot and Steel argued:

> There is no less a demand in the English regions for greater opportunity to participate in government and for greater democratic accountability in the administration of government, even though the demand, because it is not associated with strong feelings about separate national identity or language, may not be so vocal or so clearly defined. Any arrangement which fell short of the devolution of executive powers would do nothing to lighten the load on Parliament and the central government. (Royal Commission on the Constitution 1973: para. 1192)

The mantle of intellectual regionalism in the north east during the 1960s passed to Henry Daysh's successor as professor of geography at Newcastle, John House, who later became professor of geography at Oxford. House pursued a more avowedly academic approach than had Daysh, but contributed nevertheless to policy debates and was a member of the NEPC. Like others before him, he strongly endorsed the regional concept, acknowledging that he had been 'reared on the contribution of C. B. Fawcett' (House 1970: 11). He saw the region as becoming more relevant as modern society developed. Contemporary social and economic changes, according to House, were generating 'community-forming forces at higher scale' than the locality and 'prospectively creating a corporate sense out of what were initially no more that a set of functional relationships' (*ibid.*: 7). For him, the 'province' was one of a number of inter-related 'concepts of community' (*ibid.*). The creation of bodies such as the REPC both reflected and contributed to the growth of regionalism. But regionalism was also a product of growing personal mobility and a less parochial sense of life. House maintained that 'provincial level loyalties' in England were fostered in the 1960s by the emergence of regional television (Tyne Tees Television first broadcast in 1959), industrial promotion policies and regional marketing strategies, and the emergence of bodies such as regional arts associations which, in particular, had contributed to a 'strong sense of provincial community in the North East' (*ibid.*: 11). These developments, together with the growing importance of regional planning, raised the question of regional governance. House endorsed the view of Lewis Mumford that 'the reanimation and rebuilding of regions as deliberate works of collective action is the grand task of politics in the coming generation' (*ibid.*: 11). Regionalism was by now firmly linked to the agenda of modernisation (Allen 1966).

The fate of north-east regionalism remained attached to the powerful figure of Dan Smith. The ignominious end to Smith's career – he was convicted and jailed on corruption charges in 1971 – was a damaging blow to regionalism, especially inside the Labour movement. The emerging left was suspicious of regionalism offering the analysis that 'regional problems are no more than constellations of social-structural problems' (Cousins *et al.* 1974: 143). At the same time, however, during the 1970s rising Scottish nationalism meant that the devolution debate continued to exercise the attention of the region's political elite – the rise of Scottish nationalism was generally viewed, with some exceptions, as a threat to the region. Local authority leaders in the north east and the Northern Group of MPs were the chief opponents of the Scotland Bill in 1977. The Northern Group of Labour MPs was disproportionately represented among those who rebelled in the House of Commons on the guillotine proposals motion on 22 February 1977, which effectively killed the Bill (Guthrie and McLean 1978).

Structures and opportunities

The growth of interest in regionalism among sections of the Labour Party and its leadership through the 1980s and 1990s built on a long debate that could be traced back to at least 1919. Voices in peripheral regions, notably the north east, were particularly noticeable in these debates, and found themselves once again at the forefront as interest in the idea rekindled. At the end of the 1970s the idea of a powerful government in Edinburgh – which, after all, is the capital city nearest to the north east – had been regarded as a threat by most economic and political interests in the north east. For a variety of reasons this attitude gradually changed during the 1980s. The region struggled to cope with rapid de-industrialisation and its social fallout. It found itself politically and culturally at odds with Margaret Thatcher's supporters in middle England and its Labourist voting traditions were reinforced. Local authorities, trade unions and business, stimulated partly by European pressures, sought to co-operate and develop the region's distinctive institutions in order to attract new industry. In short, a series of factors reinforced the 'regionalism of dis-content' identified by Daysh half a century earlier.

Attitudes among sections of the regional elite in the north east were trans-formed during the 1980s, such that by the early 1990s the regional Labour Party had endorsed the idea of an elected assembly as its policy. Leading figures in the regional Labour movement had recognised that, despite the defeat of 1979, Scottish devolution was unlikely to disappear from the polit-ical agenda. At the same time, the Miners' Strike of 1984–85 and a series of high-profile battles to save shipyards and steelworks looked like old class struggles, but their failure cast doubt on the traditional approaches of Labourism in the face of social and economic change. Such defeats high-lighted the extent to which they were an expression of regional, as well as class, concerns. Thatcherism provided a cold political climate for the north east (and vice versa). By 1997, Labour held 28 out of 30 parliamentary seats in the region.

Following their fall from grace under Dan Smith, regionalist arguments were thus redeemed inside the Labour Party. In the 1980s, it was the younger left-wing critics of the Labour old guard in Parliament and at the local level who attached themselves to regionalism and linked it to a radical analysis of the north east's socio economic and political weaknesses. A significant contri-bution came from Alan Milburn, later Secretary of State for Health, who drafted the regional party's policy (Milburn and Corrigan 1989). These efforts were connected to – and helped to influence – a wider debate in the Labour Party, in which such future ministers as John Prescott were involved.

Thus the increasing constellation of regional institutions and groupings that grew up under the Blair Governments, like the ideas that inspired them, had a long pedigree in the north east. The debate moved outside of the increas-ingly narrow confines of the Labour Party with the formation of the Campaign for a Northern Assembly (1992) and the North-East Constitutional Convention (1999), both having an explicitly cross-party character and casting the argument for a regional assembly in cultural as well as economic terms (Forbes 1992, Tomaney 2000b). The same was true of the RDAs: though established across England in 1999, they were the latest in a long line of independent economic development institutions in the regions (albeit with far greater resources than their predecessors). Far from being the 'pet project' of John Prescott, the Deputy Prime Minister, impulses towards regionalism in the north east at least are rooted in the life and history of the region.

Notes

1 Churchill, then a Liberal, floated the idea of regional parliaments in England in response to the proposals of the 'Round Table' on Home Rule in 1911.
2 A later avowed regionalist claimed that the establishment of NEDA 'was one of the earliest occasions when people from the North had gathered together and talked of the Three Rivers Country. It was one of the first times that Northerners had voiced the notion that there was such a thing as a region' (Smith 1970: 104–5).
3 Brian Fullerton, personal communication, August 2003.
4 *Ibid.*
5 Percy was Conservative MP until 1937 and then became rector of King's College, University of Durham, from 1937 to 1956 (see Percy 1958).
6 The new regional policy of this era focused on the attraction of branch plant investments to regions like the north east. The REPC expressed doubts about his policy, calling for more investment of research and development and skilled employment. The weaknesses of branch plant development had in fact first been raised by Colonel Methven, the first managing director of the Team Valley Trading Estate in 1944 (see Loebl 1987). An alternative to the attraction of branch plants based on the promotion of 'industrial clusters' was included in early draft of the Hailsham Report, but omitted from the final version. From an early stage a critique of Whitehall regional policy was being formed in the region (Hudson 1989; see also NEPC 1966).

9

Facts on the ground: the growth of institutional answers to the English Question in the regions

Mark Sandford

If the answer to the English Question does turn out to be a form of regional government, what will it look like? At present we do not have either very comprehensive or satisfactory answers to this question. Public debate frequently starts with the fixed points of the Scottish Parliament and the National Assembly for Wales, neither of which are at all helpful for assessing what can or might happen in the English regions in the immediate future. Nor, indeed, are they relevant for understanding what has happened in the immediate past.

There are many more reliable sources of information through which to make educated guesses about how regional government will seek to answer the English Question. One source, too often ignored by scholars and researchers, is the GLA: although a unique city–region, structurally and constitutionally there are considerable affinities between the GLA and the regional structures in England. In its strategy-writing responsibilities, its quite onerous consultation duties and its reliance on executive power in a tightly limited number of policy areas, the GLA offers a glimpse of many aspects of the likely operation of elected regional assemblies (Sandford 2004a; Travers 2004).

Besides the GLA, however, a vast range of activities and initiatives has been taking place in the English regions since 1997. The establishment and growth of regional chambers, and associated fora and networks, have been relatively neglected by scholars: at best, the regional chambers have been treated as a sop to the English regions, a shadowy version of the real thing of elected regional government. Attention from economics and political economy has been focused on the regional aspects of Treasury macro-economic policy, the 'new economy' and policy divergence in the devolved nations.

This chapter's argument is that the barely visible capacity-building activities of the existing shadowy regional structures are of much more significance for future developments than might be assumed (see by comparison Adams, Robinson and Vigor 2003). A degree of institutional capacity is developing in the English regions which has, on the one hand, the potential to permit policy transfer to elected structures, should they be revisited in the future, and, on the other, to provide the institutional space for the development of networking capacity by regional sectoral fora. English regionalism at the moment exhibits many of the tendencies associated with network governance, reliant on (often personal) relationships and the availability of information.

But there is a strong degree of contingency to the institutional history of the English regions. Much of the activity which has occurred so far has been enabled, rather than driven or structured, by specific decisions from individual departments of New Labour's Government. Much has also been the result of initiatives which have derived from the regions and localities themselves. The story of regionalism thus far in England is the story of the interplay between small-scale enabling initiatives by government and the development of *indigenous* policy-networking capacity by regional elites and activists. Without asking a clearly defined 'English Question', this interplay is creating an answer to it: a form of regionalism, if not by stealth, then certainly by default.

This chapter seeks to do three things:

- Firstly, it will explain the institutional development of English regionalism since 1997, and it will explore at whose initiative those events have taken place.
- Secondly, it will assess the reasons and reasoning behind the developments, and how significant the developments so far are.
- Thirdly, it will suggest possible outcomes of the establishment of directly elected regional assemblies – and, indeed, examine the likely outcome in the absence of them.

Although the emphatic rejection of the North-East electorate on 4 November 2004 for the time being puts paid to plans for elected assemblies, the implication of the developments set out in this chapter is that English regionalism has not gone away. Administrative and planning perspectives have forced it to return, in a variety of forms, again and again over the last forty years, and there is no reason to suppose that this will change.

The Government's agenda for the regions of England

The Government's ostensible policy agenda for the English regions has been well documented elsewhere (Jones 2001; RSA 2001; Balls and Healey 2002;

Cabinet Office–DTLR 2002; Tomaney and Mawson 2002; Amin, Thrift and Massey 2003). It has been an incremental agenda, as has in practice been typical of the Labour Government's constitutional reforms. Events have reflected a somewhat watered-down version of the policy agenda set by the Labour policy documents *Renewing the Regions* and *A New Voice for England's Regions* (Straw 1995, 1996). Faced with a welter of policy priorities (for instance, health and education, as well as devolution to Scotland, Wales and Northern Ireland), and following discussion in cabinet committees, the Government elected in 1997 chose not to make English regions a priority.

The degree to which *regionalism* (as opposed to regional structures) is considered, by much of the public and many commentators, to be alien to England cannot be overstated. Large quantities of hostile press coverage and commentary have been generated as the regional agenda has expanded in England. In particular, a number of groups claim that regions have been imposed on the UK by the EU, a claim which is not backed up with any convincing evidence but which attempts to tar the regional agenda with the brush of anti-Europeanism. Under the circumstances the Government's caution in introducing elected regional assemblies was understandable; unfortunately, it led to a heavily neutered set of proposals which strongly fuelled claims that the assemblies would produce bureaucracy and achieve nothing substantive.

Adopting Michael Keating's typology of regions, outlined in chapter 7 of this volume, the English regions at present can be described as functional spaces and a confusing crowd of institutions. They are not political or politicised spaces, despite the presence of political parties in regional chambers: the emphasis on all sides in the chambers has been on co-operation and consensus. Neither, with the possible exception of the North East, are they cultural spaces. As the cultural–national question played such a major part in the public debate over devolution to Scotland and Wales, opponents of regionalism in England see the relative absence of regional culture as a *prima facie* case against political or institutional regionalism (Conservative Party 2001; *Daily Telegraph* 2002; Jenkins 2002). Nevertheless, the existence of regions as functional spaces in England is a considerable development, driven by the increasing convergence of regional boundaries since 1990. In the last few years, with the arrival of regional chambers, interest groups and regional elites have joined the crowd of institutions, but have lacked the policy discretion to use the chambers as political spaces.

Table 9.1 sets out the chronology of the main institutional developments in the English regions. The GOs were set up in 1994, and began to act as single points of contact for businesses and development initiatives; they also

Table 9.1 A chronology of institutional regionalism

Year	Event
1994	Government Offices for the Regions set up
1997	Election of Labour Government
1998	Regional Development Agencies Act passed Referendum on the creation of the GLA
1999	RDAs established (April) Regional chambers designated by Secretary of State (May–September)
2000	First elections to Greater London Authority *Reaching Out* report published by PIU – Regional Co-ordination Unit set up RDAs guaranteed boost in funding
2001	Regional chambers receive £5m collective funding
2002	RDAs' 'single pot' established Publication of White Paper on elected assemblies (*Your Region, Your Choice*)
2003	North East, North West and Yorkshire & The Humber selected to have referendums in 2004 Regional chambers begin inputs into Spending Review 2004 Boundary Committee begins local government review in those regions
2004	North west and Yorkshire & The Humber referendums postponed (July) North east votes 'No' – 78 to 22% (November) North west and Yorkshire & The Humber referendums called off (November)
2005	General election

took on responsibility for assessing bids for the single regeneration budget. GOs have been permitted to structure themselves to meet regional circumstances, at the discretion of regional directors (Mawson and Spencer 1997). In their early years GOs had to steer a difficult course between attaining a degree of regional coherence between policy silos and not moving regional priorities too far away from the (sometimes conflicting) priorities of their four parent departments.

The thin layer of institutions was increased when RDAs were established by statute in 1998. They brought together a number of extant regional agencies, principally involved in regeneration, land preparation and business support. RDAs have enjoyed a considerable boost in funding since their establishment, now spending some £2 billion per year collectively, but that is dwarfed by sums available to other comparable bodies such as the Rural

Development Service, LSCs (some £9 billion) and indeed the GOs themselves (some £8 billion). Moreover, the RDAs had to wait until 2002 before they could treat their funding as a block grant (the 'single pot'), being previously obliged to account separately to the different departments from which their funding streams originated. This was a considerable obstacle to them taking regional specificities into account: one respondent stated in interview that 'the creation of the single pot will be of greater significance than the creation of the RDAs themselves'.[1]

The RDA Act also permitted (but did not oblige) the establishment of regional chambers. These bodies, conceived as relatively influential in pre-1997 Labour Party policy,[2] do not have a clear basis in the Act, and initially had no definite powers or funding. Under the Act, they were to be 'designated' where they existed, and permitted to monitor and comment on the strategy of the RDA.[3] Chambers in all of the eight regions achieved designation in 1999; in many cases they were established on the back of existing skeleton partnerships or the regional local government association.

Through 1999–2001 this tripartite system of regional government gradually got to grips with its remit. All of the new regional bodies were subject to considerable criticism, often justified, but each could point to institutional limitations (Robinson 2000). RDAs, for instance, were formed from a number of predecessor organisations, and inherited their budget streams and existing programmes. Furthermore, related functions remained outside the RDAs, such as the Small Business Service, English Partnerships (partially) and the then Training and Enterprise Councils. The RDAs control less than 1 per cent of the public spending in their region. RDAs' own performance was also attacked: their initial regional economic strategies, for instance, were indistinguishable from one another.

The announcement of the 'single pot', and a substantial budget increase, in 2000, appears to have resulted from substantial joint-lobbying by the chairs of the RDAs themselves (Hall 2000). All of them had considerable business experience, which may have strengthened the weight of their opinions. But, importantly, they had shown their willingness to act as a team on behalf of the regions. This was one of the first signs of a gradual development of *indigenous* capacity, with statutory bodies being willing to lobby government on a territorial basis.

GOs were considerably strengthened following the Cabinet Office–Performance and Innovation Unit report *Reaching Out: The Role of Central Government at the Regional and Local Level* (2000), which documented huge numbers of overlapping regional and local initiatives and equally huge confusion from their users on how best to access them. Among its recommendations was:

> The Government [should] give Government Offices a strongly enhanced role in supporting and evaluating local performance on strategic and cross-cutting issues, especially to ensure that the necessary connections are made between different policy areas of central Government Departments. (Cabinet Office–Performance and Innovation Unit 2000)

Following *Reaching Out*, four departments relocated staff into the GOs: Culture, Media and Sport; Agriculture, Fisheries and Food (now DEFRA); the Home Office; and Health (public health teams). GOs now manage a total budget (across all regions) of some £8 billion, four times that of the RDAs.[4]

This growth began the process of establishing regions as a fundamental, if under-utilised, facet of departmental organisation rather than being a minority pursuit. The creation of the RCU within the Cabinet Office (subsequently moved to the ODPM) at this time enhanced the emphasis given to the regions by the centre. The RCU's impact has not been huge, but its existence within Whitehall indicates that regional concerns are gradually, if not marching, certainly creeping through the institutions of Whitehall in a way previously unknown.

A second significant move was the publication of the consultation paper *Strengthening Regional Accountability* in March 2001. This awarded £5 million funding per annum collectively to the regional chambers for the following three years. The granting of this funding has made an enormous difference to these fledgling organisations, most of which had had staffs of only a few people and had accepted assistance in kind from member local authorities (meaning the evenings of particularly dedicated staff). The new funding was to be spent on the regional accountability, or 'scrutiny', role, but the DETR made explicit that it would interpret this broadly:

> The way forward could involve the chambers establishing a stronger analytical or research capacity to monitor and evaluate the RDAs' plans in relation to the region's performance . . . In doing so they will, for example, need to lock into the work of the Regional Observatories and consider the links with the work on monitoring implementation of Regional Planning Guidance. (DETR 2001)

This was a sensible approach, permitting chambers to develop general 'regional capacity' – meaningful oversight cannot take place without it. Many of the chambers have since doubled their staffs, creating economies of scale via links between the functions of planning, transport and monitoring the RDA. This has been vital in enabling some of them to take a more rounded approach to regional policy.

Most chambers now have staffs of 25–50. Planning and transport, and related policies, form the majority of their tasks. In some cases more staff have been hired to carry out regionally related issues: some chambers have been eager to influence a wide range of policies, while others have concentrated on their core responsibilities of transport, planning and scrutiny. For instance, the North-West Regional Assembly has obtained some £1 million of funding from the EU to run programmes relating to e-government. The South-East England Regional Assembly is located in the same offices as the regional voluntary sector forum (RAISE), and funds two officers to provide secretarial support to the stakeholder members of the Assembly. The South-West Regional Assembly has merged with the provincial employers' association, raising staff numbers to fifty-five and bringing in a stream of (non-virable) consultancy income.

The regions strike back

The very limited nature of regional responsibilities has led to criticisms – in many ways accurate – that the Government's *regional* policy is really a national top–down policy which has very little relationship to the needs or desires of individual regions. This is magnified by the considerable interest taken by the Treasury, under Gordon Brown, in regional economic policy. But an unexpected feature of the English regional debate began to creep in from about 2000 onwards. The fledgling regional institutions began to take on a life of their own, exploring new policy directions and challenging government.

In some regions, stakeholders and local government had a considerable heritage of joint working. The three northern regions, for instance, had had development associations working on joint strategies and regeneration projects throughout the 1990s, though this had always taken place on very limited resources. However, following 1997, capacity-building and policy responses began to emanate from other regions with less regional identity and fewer economic problems than the northern ones. The East Midlands produced an 'integrated regional strategy' in 1999, and the South East made it an early priority to produce and circulate policy documents, relating subjects such as health and sustainability to economic development.

The consequence of the regional chambers' development of capacity was their ability to engage with and sometimes challenge, rather than simply follow, government priorities (and in some cases this occurred even when chambers were no more than alternative hats worn by regional local government associations). Anecdotal evidence available to the author suggests that this came as a surprise to the centre. The *indigenous* desire to create a coherent regional policy and capacity has led to chambers' frustrations with the continuing lack of joining up between different departments' regional policies. The lack of links between transport and housing, and between culture and economic development, have been particularly noted by both regional chamber and other staff. For instance, in 1999 the regional cultural consortiums and the sustainable development round tables were established, by the DCMS and the DETR, respectively, as separate bodies; they have much in common, both in terms of aims and organisational structure, with regional chambers.[5] The same is true of regional health observatories, which in some regions (such as the South West) are co-located with the regional chambers.

Scrutiny taken seriously

Regional chambers' role of monitoring, outlined in the RDA Act 1998, metamorphosed into the fashionable but ill-defined role termed 'scrutiny' which was instituted in local government and the GLA in 2000–1. The single quasi-statutory role of the chambers was to hold the RDAs to account within their regions, but with no resources or guidance as to how to do this.

The use of the term 'scrutiny' caused considerable disquiet in both the RDAs and the chambers, with its connotations of adversarial and forensic questioning. Many of the chambers have chosen alternative terms: for instance, the South East and the South West hold 'select committees', the North West has a 'regional review board', and the East Midlands an 'economic review group'. In each region it was necessary to reach a *modus vivendi* with the RDA, a process which took some time:

> In every region the Assembly has adopted a collaborative approach to regional scrutiny and there has been a very purposeful attempt to avoid conflict and an adversarial approach . . . This desire to construct a positive relationship also explains the almost universal dislike of the term 'scrutiny' . . . 'Scrutiny' is viewed as inappropriate since it has adversarial, competitive and negative connotations. It was particularly disliked by RDA interviewees. (Snape *et al.* 2003: 23)

The RDAs' suspicions of the 'scrutiny' process may have been exacerbated by the very public spat between the regional chamber and the RDA in the east of England in early 2001, where the chamber rejected the RDA's economic strategy twice. There are no procedures for dealing with continual disagreement of this kind, and in the end ministerial reassurances behind the scenes were made to ease the problems. This event is often cited as the first evidence of an indigenous impulse in the English regions (Tomaney and Hetherington 2001: 16–17). But, although it was certainly important in establishing the chambers' legitimacy, it is likely that scrutiny processes and joint working since then have had more impact on policy developments. The impetus of the east of England arrangements was reflected in early 'select committees' in the south west, where, alongside the RDA, bodies such as the Environment

Agency and the local LSCs were invited to answer questions on their role and performance. The regional chamber had no right to invite them, and they were under no obligation to attend, but they did so nevertheless. This reflects a growing self-confidence on the chambers' part.

The co-operation of regional bodies in chamber processes also reflects that many regional and local executive agencies are keen to co-operate strategically with the regional chamber and with other bodies. Many officers in those agencies are aware of the problems of poor regional co-ordination and lack of democratic oversight. Surprisingly, there have been very few examples of unco-operative executive agencies or of major disagreements – perhaps reflecting a reservoir of goodwill towards more effective joint-working arrangements.

Forums and partnerships

The increasing voice of regional chambers is complemented by the emergence of a series of forums and informal partnerships in the regional assemblies. I have already referred to regional cultural consortiums, sustainable development round tables and regional (originally public health) observatories. All of these bodies have begun to carve niches for themselves, typically employing one to three full-time staff, appointing a board of regional elites,[6] and applying for grant funding to produce strategies and hold networking events. These bodies are developing a capacity and a focus for policy-making, and concentrating minds on regional issues, rather than being advocacy coalitions which have fully formed solutions to all identified regional policy problems. The development of regional capacity through these small organisations is a significant form of 'institution-building'.

These independent bodies have been joined by regional housing forums, set up in most regions in 2001–2, and regional rural affairs forums, set up in the wake of the foot-and-mouth disease outbreak in 2001. These forums are supported from within the GOs. They enable a range (normally several dozen) of regional actors to meet, discuss and feed in policy concerns to GO staff. These policy forums rarely contain elected members (either from local government or from Parliament) and are frequently constituted via invitation.

Facts on the ground: the growth of regional networks

The importance of these facts on the ground – myriad small organisations, set up by different government agencies, which have established a complex web of interactions and policy debate – lies in the degree to which they are entrenching regional answers to the English Question. The existence of comprehensive structures of regional governance suggests that, despite the rejection of elected assemblies, a form of regionalism will still form an answer to the English Question.

How far this entrenchment goes can be gauged by considering possible alternative answers to the English Question which do not involve regionalism or indeed involve dismantling regional structures. The Conservative Party remains resolutely opposed to elected regional assemblies, and has previously made commitments to abolishing the RDAs and the regional chambers on the grounds of bureaucracy, but there are indications that the RDAs would be saved by the support of business, and that at least some form of regional local government forum would be maintained, under a future Conservative government.[7]

Either way, much of the content of regionalism at present consists of policy decisions devolved to regional offices, of networks, forums and joint working, none of which is central to the mission of any of the agencies involved. A Conservative government would be unable to abolish voluntary networks and forums, which normally exist with the overt aim of improving policy delivery by the organisations which send representatives. Indeed, regional chambers are not statutory organisations and could not be abolished by a government (although they could be resolutely ignored and deprived of funding). It is yet one more curiosity of the networks of English regionalism that they have been catalysed by the policy entrepreneurship of a combination of executive agency officers and civil society activists.

The actors from public, private and voluntary organisations who take part in these networks are among the strongest supporters of regional government in England. The networks appear to be effectively driven through a form of self-interest. One chamber member said:

> You don't have leaders of county councils turning up if this isn't about power. [They] are very busy people. They get something out of it . . . We are in a very privileged position to actually be allowed to play. I think some people don't actually understand that. (Interview with the author)

What does this mean for the institutions of English regionalism? The visible institutions – RDAs, GOs, regional chambers, and the large executive agencies – exist in a bed of indigenous networks. These networks are vital in that they transform what would otherwise be a series of loosely connected central government initiatives into a capacity for strategic thinking that is based *in* the region, with staffs and membership which are interested in regional, not national, planning and needs. The networks do not suffer, for instance, from the dual loyalty of the GOs (speaking to the regions for the centre and to the centre for the regions) nor the confused lines of account-ability of the RDAs.

The networks described here are emphatically policy networks, of the type first postulated by Hugh Heclo in 1978. They are the means by which this new tier of government – a greenfield site in policy terms – is 'open to penetration by new social interests' (Keating, chapter 7 this volume). Their members can be roughly typecast into two main groups:

- On the one hand are the members for whom, as Heclo (1978: 102) describes it, 'any direct material interest is often secondary to intellectual or emotional commitment'; these members are in the main from public agencies or from the voluntary and community sector – networks that offer them a voice at a new tier of governance which appears to promise increasing importance in the future.
- On the other hand are business and private-sector members, the majority of whom attend with what one described as a 'watching brief' – in effect, because the presence of the former groups gives networks a credibility that means they must be at the table. It is this characteristic business reluctance which most clearly emphasises that the networks of British regions are not the networks of industrial innovation described in the literature of the 'new regionalism': rather, they are sectoral public policy networks.

Network governance has made inroads into more conventional forms of democratic government in the last two to three decades. States in the devel-oped world have recast themselves as enabling rather than directing and dic-tating public policy: the reach of public policy (as Heclo predicted in 1978) is becoming wider but thinner, as states lose or abandon their monopoly on public policy in favour of an interdependent partnership with non-state actors.

Unusually in the EU, the English regions are developing policy networks in advance of democratically elected government. The 'policy network', however, is not quite an adequate concept to describe the types of activity underway across the full gamut of regional institutions. Regional chambers act not only as the focus for a variety of regional policy networks but as a kind of region-wide advocacy coalition. They have essentially invented for them-selves the role (with central government's tacit acceptance) of representing the views on a range of policy issues of regional stakeholders and local govern-ment. These include conventional policy topics such as the environment and sustainability, transport and housing, but strategies have also been produced for cross-cutting issues such as flooding, farm diversification, climate change and public health. Of interest for this discussion is not the effectiveness or oth-erwise of this 'voice of the region' role, but the fact that networks, mostly (though not all) centred in regional chambers, are allowing regional policy communities to develop which are not dependent for resources or agenda on central government (or the GOs).

Experience of joint working between public institutions and civil society can be valuable to new elected tiers of government. The example of Brittany is instructive here. Well before the establishment of elected regional government in France, a joint group known as *Comité d'études et de liaisons des intérets bretons* (CELIB) was established, with the aim of 'develop[ing] a comprehensive and integrated understanding of economic and social conditions in Brittany, producing in the process a new representation of the region's territory and its development. This, in turn, they used to put effective pressure on national authorities' (Pasquier 2003: 75). This organisation existed from the mid-1950s and played a significant role in the transformation of Breton economic fortunes, particularly in agriculture, through to the mid-1970s. Actors on the political left and right, and from a range of different backgrounds, became accustomed to working together, building a tradition of civic co-operation which has helped the elected regional government (established in 1986) to establish a successfully integrated role. Many other regions in France have remained prisoners of inter-departmental rivalry and localism, despite having similar cultural resources available of which to make use.

Elected assemblies: the icing on the cake

The publication of the White Paper *Your Region, Your Choice* (Cabinet Office–DTLR 2002) set out a route to achieving elected regional assemblies, putting flesh on a policy proposal which few had expected to see the light of day. The process set out by the White Paper is very slow: the first referendums, in the North East, the North West and Yorkshire & The Humber, were scheduled for November 2004, meaning that the first regional elections would not have been held before 2006. The powers which were proposed for elected assemblies are thin. They would have had executive control over the RDAs, regional housing capital funds, EU structural funds, and a number of smaller executive agencies such as the regional tourist and arts boards. The powers proposed cut across policy areas, and the budgets proposed amounted to 3–4 per cent of regional public spending (Adams and Tomaney 2002; Sandford 2002a). The Government remained confident that the ten statutory 'strategies' that the assemblies would have been required to write would have permitted them additional leverage over regional policy. It was unmoved by criticisms of this faith in network governance and strategy-making, both from business and other stakeholder groups and from campaigners for regional devolution.

Strikingly, there has been relatively little connection between the wide range of institutional developments in the English regions and the work of the campaigns for directly elected regional government which have been set up in many of them. Constitutional conventions have been set up in six of the English regions, with a seventh campaigning for a separate regional assembly in Cornwall. But the character of these conventions varies considerably. Two of them (the North West and the East of England) are run in-house by the regional chamber. The North-West Constitutional Convention produced a final report in 2001 recommending the transfer of a range of responsibilities to an elected north-west assembly, but has since been inactive (although the North-West Regional Assembly, i.e. the regional chamber, has vociferously supported direct election for some time). The East of England convention has been unable to explore direct election due to the presence of Conservatives, who are opposed to it, on the convention steering group.

The other four conventions – the North East, Yorkshire & The Humber, the West Midlands and the South West – have held a continuing series of public meetings and published documents exploring options for directly elected assemblies. However, they have only a weak degree of influence on the day-to-day functioning of the existing regional networks. They appear to perceive regional chambers as a step on the way to the real thing of elected assemblies, a perception that is not shared by most of the staff, members or networking organisations involved with the chambers. The regional chamber is perceived as a useful agency in its own right: one officer described it as the 'regional LSP [local strategic partnership]'; another said: 'If you ask me what the East Midlands assembly [chamber] does, I would say, "Nothing." We're the glue – we hold everything else together' (interview with the author).

Some regional chamber stakeholder members have suggested, in interviews with the author, that the chambers should be given substantial budgetary and executive powers without acquiring the legitimacy of direct election – a technocratic imperative justified, as it were, by having all the 'main players' on board. Interestingly, the White Paper showed limited awareness of, or interest in, patterns of regional networking. Many of its conclusions assume that the GO is still the fount of all things regional, a perpetuation of the centralised character of early Labour regional policy.[8]

The support for the stakeholder–network model of regional governance at present is significant for the future development of the regional tier. Those organisations which have joined or formed the existing networks may be able to act as advocacy coalitions for their particular policy preferences, and may be able to lock in their preferences in the early formative years of an elected assembly (Dudley and Richardson 2000: 30–1). Interviews with stakeholders suggest that the picture of regional chambers being run primarily by existing elites is realistic: one claimed that their impact has been through

> our ability to sit in the middle, not be too politically driven and say, 'That's good for the region, that's not good for the region.'. . . It's because we don't have a particular axe to grind that we tend to take a broader view . . . It's like a private-sector board.

Stakeholders in many regions, indeed, reacted very negatively to the proposals for elected assemblies precisely because of the perceived threat to existing networks and relationships. Of his regional chamber, one of those interviewed commented:

> We're totally integrated. The White Paper wants to dis-integrate all this. It's a disaster. All of the four options[9] are an insult. If we're going to be there willingly, we want to be full partners. Most of the partners are . . . as democratic as local authority members who get elected by about 20 per cent of the electorate.

It is perhaps no accident that the environmental and voluntary sectors, which have never before had access to strategic policy decisions of the kind offered by the regional chambers, have become among the stoutest defenders of the chambers. The stakeholder options offered in the White Paper were an important catalyst in the set-up of a national group for social and economic partner members of regional chambers, which meets quarterly to discuss issues of mutual interest.

Elected assemblies: a crystal ball

It is possible that elected assemblies will be open to a degree of capture by the interest groups – local government, business, voluntary and environmental sectors – which currently hold a near-monopoly on the regional agenda in England. However, it would be wrong to suggest that elected bodies would have led to no change. They would have brought the RDAs under closer democratic control, along with substantial housing funding responsibilities, and a raft of other small bodies.[10] The RDAs command considerable business interests, and most have their own stakeholder networks. In essence, an elected assembly would put politicians back in the driving-seat in the region, though they would not have the road to themselves. As is the case with the mayor of London, considerable duties of consultation with regard to strategy-writing and policies would be involved. Assemblies would also be entitled to co-opt stakeholders on to scrutiny committees, though this would not of course mean decision-making status. A regional cabinet of elected members could alter the balance between political priorities and listening to stakeholders or members could quietly ignore some of the networks described. They could gradually have moved their own appointees into positions of power (for instance, appointments to the Environment Agency or to LSCs' boards). Alternatively, like the Mayor of London, they might have concentrated policy, interest and cash on the issues over which they have executive control, such as housing and economic development (Sandford 2004a).

It is also possible that the presence of elected regional assemblies, with a strategy, research and publicity capacity, would begin to contribute to the development of a kind of regional identity where previously there was either none or only diffused sentiment. The argument put forward by Michael Keating in chapter 7, that identities can be operationalised by actors in pursuit of interests, can also apply, I suggest, in reverse. Actors in pursuit of interests, together with territorial institutions with specific governance responsibilities, can themselves develop a regional identity. 'Identity' is of course a contested concept: a future regional identity might be a sense of shared economic interest, stronger consensus over regional boundaries, a sense of shared features of territory, landscape, political orientation, or a regional version of the 'rewriting of history' associated with nineteenth-century nationalist movements. Where they occur, such developments are long-term phenomena, not the result of year-long advertising campaigns, but they are not inconceivable. The case of Greater London is a case in point: once regarded as the 'county of London' joined with a range of parts of surrounding counties, in the forty years since the creation of the GLC and of 'Greater London' in 1964 it has become accepted as a city–region in its own right (Travers 2004).[11]

Regions without election

The institutions of English regionalism therefore resemble a gradual growth of ivy around the lattice of government's initial interventions. From inauspicious beginnings, it is clear that the regional chambers are perceived increasingly by the Government as institutions with clout. All of them have taken unilateral decisions to rename themselves 'regional assemblies', without protest from the Government. Chambers in the southern and midland regions have been particularly vocal in supporting the model of 'partnership assemblies'. (This term, used by the chambers themselves, implies that they are different from, not inferior to, elected models.) Most significantly, the chambers played a leading role in co-ordinating a regional input into the 2004 Comprehensive Spending Review. As leaders of many regional strategies and of increasingly good quality social, economic and environmental data, they are ideally placed to carry out this work. One chamber's chief executive suggested to the author that a useful future development would be a 'summit' between the region and a range of central departments. Such an aspiration demonstrates the rise of network regionalism in the last five years.

As elected regional assemblies are now indefinitely shelved, it is almost certain that the English Question (or at least its sub-national variant) will be answered through non-democratic means, and the most likely prognosis at present is for a gradual development and extension of the current position through the lifetime of this Government. Non-elected networked regionalism is a convenient mixture of government framework policy, administrative incentive and grassroots elite activism. Peace and goodwill between all actors in the networks and forums of the English regions is the order of the day: this form of regionalism has not yet arrived at the point where serious differences in policy, or lack of tangible outcomes, jeopardise this state of grace.

Non-regional futures?

Given the Government's current state of relative weakness, it is salutary to remember that there is not only one sub-national answer to the English Question. Regional government, indeed, was far from the most obvious choice as an answer even in 2000, being viewed as a poor second in government priorities (Hazell 2000b). Arguments that elected regional assemblies were no more than an attempt to ape the devolution settlements in Scotland and Wales, within a country where they made no geographical or cultural sense, were common (Stoker 2000).

It appears that a policy shift took place throughout 2000 and early 2001, linked to a range of events within government. Prior to this shift, the modernisation and revitalisation of government in England had been strongly linked to the creation of local authority elected mayors. Tony Blair was known to be strongly in favour of this policy, and he was instrumental in inserting a directly elected mayor into the plans for the new GLA (Pimlott and Rao 2002: 57–8). It was expected that elected mayoralties in the major English cities, as well as London, would lead to high-profile individuals, sometimes politically independent, running for office, renewing public interest in local politics and bringing new ideas and priorities to local administration.

The gradual move away from elected mayors coincided with the replacement of Hilary Armstrong, a strong supporter, with Nick Raynsford as minister of local government in 2000. Throughout 2000 it also became clear that most of the major English cities were unwilling to hold referendums on the issue. There was also a lack of interest from the public, despite the entitlement in the 2000 Local Government Act to call a referendum on having a directly elected mayor via a petition signed by 5 per cent of the local authority's electorate. A groundswell of support suggested by earlier opinion polls did not materialise: of some forty referendums through 2000–1, only eleven 'Yes' votes were obtained. Nick Raynsford's decision not to compel Birmingham and Bradford to hold referenda appeared to be the nail in the coffin of the policy (Sandford 2004b).

It is entirely possible that the idea of elected mayors will be resurrected at some point in the future, should the existing eleven incumbents make a demonstrable difference in their authorities. At best, however, it is a partial answer to the English Question. Mayoral authorities do not have any more powers than non-mayoral authorities, only a slight increase in prestige and media attention. A more likely alternative to regional government is another round of some type of local government reform.

Local government

Ever-increasing levels of centralised control, through processes such as the Comprehensive Performance Assessment and an increasing use of hypothecated grants and minimum funding levels, emphasise the degree to which government policy is still, and will continue to be, delivered through local government. Since 1997, there have also been considerable reforms to the political process within local government. The most obvious change is the introduction of the executive–backbench split, a reform of which the introduction of elected mayors was a part. Other reforms include: the requirement that councillors sign a code of conduct; the requirement that councils must have a written constitution; and access to information provisions.

Furthermore, regions which vote for an elected assembly must move to a pattern of unitary local government, meaning yet more reorganisations are threatened in the north. The fragmented system of counties, city unitaries and metropolitan boroughs left *in situ* after the last round of reorganisation by the Local Government Commission in the 1990s remains in place, though rumours have circulated that the Government will seek to impose unitary local government across England during its third term in office, regardless of the progress of the regional agenda.

The current fragmented and illogical boundaries of local government pose a problem for any suggestion that local government could become an answer to the English Question. The Conservatives, for instance, have advocated passing RDA powers back to local government, but do not explain how tiny unitary authorities such as Torbay, Bracknell Forest or Rutland could exercise economic development powers of equivalent effectiveness to those of the RDAs. If a future government looked to expand the powers of local authorities, their options are limited. Economies of scale would make it very difficult to transfer the powers of authorities such as local LSCs or tourism boards to local government across England.

One solution might be to recreate an all-encompassing pattern of counties approaching the 1974 settlement; another, which has been mooted in the recent past, might be the creation of 30–40 new 'city–regions' based on travel-to-work areas without reference to traditional boundaries (Coombes 1996).[12] But either of these ideas would lead to yet more reorganisation, something for which few governments have much appetite. The former implies subsuming cities back into counties in several parts of the country, with the attendant political battles, while the latter has consistently failed to make any political headway.

In the wake of the North-East referendum, some members of the 'No' campaign have suggested a select committee of north-east MPs in the House of Commons, a minister for the North East located within the Treasury to 'shake up the Government and get us the results we expect';[13] others have made vague noises about 'getting more out of our MPs'. But there is very little reason to think that any of these ideas would make a substantive difference to government action. Existing departmental select committees have no leverage over government and never force significant policy change on government departments. It is barely conceivable that a regional select committee would be able to change regional policy.[14] It could certainly write interesting reports and issue declamatory press releases, but this is not a particularly effective means of 'standing up for the region'. Likewise, it is implausible to expect a minister for a region to be able to change policy decisions, which are actually located in mainstream departments, on the grounds that a particular policy is not suited to a particular region. Decision-making powers on matters such as transport and skills are indivisible within the Westminster system: they rest within their departments and are not susceptible to being 'shaken up' by a minister from elsewhere. If a minister for a region had his or her own regional department, with responsibility for all or most of the main public spending areas, in the manner of the Scottish and Welsh Offices prior to devolution, that would represent *real* power: but the chances of it happening are equally remote.

The short life of the metropolitan counties, which were surrounded at their inception with rhetoric about 'strategic government' similar to that which surrounds the English regions today, perhaps shows that there is no guarantee of a long-term future for ill-designed elected bodies which rely on partnership and goodwill from other tiers of government. Although the metropolitan counties' roles were very different from those of the proposed elected regions – they controlled fire, police, transport and waste – they, too, were expected to exercise a strategic influence not available to their constituent boroughs or districts. Whether elected regional assemblies are sufficiently qualitatively different from the rounds of local government reorganisation which have dominated the last thirty years remains to be seen.

Conclusion

This chapter suggests that the current development of institutions and networks of governance considerably strengthen the likelihood that regional government will be the answer to the English Question. That does not necessarily mean elected regional assemblies: it could simply mean that the Treasury's erstwhile interest in regionalism, and the promises made in the White Paper of 'regional awareness training' for civil servants, will entrench a process of 'region-proofing' policy within government. A large number of vested interests have been created already in and around the regional structures, and a future Conservative government (for instance) might not find it so easy to sweep all of these away: their natural supporters can also be found there, often converted to the benefits of some form of regionalism but not to the benefits of democratic accountability through an elected assembly.

The core of regionalism in England is an ongoing, but rarely clearly expressed, debate about the appropriate scale of public administration. It has not caught the public's imagination on the grounds either of identity or of democratic renewal: it has remained a technocratic activity. So far as it answers the English Question, it will do so in a quiet, unobtrusive way. The emphasis on civic engagement, networking, and long-term strategic thinking, though appearing wispy in the current structures, has the potential to lead to changes in the way in which England is governed which equal the effects of most other constitutional reforms since 1997. The English regions could become crucibles of innovation in governance, the outcome of which will have a lasting effect.

Notes

1 This interview – with a middle-ranking RDA staff member – took place in early 2001.
2 See Regional Policy Commission (1996), *Renewing the Regions: Strategies for Regional Economic Development*, Sheffield: Sheffield Hallam University, for the clearest expression of regional policy (including RDAs and chambers) prior to the

election of the Labour Government in 1997. Many of the recommendations found their way into policy in watered-down form.

3 Although all of the regional chambers have now re-styled themselves 'regional assembly', I am referring to them collectively as 'regional chambers' to avoid confusion with elected regional assemblies. Where a single chamber is referred to I have used its actual name.

4 This is not a meaningful cumulative figure, as regional directors do not have discretion to vire funds between programmes: it simply indicates the total spend passing through the GOs.

5 In Sandford (2001), I argue for the merger of these functions with those of the regional chambers.

6 A number of board members of these organisations are chairs or chief executives of other regional organisations, often with spending duties. Others may be long-time actors or activists in the policy field or in closely related policy fields, facilitating joint working.

7 A survey carried out by the author on MPs and local authorities in the south-west region found considerably less hostility to the existing regional chamber from Conservative councillors who sit on it than from the region's Conservative MPs. Some of the MPs favoured abolition of the regional chamber, while most Conservative councillors surveyed stated that it worked well – and should not therefore be replaced by an elected assembly. It is not known whether this distinction exists in other regions.

8 See in particular pp. 26–9, and box 2.5. Four of the five changes for regional chambers announced in box 2.5 – scrutiny of the RDA, coordination of regional strategies, becoming the regional planning body, and 'discussing work' with GO directors – were already in place in most regions when the White Paper was published. The GOs, by contrast, are given a more expanded role on pp. 28–9.

9 The four options for stakeholder involvement in the White Paper – see p. 54.

10 At the time of writing, indications are growing that the Government is willing to listen to the case for additional powers to those proposed in the White Paper. Pilots of pooled budgets between RDAs, and LSCs and Business Links (both outside the competences proposed for elected assemblies), are underway in many regions, which may increase the case for bringing these budgets under one body.

11 In the 1998 referendum on the introduction of the GLA, every borough voted in favour. The lowest support was recorded in Bromley, traditionally regarded as the borough least happy about being part of Greater London, where 57 per cent of those voting supported the introduction of the GLA.

12 The 'city–region' idea can be traced back to Derek Senior's dissenting memorandum to the Redcliffe-Maud Committee, which drew up a plan for reorganisation of local government in the early 1970s.

13 'No group wants north minister', *Newcastle Journal*, 6 November 2004; 'It's up to us now, say north's MPs', *ibid*.

14 This would be doubly true, in the North East, when a non-Labour government is in power. A regional select committee dominated by Labour (reflecting political balance in the region) would merely be an opposition committee, and would be either resolutely ignored or disbanded.

10

A very English institution: central and local in the English NHS

Scott L. Greer

While few in England think of it as such, the National Health Service is a very English institution. Like much else in English life, it is often mistaken for an institution of the UK, and like much else in English life it is actually a distinctly English institution in jurisdiction, history and politics. Its borders, history and present administration stop at the Scottish and Welsh borders, as do much of the politics and policy debates that they create. And it operates on the level of England, with no significant regional level and only a weak local level, all of it disconnected from formal accountability to anyone but voters (or maybe MPs) via the Government.

That means study of the English NHS can help explain one of the basic questions of English politics and life: why is the country so centralised? What did policy-makers think they were doing when they made it thus, and what do they and the public think they are getting out of it? England is an anomaly for its absence of a regional level (which distinguishes it from countries of a similar size such as Canada, France, Spain, Italy or Germany) or a meaningful strong local government (as in Scandinavia). This applies to health services as much as to other areas of government. In most countries with health services comparable to the UK's there is a regional level of health services (with populations of around 5 million people in the larger countries; see table 10.1) that is both a major player in the delivery of services and some kind of a countervailing power to the centre within the system. England has no such thing. This chapter discusses the (comparative) anomaly of a unified health service for over 49 million people in the light of the trajectory of organisational change in the NHS – or how the NHS in England has dealt with its problems (central overload, value for money, etc.) in a way that reduced local autonomy without creating a regional level. It is a story of the laborious construction of a market-based functional alternative to the local and professional autonomy that for so long structured English public administration and health services, and regional autonomy happens to have been the ordinary European alternative. How did England come to do this?

Table 10.1 Member states in federal constitutions

	Number	*Average population*
Swiss cantons	26	248,000
Austrian länder	9	849,000
Australian states	6	2,495,000
Canadian provinces	10	2,533,000
German länder	16	4,905,000
North American states	50	5,008,000
Autonomous regions		
Greek	16	1,081,000
Spanish	17	2,142,000
French	22	2,521,000
Italian	20	2,833,000
Belgian	3	3,286,000
United Kingdom		
England		49,138,831[a]
Scotland		5,100,000 (5,062,011[a])
Northern Ireland		1,685,267[a]
Wales		2,903,085[a]

Note: [a] Data from UK 2001 census, available online:
news.bbc.co.uk/1/shared/spl/hi/uk/03/census_2001/html/population.stm; all other data
are from www.scotland.gov.uk/cru/documents/con-status-13.htm.

Tying the English Question to policy affords a useful perspective: policy is, after all, what governments (especially regional governments) do, and control over health services is both a political prize and a curse. The NHS is a good case for the study of English public services and the shape of governance in England. It matters, on every level: it is a huge service directly dependent on state funding and responsible to the political authority of government, which makes it both a prize to play for and a curse for whoever accepts responsibility for it. It touches the lives of everyone in England at some point. It is the agent of one of the great citizenship rights of the modern welfare state in Europe, namely the right to health care. And for all that the public (and a surprising number of people in politics and government!) might not have noticed, it is also organised on the level of England. If we want to see how English politics handles serious issues, and if we want to see how England, from a base of considerable local autonomy, became so centralised, then the NHS is as good a case study as any. Moreover, it is a good case because the politics of public policy can feed back into pressure for constitutional change. If a player repeatedly loses the game, then it might pay to think about trying to change the rules. Frustration with the centre's policy decisions contributes to pressure for decentralisation in many places, including pre-1998 Scotland and Wales, and in the politics of states like Belgium, Canada, and the USA (McEwen 2002; Greer 2005a; Jeffery 2005). If the operation of the NHS – or of English public services that are subject to the same dynamics – systematically creates discontented groups, then it might be systematically creating the constituency for a new regional or other territorial dispensation in England (see also chapter 9). In the meantime, the career of the English NHS is a story of how tax funding, state ownership, and the centralisation of power and public accountability eroded local and professional autonomy in favour of accountability to the centre, that is, the Government and the Department of Health. It is a story of the nationalisation of a part of English life, its recency and its consequences.

From local to national and from territorial to functional

The history of the English NHS contains many forces and pressures and interesting policy debates, but it includes no politically important pressure from regionalists or English nationalists and it contains no moment when the State tried to solve its legitimacy or policy problems with regionalisation. The former should not be surprising in the light of the overall homogeneity of English national identity; the latter is interesting, and requires some history. There have been plenty of crises in English health policy and English politics, but at each juncture a different solution to problems of weak central legitimacy and central policy problems was chosen. The result is that a system that originally operated with a high degree of local autonomy shifted to one based on professional autonomy, and then to one based on centralisation and markets, including central efforts to make markets. At each point England's elites opted for a *functional* rather than a *territorial* solution; indeed, the history of reorganisations shows a steadily diminishing role for regions, and the progressive weakening and abolition of autonomous territorial levels. This comes with what might be a decreasing lack of respect for regional networks or economies of scale, combined in more recent years with the assumption that if they are rational and functional they will be produced by managers responding to appropriate incentives. If there is a trend throughout the various reorganisations (and implicit in their number), it is centralisation.

The story begins with the basic decision taken with the creation of the NHS (at the time an England and Wales service, with parallel legislation for Scotland and Northern Ireland coming along 'step by step') by the Attlee Government. This was the decision to create a single service in England, owned by the State, with its employees either paid directly by the State (if in hospitals) or contracted by the State (if in primary care). This made the NHS an effective monopsony; that is, a system with only one buyer of the services (see table 10.2). That in turn promoted cost containment and made reorganisation easier, while also reducing other important actors such as the unions, local government and the professions to the status of lobbies. Legislative centralisation, though, turned out to be a necessary but not a sufficient condition for central control. It is quite possible to legislate centrally and run affairs locally, and for decades the NHS in England, like much else in England, ran that way. The NHS of 1948 was the property of the State, and formally the Government could do what it liked. It was in many respects another application of the idea of a dual state in which the local level and the centre co-existed without much mutual influence.

The second part of the section analyses the shift since 1983 from centralised finance to centralised organisational control. This is a change quite possibly mirrored across British society. By 2004 the English NHS was a far more centralised organisation, with little if anything left of its old culture of local autonomy and far more effective central control. This series of reorganisations and changes meant that the government of England moved, in good part unintentionally, from paying for a comprehensive but locally autonomous and highly variegated set of organisations to controlling a complex but accountable organisation. In other words, the centralisation of the English NHS was in 1948 something of a sleight of hand, a change in the financing of a group of highly autonomous local organisations, and the unity of the English NHS was on the level of finance and ownership rather than control over what happened in given places. This extreme local autonomy, polytheistic management in a theologically monotheistic system, was slowly undermined from the 1970s and collapsed in the 1990s. It was only in that decade that England finally began the most serious phase of its experiment of having one minister running one of the world's largest health service organisations on behalf of one of the world's most diverse populations.

The legislative centralisation of the NHS

The first question to answer, then, is how the English NHS became centralised in legislation and finance if not necessarily in organisation. The story starts with the decisions made in 1948, when the Attlee Government created it. In part, the establishment of a unified tax-funded system (rather than one in the hands of local government, or an insurance scheme) reflected the overall tone of management thinking in the 1940s. There is something of a consensus among students of the NHS in politics that it was born of a pre-war and wartime rationalising trend. During the Second World War the health system

Table 10.2 Staffing of the four NHS systems

		Medical and clinical					
	Medical and dental %	Qualified nursing, midwifery and health visiting[a] %	Qualified scientific, therapeutic and technical %	Support to clinical and other direct care staff[b] %	All medical and clinical staff %	NHS infrastructure and support staff %	Total staff[a] (= 100%) (1,000s)
England[c]	7.7	31.7	11.2	31.5	82.1	17.9	882.1
Wales	6.9	31.2	13.5	26.3	77.9	22.1	60.1
Scotland	8.0	32.8	11.9	18.3	71.0	29.0	113.6
Northern Ireland	6.8	29.8	10.1	13.6	60.3	39.7	40.0

Notes: [a] Figures for nursing, midwifery and health visiting exclude student nurses; Northern Ireland does not have any healthcare assistants. [b] Includes qualified ambulance staff. [c] The Northern Ireland figure includes administration and clerical staff working within Personal Social Services. [d] Directly employed whole-time equivalents; the Northern Ireland figures exclude bank staff. [e] Data include staff not allocated to individual region.
Sources: Department of Health; National Assembly for Wales; Information and Statistics Division, NHS in Scotland; Department of Health, Social Services, Northern Ireland.

was effectively under the control of the State as part of its war effort, and the Government took the opportunity to both re-allocate some services and start considering ways to reorganise health services for greater efficiency and equity. The NHS, runs the argument, emerged from this environment of recent experience with state planning and designs for more equitable and efficient health systems (Eckstein 1959; Webster 1988; Hacker 1998; Moran 1999; Tuohy 1999; Klein 2000; Mohan 2002). Following this line of argument, it is not a surprise that the rationalising policy included the simple establishment of direct control over the health services rather than maintaining or extending the previous web of insurance funds, charities, independent hospitals and local government facilities.

This *tidying-up* view of the NHS can be overstated.[1] Labour anticipated much of the Beveridge Report and Bevan's NHS went considerably beyond what the Conservatives had thought to be worth a fight (Morgan 1984: 16, 151–63). A broad post-war consensus on the desirability of a neater, better-planned and more equitable health service was not the same thing as a centrally funded nationalised service accountable to a minister; there were alternative ideas (Rintala 2003: 48).

The subsequent organisational, territorial, story of the English NHS falls into two parts, with the story told in greater detail in classic texts (Rivett 1998; Klein 2000; Ham 2004) and its territorial aspects analysed in the valuable works of Powell (1997) and Mohan (2002). The first is from 1948 to 1983, when the system operated with a very substantial degree of local autonomy. It was impossible to govern the English health system *directly* because the centre lacked the implements with which to intervene in medicine or most aspects of management. The real power of the centre was indirect at best, and it tended not to intervene. The only major division in this period is between the 1948 model, which more or less incorporated the organisation of health care before the NHS into the NHS, and the reorganised NHS of 1974, which placed a clear bet on professionals as the agents of government. The second half is the period after 1983, when the system became much more centralised and much less territorial. These years are the story of the hard-fought long-term transformation of the NHS from a territorially organised institution with a very high degree of regional, local and professional autonomy into an organised ecology of firm-like trusts tightly bound to the centre (see figures 10.1–4).

1948: THE ENGLISH ALTERNATIVE

Organisationally, in 1948 the State effectively took over almost all of the pre-existing pre-war providers of health care. The fight to take control of the system and enhance its accessibility was enough for the Attlee Government,

Figure 10.1 Structure of the NHS, 1948–74

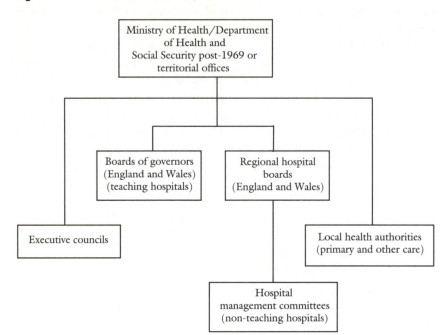

and the system appeared to work well enough to remain below the radar for subsequent decades with very little change. The result was that a hospital that had been voluntary, and governed by a board prior to 1948, would probably keep its board in 1948, but now be publicly owned and have a board appointed by the Secretary of State. A hospital that had been owned by a local authority would have a board created for it by its new owner, the State. The Government nationalised but did not thoroughly reform the health sector, just as it nationalised but did not thoroughly reform the railways or the mining industry.

Territorially, there were fourteen regional hospital boards, including Wales as one. Otherwise the map was designed wholly around acute services in a territorial expression of what Fox (1986) called 'hierarchical regionalism'. Built around the catchment areas of treatment facilities, they did not match up with other regional breakdowns of the UK. Beneath the boards there were bodies governing each of the different inherited parts of the systems: 36 boards of governors (for the teaching hospitals), 388 hospital management committees (reflecting the lesser independence, but continuing personalities, of the different inherited hospitals), 38 executive councils and 147 local health authorities. They were a patchwork quilt because the institutions nationalised in 1948 were a patchwork quilt of different providers

Figure 10.2 Structure of the NHS outside of Northern Ireland, 1974–82

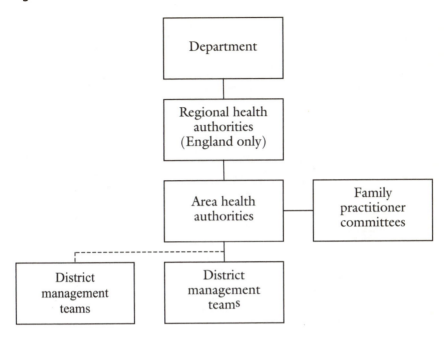

with different owners and orientations including local government and charities of many kinds. The result was that regional health boards, with their important members and their large scale, looked to Whitehall like the commanding heights of the system; they had the largest flexible budgets, and had a great deal of influence over the policy decisions of the autonomous but dependent lower tiers. As ever in health services, this could look to those below like a function for fixers – what can look like budgetary power from above in a system with that level of professional autonomy can look like a high-level accounting operation and source of capital to the professionals below.

The crucial aspect of the English NHS (integrated until 1974 with Wales) was the autonomy left to these local organisations over their operation, decisions, hiring, and general organisation. The finance was central, as was the legislative framework, but that did not mean that the Department of Health (not even a cabinet department in those years) was involved in 'running' them. If ministers chose, the regional hospital boards could shield them from even the largest decisions about investment, planning and service organisation. In other words, while on paper the system was 'Stalinist', in reality there is very little evidence of central control (see Paton 2005). The best evidence for this is simply the weakness of central tools for intervention: while the boards of all

Figure 10.3 Structure of the NHS in England, 1991–96

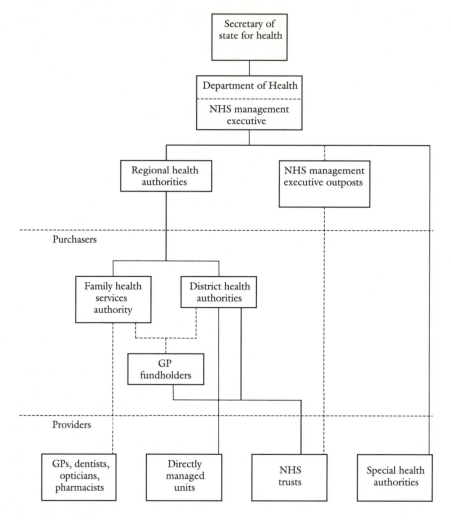

the different organisations were appointed by the minister and their plans required approval, there was little information at the centre, expertise in developing alternative plans, or civil service depth to implement decisions. A small department outside of the Cabinet, meanwhile, was unlikely to do much, whether in reorganising services or in top–down planning.

1962

In 1962, though, the Government made a stab at real central planning of health services, led by Health Minister Enoch Powell, who boasted that this large-scale building scheme, based on centrally determined understandings

Figure 10.4 English NHS, January 2005

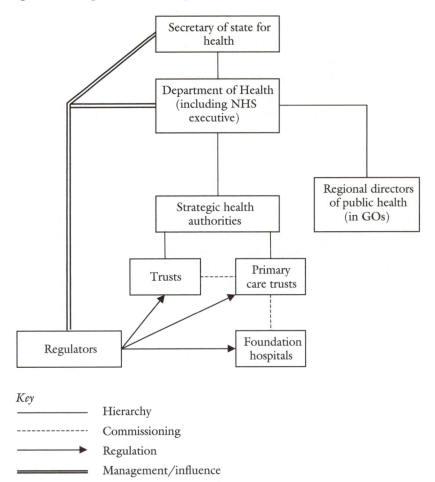

and projections of need and resource allocation, was the largest centrally pro-grammed building scheme 'this side of the Iron Curtain' (Mohan 2002: 1–2).

The 'Hospital Plan' (HP) was an effort to increase productivity and overall efficiency, and address inequalities of provision left over from the pre-NHS profiles, through significant capital investment according to a national plan. This involved, for example, efforts to guarantee a broadly equal distribution of hospital beds across all parts of the country. It was an optimistic document, proposing to use a well-thought-out projection of demand and inequalities of service to guide significant investment that would produce a more efficient and territorially equitable system. The chief instrument of this was to be the devel-opment of the district general hospital (DGH), of 600–800 beds serving populations of 100,000–150,000. The DGH would be a facility with the critical mass to carry out most procedures and operate good accident and emergency services. The distribution of DGHs would increase territorial equity by creating good facilities in underserved areas and improve efficiency by replacing groups of obsolescent facilities in others. The NHS would plan and then build its way to efficiency and territorial equity.

The striking thing about this episode of top–down central planning, though, was the extent to which it was not really top–down. The notion of the DGH, one that was not particularly opposed, essentially involved building new hospitals but even their number and location were not, by and large, centrally programmed: 'The Plan itself was an aggregation of the individual intentions of the RHBs' (Mohan 2002: 124), even if departmental officials did complain of the poor quality of some plans. The centre itself lacked the analytical capacities to plan or analyse issues, and the minister, Powell, found himself criticised for 'pseudoprecision' (Mohan 2002: 122, 116). The implementation of the HP, meanwhile, was less than perfect (Webster 1988).

The point in terms of the relationship between structure and territory of the NHS is that the 1962 HP was not in a significant sense top–down; nor was it even a case of central planning. It relied on information and proposals from the regional boards (and, in some cases, their subordinate units) and was leavened with significant extra money. The Department's ability to turn down requests for new money was certainly significant, but that is nonetheless a limited power compared to what the centre would later attain.

1974

If the structure of 1948 was an English alternative to centralism based on de facto local autonomy, that of 1974 was a second English alternative to centralism based on explicitly worked out local autonomy and a compact with the professionals in which they did many of the things that Whitehall might otherwise do. It also went beyond the 1962 HP, with its implicit changes, to be the first functional reorganisation of the NHS – the first one based on the centre's understanding of medical work and organisation rather than inherited institutional forms.

The 1948 organisation was part of the careful set of compromises of medical and parliamentary politics intended to preserve the autonomy or power of some group in medicine or local areas and thereby ease in the creation of the NHS. As the NHS bedded down, those compromises went from being bulwarks of one group or another to being impediments to working. Hospital management committees, for example, ran hospitals with considerable autonomy but lacked funds or scale to restructure services well – they could not, for example, respond to population shifts across districts.

Organisationally, in 1974 the State moved to clear away these many different organisations and reorganise the NHS so that its internal divisions reflected efficiency and its services rather than the inheritance of pre-war provision. The Government decided to reform the system under Keith Joseph on the basis of close study of the actual processes of work involved in the provision of health services – a largely unreplicated example of evidence-based policy-making (Hands 2000). It commissioned a study of health services and recommendations from Brunel University sociologist and psychiatrist Elliott Jaques, known also for his work on organisational culture and the mid-life crisis (Jaques 1976, 1978). Based on Jaques's design, after 1974 the UK State contracted with professionals through a system called consensus management which essentially placed most policy decisions within the organisations (hospitals, districts) in the hands of committees of professional representatives who had to agree decisions. It was an under-researched system that appears to have been successful in maintaining morale and in rationing legitimately (Schulz and Harrison 1984; Harrison and Schulz 1989). As in 1948, this entailed great local autonomy with local groups of professionals and organisations taking decisions rather than the centre. The difference was that the autonomous groups were now local area groups dominated by professionals rather than the various local boards that the NHS took over in 1948 or created to govern former local authority facilities. The logic was clearly spelled out, and in almost the same words as now are used to characterise 'subsidiarity'. Every function was to be performed as close to the patient as possible, with as much authority as possible devolving to to the patients' personal doctors and very little (by way of high-end tertiary services) being run from Whitehall. The idea was simple and in good part was implemented; services were administered and planned at the level of the smallest feasible area on the basis that local professionals could best spend scant resources.

Territorially, this meant several levels and 'tears about tiers'. The new organisation had 14 RHAs, 90 area health authorities (AHAs) responsible for working with local government (but in control of little) and 192 district health authorities (DHAs) responsible for co-ordinating local health care. The DHAs were the key tier for service provision, taking over hospitals and ancillary services on a territorial basis. Apart from AHA coterminosity, there was no effort to design a map around anything other than health service provision. Regions (now minus Wales, the Welsh Office having taken over the Welsh health board's functions) reflected the catchment areas of large medical centres and patient flows. The regions, while they underwent some changes in their borders and functions, remained the high-profile organisations: districts ran and co-ordinated the services, making them crucial to day-to-day work, but regions had the critical mass to make policy. The reliance on professionalism and consensus management, however, meant that the power of all of these structures was both interpenetrated and curtailed by the professionals: the autonomy of a hospital or a district was not that of the local community; it was the autonomy of the professionals on the consensus committee.

Meanwhile, the 1974 reorganisation, pushing its functional logic rather far, eliminated the medical officers of health (MOHs). These were the storied public health officers who were responsible under the UK's nineteenth-century Public Health Act for the maintenance of health standards. They were appointed by local government and controlled large staffs: environmental health, large parts of primary care (such as health visitors), port (including airport) health control, food safety and public health campaigns were all within their remit, even after they lost control of the Poor Law hospitals in the 1948 creation of the NHS. A big city MOH might have 5,000 or more employees, and while it is easy to romanticise them, they were powerful, often effectual, local and focused on health improvement rather than health service provision. From 1974, local governments would administer health protection such as environmental health. They had been shorn of much of their expertise and their status, and of a focus on population health, and were accordingly prone to become mechanistic in operation. Low-status professions such as home visitors would be orphaned in the larger NHS without their powerful MOH protectors. Local government and local electors would lose control over public health promotion. The newly medicalised public health doctors would find themselves few and far between, with less coherent staff, a basic focus on infectious disease outbreaks rather than health protection or improvement and a strong tendency to be pulled into management – for their knowledge of population data (Tuohy 1999) – or a more or less successful career as a sort of freelance political activist. The functional logic of 1974 was built around health services and health professionals, but when taken too far, as was the case in the separation of public health medicine from local government public health, it gutted the last institutional reserve of resources, power and responsibility not subject to the centre (as well as doing severe damage to the coherence and utility of public health promotion activity).

1974 may have been good for the health service, but the task of reorganisation was a new experience for the NHS, and in retrospect was the first of many reorganisations that turned out to be unintentionally conducive to centralising. The Department of Health published a large document specifying how each of the new tiers would function and be organised. This meant that the Department's civil servants and consultants had to figure out how the NHS worked in order to identify and re-allocate tasks. Even if they did so, ironically enough, as part of a strategy that entrenched professional power, the act of reorganisation increased the Department's knowledge and its capacity to reorganise. They had now created a far less idiosyncratic and locally varied set of organisations than had existed, and demonstrated that they had the capacity to enact major reorganisations. The result, then, was a successfully executed reorganisation and the replacement of the detritus of pre-NHS local politics with a functionally designed organisation that very clearly located the autonomy in professionals, organised around their hierarchical regions.

Centralisation starts in earnest

Until 1982–83, in short, the English NHS demonstrated that the necessary condition of centralisation – legislative and financial power lodged at the centre – was not a sufficient condition for central control. From 1948 to 1974 the centre funded, broadly, pre-1948 arrangements with a high degree of autonomy for local areas and individual institutions and hence extreme variation in practices, organisation and consequences. From 1974 to 1982, though, the model changed; now the State both formalised and made rational (and evidence-based) its territorial organisation, and enlisted the providing professions. This gave more coherence to autonomous local levels and brought the professions more firmly into governance as rivals to any management from the centre.

1982

The first change of the Thatcher years was a territorial one, namely the abolition of the AHAs. The whole justification for the AHAs, the NHS tier coterminous with local authorities, was that they would improve the integration of care and planning between local government and the NHS. By 1982 the Government's judgement was that they did not accomplish that; the cultural gaps and differences in incentives between the NHS and local government were just too big. In an effort to reduce the bureaucracy created by the local tier and move decisions closer to the patient, the AHAs were abolished in 1982 with little mourning. Buttressed by neither local medical practice networks (rarely coterminous with local governments) nor the authority and medical logic of regions, they were weak bodies from the start. New DHAs, quite similar to their predecessor districts and similarly charged with overseeing local health systems, were put in place. 'If 1974 had been a triumph for coterminosity between health authorities and local government, the restructuring of April 1982 . . . restored the district as the functional and key tier' (Rivett 1998: 350–1). The NHS now had no tier or set of organisations designed to work easily with local government; the organisation was purely functional, about providing professional services. That said, the regions still remained the home of high-profile planning and politics, even if their borders still matched no other part of the English administrative map.

1983

The professionalist model of consensus management from 1974 lasted into the 1980s, when transformation in politics and the economy shifted most of Britain to a very different organisational model, that of the private sector (retail) business (Pollitt 1993). In the health service, it took the form of the Griffiths Commission, led by an executive from the Sainsbury's supermarket chain. In 1982 Griffiths was called in to advise on the management of the NHS and was struck by the absence of management as it its commonly understood. In the short letter from Griffiths to Thatcher that is often referred to, wrongly, as a report, he famously wrote that if Florence Nightingale were to walk the corridors of the NHS with her lantern, she would be looking for the people in charge (NHS Management Inquiry 1983).

The introduction of general management was initially an organisational change without necessary territorial implications. Griffiths suggested the establishment of a general management function within the NHS to centralise decision-making and strategic thinking at all levels, with management and policy boards at the centre to make operational and strategic decisions. This model of the NHS would be signally different. It had been difficult for the centre to influence the professionals on the committees that made decisions in the districts; now at least there was a management hierarchy that could transmit the order from top to bottom and enforce it (Hunter 1994). On paper it did not entail reorganisation of the NHS, since the units continued to exist but under new management. The only new creations were epiphenomenal boards at the top that were intended to rescue the minister from close involvement with the NHS Management Executive. The Executive was comprised of the managers implanted into all the different NHS organisations, with its headquarters in Leeds. The districts shut down their committees of professionals to make way for new chief executives and boards, and regions hired new managements to complement their boards. The creation of the Management Executive effectively hollowed out the old Department of Health, with its out-of-favour civil servants and ties to the hospital 'administrators' from the days of consensus management. The Government had successfully created an instrument, the Executive, with which it could try to control the health service and execute policy. While there were real questions about what managers could really do there was now a chain of command from the Secretary of State to the ward. The existence of management gave the centre a real claim to control that it could not have made before.

While the introduction of general management did not change the territorial organisation of the NHS, it did achieve two things. First, it was another reorganisation. The exercise of approving job descriptions for chief executives at every tier, for example, both increased the centre's knowledge of what happened in the system and created a new set of administrators with functions defined by the Department or the Executive. Second, the whole point of general management was that the Government would now have a tool with which to enunciate and implement a strategy, unencumbered by local or professional resistance. If policy, finance and organisation were all in the hands of the Executive, and therefore in the hands of managers paid to achieve the goals sent down from above, then the Government had a tempting new tool with which to intervene in the organisation and incentive structures of the NHS down to the ward or the operating theatre level. Managers, unlike professionals (or the local boards of pre-1974 memory), were chosen to respond to central strategic direction and incentives.

1989

The next set of blows to local autonomy came with the establishment of the internal market, 1989–91. This had serious consequences for the territorial organisation and overall structure of the NHS. This set of reforms involved dividing the NHS into purchasers and providers in order to introduce greater accountability, market discipline and therefore, presumably, enhanced cost-effectiveness and experimentation. It did not create a market, because it was merely a way of allocating resources within an envelope fixed by the UK Government's budget. Nor could it be a market, because the NHS lacked the over-capacity or easy entrance into the market necessary to truly let weak providers go to the wall. It arranged the purchaser side into health authorities or 'fund-holding' practices which could purchase acute services for their patients – general practitioners were offered the opportunity to become fund-holders: 7 per cent took the opportunity in 1991–92, but by 1997–98 as many as 59 per cent had done so.

The provider side was organised into firm-like trusts, at first generally based on the hospital. Initially this was voluntary, but as no hospitals of note applied, the Government cajoled the high-profile London institution Guy's Hospital into trust status. Once the Conservatives won the 1992 election the whole system moved to trusts. Notes Rivett, 'in place of the traditional authorities tiers an industrial model of governance was substituted. This was technocratic and, while it might promote efficiency and responsiveness, it also increased insecurity, the authority of the centre, and short-term decision-making' (1998: 422).

The industrial model also finally removed the fundamental link between local or regional territory and provision. The districts, prior to the coming of the internal market, had been the key units for service provision (especially acute hospital services), while the regions were key to planning and budgeting. The creation of trusts hollowed out the districts by taking away their responsibility for direct service provision, while the growth of fund-holding reduced their role on the purchaser side. The regions were charged primarily with constructing the new market. They would naturally lose their regional planning role in the new internal market, since market logic rather than planners' designs would dictate resource flows. In practice, the internal market did not provide meaningful capital, which continued to be allocated by organisations higher up, but the regions had lost their claim to be the most important decision-makers in such large resource-allocation decisions. From this point onwards, the trusts would be the heart of the NHS, and acute care trusts responded to a more functional than territorial logic.

1996

The Conservatives' final reorganisation of the NHS of their eighteen-years in government was in 1996, and amounted to cleaning up territorial components of the NHS organisation that were losing their functions as quasi-markets developed. As fund-holding in England increased, there was less role for the DHAs as purchasers and the Government had begun to merge them. First, it merged them with their family health equivalents, then by 1995 the districts themselves were merged into bigger districts; only half of the initial total remained. The regions now came into the line of fire. They were fundamentally hold-overs from an earlier day in which there was region-level resource allocation. In a market context, however, they were weak. They did not control most of the money and the more enterprising purchasers and providers resented their interference. The Government responded in 1996 by merging them into eight regions[2] and making them components of the NHS Executive rather than autonomous boards. Their job would be to co-ordinate services and act as freelance executors of departmental policy.

Turning boards into mere components of the NHS Executive eliminated the last vestiges of the old NHS model, with its considerable local autonomy vested in various territorial organisations and responsible for both the purchasing and provision of services. The NHS, from this point on, did not have an autonomous regional level anywhere; it was now made up of trusts, DHAs or GP fund-holders, with a centrally controlled Executive looking for a role. This is how a market should work, at least in theory, since if it is a self-regulating market there is no need for a managing authority. In practice, the NHS was not and has never been a market, and the regions quickly became instruments that the Department and the Executive used to intervene to change provider behaviour.

1998 AND 2001

Labour completed the market pattern when in 1998 it began reorganising the purchasing side into primary care trusts (PCTs) encompassing all primary care and commissioning (the Labour commitment to ending the internal market translated into ending GP fund-holding – and insisting that the word 'commissioning' replace the word 'purchasing' in NHS jargon). The idea was to build on the aspects of the internal market that *worked*, above all commissioning, while reducing inefficient competition and the supposed incentives to two-tier treatment (Greer 2004; Ham 2004). This meant merging the residual purchasing functions of the DHAs with those of the fund-holders (who often resented their loss of status) into primary care groups (PCGs). PCGs were sub-committees of the DHAs charged with deciding how the DHAs would commission, and the Department of Health hoped that they would become trusts with a fixed population-based budget that would handle around 85 per cent of the commissioning (Department of Health 1998). The whole NHS was now an ecology of 576 firm-like acute and primary care, or other, trusts, each with a manager and a board, each subject to Labour's new regulatory agencies and each with its own identity, letterhead and internal management hierarchy. On paper, it looks like a textbook quasi-market; in reality, however, it is still doubly centralised. The regulatory agencies, currently being consolidated tightly prescribe much of what must be commissioned and provided, and have work programmes largely set by ministerial decision. And all of these trusts have one shareholder, the minister, and are subject to both specific interventions and intense central control (the number of targets issued by the Department of Health to acute trusts is unknown, but according to one minister in early 2003 the officials' best count was at least 450).

In the run-up the 2001 election the Secretary of State for Health Alan Milburn abolished yet more of the territorial organisations left behind by the advance of the market. This programme, announced in a surprise speech, was called 'Shifting the Balance' and arranged the DHAs into 28 strategic health authorities (SHAs) at a ratio of roughly 3:1, abolished the NHS regions, merged the Department of Health's top leadership with that of the NHS Executive (to the detriment of the former), and introduced four new Regional Directors of Health and Social Care to cover the remaining regional functions. (These last were abolished in 2003.) The result is that the NHS today has a thriving ecology of trusts, a layer of SHAs with populations of around half a million whose purpose is somewhat confused, but which the

Department of Health views largely as its agents for performance management, and a high-level infrastructure of auditors, inspectors and agencies with special missions such as modernisation or patient safety. The only local dimension is that the primary care trusts are responsible for population health in their local areas. This is laudable but is overshadowed by central regulation dictating most of what they do and the real threat that the powerful acute trusts will dominate them. The logic of this reorganisation, as with the others since 1982, is simple enough: as a system of professional management operating with the right incentives supposedly goes to work, the need for territorial tiers of management or planning is reduced and they can be eliminated, possibly to press and public applause.

Developments since 'Shifting the Balance' have simply worked out the most non-market-like ramifications of this attempt at market organisation. The most prominent has been the Labour Government's interest in a 'new localism' (as against old localism, which presumably refers to elected local governments). New localism is, according to a Labour and Co-Operative Party figure involved in manifestos and the Department of Health's NHS foundation trusts' External Reference Group on Governance, 'explicitly based around the cooperative and mutual sectors here in the United Kingdom and overseas . . . the direct descendants of the Rochdale Society of Equitable Pioneers'.[3] New localism ties up with the much stronger and well-entrenched rhetoric of markets and the managerial backlash against central control (one that is particularly intense due to Labour's centralised targeting, but which is probably intrinsic to any situation with powerful managers whose interest is to shape their trusts to their liking). The result is the foundation hospitals initiative, in which acute trusts that achieve a high ranking for quality (not just of treatment, but financially) can apply to a regulator for extra powers, such as borrowing rights, and for exemption from most of the performance management of the centre, including most of the SHAs' forms of control. They establish their own boards, in the new localist strand of the argument. Their governance, though, is a 'cacophony of accountabilities', with their local boards, their own regulator, normal NHS regulators and local PCTs charged with commissioning care and holding them accountable (Klein 2003) – and it is a good question whether the managers will dare to defy a minister. The new localist governance has thus far tended to be comic: Bradford Teaching Hospital's NHS Trust mustered 541 voters for its council, well below 1 per cent of the local population. Only specialised hospitals bound to organised constituencies did better at inducing participation (Klein 2004). In other words, the new localist strand means exempting some institutions from mid-tier performance management (SHAs) and creating a rather feeble form of non-local-government local governance while otherwise leaving them to be disciplined by centrally controlled regulators and the PCTs, which are vulnerable to both the centre and to powerful trusts. It does suggest that as the form becomes more widespread the SHAs, the last of the mid-level organisations, will lose functions and, like their predecessors, become targets for elimination.

They will be paid via a programme called 'Payment by Results'. This is a central effort to make competition and commissioning work by setting fixed tariffs for different procedures (it is modelled on the well-established but still controversial US system of diagnostic related groups, which operates on the same logic). A trust that performs a procedure for more than the tariff will lose money on each procedure; one that does it for less than the tariff will make money. The powerful centrally-driven 'performance management' structures and the independent (and budget-focused) foundation hospitals' regulator will punish trust managers, as they already do, who do not balance the books. The centre will cope with the instability created by its existing contracts with treatment centres for specific routine procedures, such as hip replacements and cataract removals.

Payment by Results, of course, is also a neat illustration of the inextricability of the centre from its quasi-market. No real market could possibly have centrally fixed prices. The problem with real competition, though, is that the system, all of it still paid for out of general taxation and all of it the Government's political responsibility, would be severely destabilised by genuine price competition (London, with its high-cost specialised centres and generally high-cost property and staff, would probably be denuded of hospitals). The result is that in its effort to disengage from the frontlines and let local initiative flourish, the Government is now obliged to set a fixed England-wide rate for payment for every procedure done in the NHS – a most complex task, and one that if done poorly could create waves of financial crisis throughout the system (Street and AbdulHussain 2004). The performance managers at the centre should not want for work as the unexpected consequences of this extraordinarily complicated agenda work through the system – there is already a substantial Department of Health budget ready to bail out the victims of the first unintended consequences. And in October 2004, a few months into the new regime, the Bradford Foundation Hospital Trust, already fingered for the local lack of interest in its new localism, had developed a yawning deficit and blamed the 'Payment by Results' programme. Department of Health finance officials explained that such deficits were expected and should be no more than teething problems, and that 'the transparency is what we want' (interviews, June and September 2004). The centre may not get efficiency – there is no guarantee that trusts will reduce costs – but it will finally have the activity rates, patient statistics and traceable financial flows that so many ministers and officials see as the solution to almost any problem.

Finally, there is the combination of *diversity* and *choice* (Greer 2005b), which amount to the hotly contested effort to introduce greater private provision (Pollock 2004). The link between GPs and patients is thus broken in order to route patients by available capacity rather than doctors' networks (known as choice) and using private providers from overseas or the UK to destroy the traditional private-sector model by wiping out waiting lists with a combination of 'assembly-line' facilities for specific procedures such as hip replacements, foreign doctors, new methods and enhanced government ability to choose with whom it will contract for services (diversity). The Department of Health has made it clear that it expects 10 per cent of commissioning to come from private providers: between the increased capacity (which reduces demand for private treatment) and the private providers' inability to compete with the foreign entrants at their traditionally high prices, it appears to be well on the way to destroying the traditional UK private sector – which is why Dennis Skinner, MP, decided that 'the government's strategy is correct' (Watt and Carvel 2004). But if we think about the NHS as the political institution that it is, this is also about central control. Simon Stevens, a former advisor to the Prime Minister, now working for a private firm (United Health) that entered the NHS market during his tenure, explained in 2004 that the 'plurality' in provision will 'expand capacity, enhance contestability and offer choice'. 'Contestability' means that the monopoly power of any given NHS provider – as the only local purveyor of services – can be reduced. This will enhance government bargaining power vis à vis managers of any NHS or non-NHS health provider.

Markets as central control

In other words, the story of the English NHS has been one of the progressive elimination of models of territorial logic in favour of a functionalist logic. First it experimented with professionalism as a model of functional organisation, essentially hiring the medical profession to run the NHS. In the second, and more lasting, set of policies, the bet is on quasi-markets. In this logic, the centre organises the health service into units with prescribed interests and then develops a structure that will regulate and set incentives appropriately. In such a model there is little role for territorial layers of either management or planning: planning will be done by the market (at least in theory), regulation will be done by special quangos, and management will be done internally, in the trusts. The promise of foundation hospitals is obviously not co-operative new localism or managerial autonomy; it is freedom from the last territorial survivors, the SHAs, and subjection only to the centre and its regulators. The unexpected consequences of most of these innovations has instead been a tighter central grip on the system.

To the extent that this dynamic holds in other areas of the public sector, it relates to a potential explanation of the weakness of regionalism in England to date by highlighting the essentially homogeneous country presupposed by such functional solutions. It is easy to assume such homogeneity if territorial differentiation has no political representation. England's regions lack the historically rooted complexes of regional organisations that underpinned devolution in Scotland (and to a lesser extent Wales) as much as they did in Catalonia or the Basque Country. And the reduction in the powers of the regions – any regions – within the NHS alongside the reduction in the powers of local government means that England basically lacks the groups created around the exercise of power and the formation of public policy whose quarrels with central government and slow divergence over time generate constituencies for more regional autonomy in places like Andalucia or Rhône-Alpes. That lack of existing regional constituencies to date probably explains why a territorial alternative in the NHS is curiously absent. Policy-makers can think they are looking out at a uniformly homogeneous country and system, and adopt one-size-fits-all models based on their understanding of what motivates managers and professionals.

The result is an English system which may not be under the firm control of the centre but in which the centre has more, and more rapidly growing, power to orchestrate and greater blame to take for problems than anybody else. In a way, this story replicates many others in British life. There is a necessary tension at work when the centre (of any large, complex and territorially dispersed organisation) wants to enact any policy. On the one side there is a focus on England-wide, organisation-wide standards set and enforced by the centre and justified both by public expectations and by the accountability to the centre that comes with funding from the centre. On the other side, there is the problem that England is a very large unit to run. Central overload is a slippery concept, but there is a circumstantial case that the civil servants and ministers of the Department of Health cannot realistically make and enforce the decisions that would provide the best available health service across the UK. It is difficult to imagine them being able to adjust policy so that there are the right kind of toxicology services for urban areas with different drug problems; so that there are the right kinds of outreach to the elderly of diverse communities with very different immigrant groups; so that the appropriate documents are translated into the appropriate languages for the population of a given area; so that the accident and emergency services in rural areas are properly designed to respond to the long travel times for many patients. This means, for example, that equality of provision might not mean equity of provision (Powell 1997; Oates 1999).

Putting the same number of consultant pulmonologists (lung specialists) per 1,000 in the different areas of England would constitute formal equality, but it would not ensure the same standard of treatment since need for their services is enormous in former mining communities with rampant lung diseases and minimal in clean areas with an agricultural economy. Regional health boards could usually allocate the resources to maintain some level of equity in provision, but even they were sometimes indifferent to real problems.

Markets would seem to displace this problem by permitting divergent, locally appropriate forms of provision while ensuring overall standards through regulation. It is for that reason that they appeal to policy-makers looking for a flexible – and ideally automatic – mechanism to reconcile national standards and local responsiveness via a regulated health services' market. In this vision, the regulatory agencies guarantee not just that public money is intelligently spent, but that the level of medical care is of a quality that the public will accept. Actual provision, then, can be liberated, whether through foundation hospitals or through contracts with foreign firms. This will disengage government and create incentives to greater efficiency as part of the discipline of the market.

Whether one comes to this view from a left-wing perspective that sees a controlled market as a device to adapt a national service to local needs while permitting experimentation and getting control of the overall health service or from a more right-wing belief in markets as devices for beneficial competition, this is an appealing vision. The problem is that it has bumped up time and time again against constraints that mean the market has worked to lodge power at the centre rather than create anything like a functioning market. Until some government successfully creates quite a lot of spare capacity – enough to allow trusts or private firms to go under – and enjoys enough political strength to let hospitals close, and finds a way to do it on the taxpayers' tab (even if it is by buying in foreign firms, as in 'diversity' under Labour), there is not likely to be much real competition in the NHS. The only guaranteed way out, given the logic of the system, is to essentially privatise the NHS, or at least the hospitals and clinics, so that someone else can bear the risk of building new facilities with which to compete for public money – a shift that would be as radical as the creation of the NHS in the first place, and while justifiably just as hotly debated would almost certainly be hideously expensive during the transition (Myles and Pierson 2001).

Removing the prospect of a realistic market means that the only discipline left is political, through the Secretary of State. It is by no means clear that a service spending enormous sums of public money on matters of life and death will ever escape close public and parliamentary scrutiny, but the fact that the main discipline in the system, and apparently the only kind that the press understands, is via the centre rather than the market probably does not help the centre avoid the micro-management it generally claims to want to avoid. It is hard for central government to disengage. Even ministers who refuse to get caught in local crises (and many do get engaged with very local problems, whether by temperament, strategy or mistake) can be forced by the logic of politics into promising a programme or decision, simply to defuse some kind of crisis. The logic of English politics, probably in any sector but certainly in health, focuses the blame on government, and this has generally been more likely to lead ministers to intervene or make new policy than to retreat behind the theoretical autonomy of their various kinds of NHS organisations. The result is that any part of the NHS is weak when compared to government, which essentially owns, designs and manages the system.

Conclusion: the English experiment with centralism

So after enormous labour, the NHS is an orrery of trusts and private providers, all on their different orbits around the powerful, controlling, centripetal figure of the minister. Localist inheritance gave way to a run of functionalist solutions – professionalist logics, then management, then markets and, now, 'diversity', 'choice', 'new localism' and 'payment by results' in the service, essentially all logics of 'contestability' and therefore central power.

The implications for our understanding of the governance of England are potentially serious. The first point is the extent to which the centralisation of England is *recent*, and the rise of English political regionalism could well be just the first reaction to the extensive nationalisation of policy-making in various spheres since 1979. Prior to the election of the Conservatives in 1979 Bulpitt's description of 'the dual state' worked well: the central state might have been formally all-powerful but it permitted the local level and professional groups a high degree of autonomy (some comparative studies of management styles and corporate organisation suggest that this was also the case in the UK's private sector). In health, certainly, something like the dual state was at work: the centre lacked the resources or habit of intervening in much of what went on. To have demanded regional power would have been peculiar, given both the real autonomy of the regional bodies, and the greater importance of the local and professional levels. Given that the real nationalisation and centralisation of England is recent, then, it could well be the case that we are only now seeing the start of pressures to democratise and improve responsiveness through regionalisation.

The second point to note is the extent to which England's alternatives to centralism have not been regional. England has had the alternatives of local autonomy (including within the public sector) and professional autonomy within the public sector. The result may be part of an explanation of the weakness of English regionalism both historically and even now. There is, of course, no tradition of regionalism in much of Spain, France or Italy (or at least the regions that have the power are not always the ones with much tradition, even in some cases in Germany), but the development of regional governments there has come with time; regional governments tend to attract allies who, winning contests at the regional level, will support increased regional powers.

The third point is that central overload may be a reality, because the market, the chosen alternative of the last twenty years, creates serious problems that have not been overcome and which may be impossible to resolve while maintaining a commitment to egalitarian values. The NHS defies most of the rules of market design that have been applied to it (as do many other public services). An economist's market has easy entry and exit, prices that are set by buyers and sellers, and private risk. None of these assumptions apply to the NHS. There can be little risk because there is little justification for taking chances with public money (and because most of the NHS cannot be allowed to go out of business!). This means that the efforts of governments to create the markets and the market participants (fund-holders, private contracts for treatment centres, foundation hospitals, trusts, primary care trusts, etc.) are always likely to founder and lead instead to more central intervention – and, if we believe Tony Blair's ex-advisor Stevens, that increase in central power, rather than a market, is what was supposed to happen. The markets and market participants are indeed set up, but when they produce an unexpected outcome the centre must step in as the guardian of English public services and of the citizenship rights of the English. The result is both central control and a large apparatus of market-like regulators and organisations.

In other words, the governments of the last thirty years may have been barking up the wrong tree when they talked of decentralisation. What they have done is pursue functional logics, above all those of markets and purchasing, with a relentlessness that has paid off in the elimination of local and regional organisation or power in the NHS. That centralisation, made possible by the centre's assumption of the country's essential homogeneity and by the absence of territorial political response is typical of much of English life. And that makes the NHS a very *English* institution.

Notes

1 'The National Health Service is a prime exhibit in illustrating the danger of making too much of the continuity between the social consensus of the war years and the post-war Labour welfare state' (Morgan 1984: 154).

2 The borders of these eight regions were similar, but not identical, to those of the 'standard regions' that were evolving in the same years. The three major differences, reflecting patterns of patient flow and service catchments rather than the logic of the standard regions, were the inclusion of South Yorkshire with the East Midlands in Trent, Northamptonshire in a giant south-east region and northern Cumbria with the north east in a northern region; otherwise the maps were almost identical.

3 See Geraint J. Day, 'Historic changes take time to development [*sic*]', online 'rapid response' (www.bmj.com) to Klein 2004, dated 6 June 2004.

11
Conclusion: what are the answers to the English Question?

Robert Hazell

In this final chapter we revisit all the possible answers to the English Question which have been identified in the course of the book, and evaluate them in terms of their feasibility and their probability. These last we gauge in terms of the support they have attracted among elites or the general public. Most are found seriously wanting in either their feasibility or their probability, and some in both. For those who regard the English Question as a quest for the Holy Grail with a magic solution to be discovered if only we search hard enough, this is profoundly disappointing. But the English Question does not necessarily have a magic solution. Like other big historical questions (the Eastern Question, the Irish Question), it is a shorthand title for an problem (or set of problems) which is not susceptible to an easy solution.

Nor can the English Question be answered purely in intellectual or logical terms. This book is written by a group of academics who have analysed and attempted to answer the question from every conceivable angle. But the question cannot be answered by academics alone. It is a political question, about the governance of England, and the answers must ultimately come from the English people. Do they want elected regional assemblies, or an English parliament? Or are they quite relaxed about devolution for the rest of the UK, but want none of it for themselves? Academics can highlight the inconsistencies and instability inherent in an incomplete process of devolution, and lay out the range of possible solutions. Politicians can do the same more selectively and promote some solutions rather than others. But ultimately only the English people can say for how long they are willing to tolerate the anomalies thrown up by devolution and whether they are ready to vote for change.

Institutional answers to the English Question

In chapter 1 we adopted a strongly institutionalist approach, explaining that the central focus of the book is on political representation for England and the English regions in the light of devolution. In seeking the institutional form that representation should take we identified two versions of the English Question:

- a UK version, about rebalancing England's place in the Union post devolution
- an English version, about decentralising the government of England.

Part I of the book discussed England's place in the Union; part II explored ways of decentralising the government of England. The institutional responses to these two versions of the English Question are summarised in box 11.1.

Box 11.1 Institutional solutions to two versions of the English Question

Solutions to strengthen England's voice in the Union:

- An English parliament
- English votes on English laws
- English independence

Institutional solutions to decentralise the government of England:

- Elected regional assemblies
- Functional regionalism
- Strengthening local government
- Elected mayors

In this final chapter each solution will be discussed in turn, as well as the interplay between them. But to summarise the conclusions, and to show how few of the solutions hold out much promise, it is helpful at this stage to set out a skeleton of the argument in tabular form. Table 11.1 sets out each of the institutional solutions in the left hand column, and in the rows opposite indicates how much elite support and how much mass support the solution has attracted, and then comments on its feasibility and its probability.

An English parliament

FEASIBILITY

At first blush an English parliament would appear to be a neat solution to the fundamental asymmetry in the devolution arrangements. It would create a federation of the four historic nations of the UK, each with a parliament enjoying significant devolved powers. But it is one thing to create such a

Table 11.1 Summary evaluation of institutional answers to the English Question

	Elite support	Mass support	Probability	Feasibility	Comments
Strengthen England's place in the Union					
English parliament	Low	Low: 15 per cent in 2003 poll	Low	UK would become federation of four historic nations. But could such an English-dominated federation endure?	English parliament would risk being as overburdened as Westminster, and equally remote
English independence	Negligible	Negligible	Very low	Technically very difficult	Hard to envisage England declaring UDI from rest of UK: more likely that Northern Ireland and Scotland would break away
English votes on English laws	Conservative Party policy	60 per cent support: table 6.3	Low	Technically and politically difficult	Becomes live issue if UK Government has small majority, but unlikely ever to be implemented by a Labour Government

Decentralise government of England

Elected regional assemblies	Labour Party policy, Lib Dem policy, opposed by Conservatives	20–30 per cent: highest in north, lowest in south and east (see tables 6.1–6.5)	Low in near future following defeat in Nov 2004 referendum in north east	Feasible: draft Regional Assemblies Bill published July 2004	Powers proposed for elected regional assemblies were very weak
Functional regionalism	Labour Party policy	Little public knowledge or interest	High: regional chambers exist	Feasible	Limits to functional regionalism, which depends on consensus: see chapter 7
Revive local government	Politicians pay lip-service, no party has strong proposals	Public seem to share some of national politicians' mistrust of local government competence	Low	Feasible: no shortage of proposals – merely requires political will	High standards and national targets for public services militate against local autonomy
Elected mayors	Low: very little support among local councillors	High in opinion polls, less when tested in local referendums	Has not yet gained momentum, no big cities have mayors except for London	Feasible and achieved under Local Government Act 2000	Might also be linked to city-regions

federation; quite another to make it work. The fundamental difficulty is the sheer size of England in comparison to the rest of the UK. England, with 80 per cent of the population, would be hugely dominant. On most domestic matters this English parliament would be more important than the Westminster Parliament. No federation can operate successfully where one of the units is so dominant. In the post-war German Constitution of 1949 Prussia was deliberately broken up into 5 or 6 distinct states to prevent it being dispro-portionately large and dominating the new Germany. Although all federations have some units much larger than others, as a general rule no unit is greater than around 30 or so per cent of the whole, to avoid it dominating the rest. If this logic were accepted, England would have to be broken up into smaller units for a federal solution to work – something which is anathema to the CEP.

PROBABILITY

The CEP has remained stuck on the political fringe. It has attracted neither elite nor mass support: in the 1997 Parliament it attracted the interest of a dozen or so backbench Conservative MPs, but no heavyweight politicians have come out in support. This is in marked contrast to the Campaign for a Scottish Parliament, which attracted support in the 1990s from two main political parties and all the political heavyweights in Scotland except the Conservatives. It also contrasts with the CFER, which (although the Labour Party is divided) has attracted support from such Labour heavyweights as John Prescott, Gordon Brown, Peter Mandelson and Alan Milburn. Perhaps because of this lack of elite support, mass support for the idea of an English parliament remains low and shows no sign of increasing. Table 6.1 shows that in the first five years of devolution support for an English parliament remained flat at 16–19 per cent, while support for regional assemblies crept upwards from 15 to 24 per cent. An English parliament is not seriously on the political agenda, and will never get on to the agenda unless serious politicians begin to espouse it.

English votes on English laws: Westminster as a proxy for an English parliament

PROBABILITY

By contrast, English votes on English laws does command some elite support and considerable mass support. Polling data consistently show that 55–65 per cent of people in England agree that Scottish MPs should no longer be allowed to vote on English laws, now that Scotland has its own parliament (see table 6.3). It seems only logical and fair, since English MPs can no longer vote on matters devolved to Scotland. Even a majority of Scots support restricting the voting rights of Scottish MPs in this way (Curtice 2001: 234).

But chapter 4 spells out just how formidable the difficulties are, at both a technical and a political level.

The technical difficulty is identifying those English laws on which only English MPs would be allowed to vote. Strictly speaking, there is no such thing as an English law, in the sense of a Westminster statute which applies only to England. The territorial extent clauses in Westminster statutes typically cover the UK, Great Britain or England and Wales. Many statutes vary in their territorial application in different parts of the Act. In theory the Speaker of the House could identify in advance those clauses or amendments which apply only to England and rule that only English MPs could take part in those divisions. But the example of the Higher Education Bill 2004, discussed in chapter 4, shows that such rulings would be controversial and some would be strongly challenged. The complexity of excluding non-English MPs from some votes but not others in the same bill would be immense, and the legislative hokey-cokey required would be too confusing to be regarded as feasible. Only with the introduction of electronic voting at Westminster would it become feasible, because that would enable the voting terminals of non-English MPs to be disabled or discounted in divisions in which they were deemed ineligible to vote.

If the technical difficulties are daunting, the political difficulties are even greater. Proponents of English votes on English laws tend to underestimate just what a huge change would be involved. It would create two classes of MP, ending the traditional reciprocity whereby all members can vote on all matters. It would effectively create a parliament within a parliament. And after close-fought elections, the UK Government might not be able to command a majority for its English business, leading to great political instability. These political difficulties cast serious doubt on the likelihood of English votes on English laws ever becoming a political reality.

English votes on English laws would suddenly become a critical issue if (as may happen) after a future election Labour formed a government with a narrow majority, and depended on Scottish and Welsh MPs to get their legislation through. There would be heady talk of a constitutional crisis, but whether in reality it triggered a crisis would depend on the reaction of the English. Up to now the English have been willing to tolerate anomalies, as part of the statecraft of managing the Union. Chapter 4 showed how there has been a kind of rough justice at Westminster, from which the Scots and the Welsh have suffered more in the past than the English. Now the English are more likely to suffer rough justice, but only when the arithmetic at Westminster is very close. A close result would put the English to the test.

The Conservatives have fought two elections on English votes on English laws (under Hague and Howard) and will try to arouse the English. On past form the English seem unlikely to respond. Although opinion polls show majority support for English votes on English laws, it is not an issue of high salience. It would become salient only if the Government used the votes of Scottish and Welsh MPs to force controversial or unpopular measures on the English. Its salience would depend on how the media reported parliamentary votes on the issue. In the 2001 Parliament the media reported only spasmodically on the contribution of non-English MPs to help carry controversial measures such as the ban on fox-hunting and student tuition fees, highlighting it on some votes but ignoring it on others.[1] In a Parliament where the Government had a narrow majority the media might make more play of the issue. But in a Parliament with a slender majority it is harder to foresee the Government introducing such measures in the first place and risking electoral unpopularity in middle England.

It is also hard to foresee the Conservatives campaigning on this issue with real conviction. They will know that English votes on English laws garnered them few votes in the 2001 election. And the more historically minded will be aware that this is a strange *volte face* for the Conservative and Unionist Party. If they seriously wanted to end the equal voting rights of all MPs, the Conservatives could no longer claim to be Unionist, but would have become an English party. An *English* party does not sound like a party of government. And if the Conservatives found themselves in government, would they go ahead and introduce English votes on English laws? A Conservative Government with a majority at Westminster would probably find that it included once again a contingent of Scottish Conservative MPs, and might take a different view.

The West Lothian Question does have two other possible answers

What gives the West Lothian Question its political edge is the mismatch between territorial and party balance at Westminster, with Labour being disproportionately over-represented in Scotland and Wales. There are two other possible solutions which would help correct this mismatch between territorial and party balance. The first would be to reduce the number of Scottish and Welsh MPs to reflect their reduced role at Westminster following devolution, in much the same way that Northern Ireland had reduced representation during the Stormont Parliament (1922–1972). During that first period of devolution in Northern Ireland the number of Northern Irish MPs was reduced to 12, compared with their current representation of 18. If a similar discount of one-third were applied to Scottish and Welsh representation, Scottish representation would be reduced to around 40 MPs at Westminster and Welsh to around 22.[2] It would not eliminate the possibility of Scottish and Welsh MPs voting on English laws, but it would further reduce the like-lihood of their votes tipping the balance.

The second solution is proportional representation (PR). 'First past the post' offers a bonus to parties whose support is geographically concentrated, and so tends to exaggerate the political differences between England and Scotland and Wales. PR would help to reduce Labour's landslide in Scotland and Wales, and so reduce the differences between their political centre of gravity and that of England.

Again, PR would make no difference to constitutional purists who believe that Scottish MPs should not be voting on matters at Westminster which have no direct impact on Scotland. However, as Russell and Lodge demonstrate in chapter 4, and McLean and McMillan in chapter 2, concerns about the question are driven primarily by party-political concerns, with purism being a secondary factor. The salience of the West Lothian Question for the Conservative Party comes largely from the fact that Labour holds an overwhelming majority of the seats in Scotland and in Wales, which could be enough to swing parliamentary votes in favour of Labour across the UK. In particular, an election result such as that of 1964, or February 1974, could see a Labour Government dependent on Scottish and Welsh votes to get its legislation through, while the Conservatives held a majority of parliamentary seats in England. These problems are exacerbated by the 'first past the post' electoral system, which in recent times has tended to exaggerate Labour's representation in Scotland and Wales and the Conservative Party's in England. At present Labour's overwhelming majority extends to England as well. But in 1964, for example, Labour won 61 per cent of the seats in Scotland on 49 per cent of the vote and 78 per cent of the seats in Wales on 59 per cent of the vote, while the Conservatives in England won 51 per cent of the seats on 44 per cent of the vote.

A change to a PR electoral system would help to ease the tensions created by the West Lothian Question. It would of course have many other implications for the British political system – central among them the likelihood of coalition governance. It was the desire to avoid coalition government that led the Jenkins Commission in 1998 to propose an only partially proportional system. However, by definition a system which was only partially proportional would be less likely to smooth out the differences in election outcomes between England, Scotland and Wales, and thus to address the grievances felt about the West Lothian Question.[3]

Independence for England

English independence is the third and most extreme institutional solution which would ensure the English have a louder political voice. If it is impossible to give the English a political voice within the Union, the argument goes, they need to break free from the Union and establish their own English state. To many readers of this book it will come as a surprise that anyone advocates English independence, but there is an English Independence Party (formerly the English National Party), which is in favour of England withdrawing both from the UK and the EU.[4] It need not detain us long, because its support is vanishingly small. It commands zero support at elite level, and minimal support at mass level. It may offer a stark answer to the English Question, but it is not an answer the English seem willing to grasp.

For the English to demand independence from the rest of the UK, the dynamics of devolution would have had to throw up political issues which created a sharp cleavage between the interests, respectively, of England and the smaller nations. Given how much power is retained by the UK's Government and Parliament under the devolution settlement (Trench 2005), it is difficult to envisage how such a *casus belli* could be allowed to arise. It is also difficult to envisage the English unilaterally dissolving the Union: losing Scotland and Wales really would be the last retreat of empire, and an extraordinary rupture from England's traditional view of her place in the world, which for centuries has been inextricably linked with that of Britain and its island partners.

If the English are denied a louder political voice, does English nationalism need some other outlet?

It is time to sum up our answers thus far to the English Question. There is no demand for English independence. There is no demand yet for an English parliament. There is broad support for English votes on English laws, but it is not an issue of high salience, and it would be extraordinarily difficult to realise in practice at Westminster. So, for the time being, the English seem destined to be denied a louder political voice. Does English nationalism, then, need some other outlet? It has become commonplace even among supporters of devolution to view English identity and lack of national institutions as problematical, and to deplore the confusion of 'English' with 'British'. We believe this concern is itself confused – and misplaced.

One of the important conclusions of this book is that weak English nationalism has not necessarily been a problem. In some ways it has actually proved beneficial – England has not blocked devolution to the smaller nations of the UK. Table 6.8 shows how strongly the English have supported devolution to Scotland and Wales, with 50–60 per cent consistently supporting the creation of the Scottish Parliament and the Welsh Assembly. Undoubtedly it helped the passage of the devolution legislation that there was no serious

opposition to it in England, and it has also helped the bedding-down of devolution that there has been no English backlash. If anything, the English have
become more relaxed: the final row in table 6.8 suggests that in England the
modest opposition to devolution declined by 10 percentage points between
1997 and 2003.

English national identity was explored extensively in chapter 3, with
Arthur Aughey concluding that it is not necessarily a problem that the English
have a weak sense of national identity. It is certainly the case that English identity is closely interwoven with Britishness. Table 6.9 shows that on a forced-
choice question almost equal numbers say they are English (40 per cent), and
British (50 per cent). And on the Moreno question in table 6.10 nearly two-
thirds say they are some mixture of English and British. Commentators have
bemoaned this confusion by the English of Englishness with Britishness. But
in our history and in our institutions the two identities are closely intertwined
and can not easily be unwoven.

Nor is there necessarily a mismatch between perception and reality. The
political institutions to which the English owe loyalty are themselves a mixture
of English and British. Westminster was originally the seat of the English
Parliament and is now the home of the British Parliament. The English regard
it as their Parliament, and do not want a separate parliament (see table 6.1).
Most departments in Whitehall combine a mixture of English and British
functions (see Lodge and Mitchell, chapter 5, this volume). There are no separate English departments and no demand from the English to have a separate government of England.

Identity and institutions mirror each other. Englishness is commingled
with Britishness in the English people's sense of identity and in their political
institutions. To combine Englishness with Britishness is not necessarily a sign
of confusion. It is a reflection of reality. We cannot readily disentangle
Englishness from Britishness in either our history or our institutions. It is
better to accept them for what they are, deeply intertwined, and allow the
English to celebrate being English *and* British. Their political allegiance is to
Westminster. English identity would start to become problematic only if the
English no longer identified with the British State and its institutions. So long
as Westminster commands their allegiance, it probably matters not if almost
equal numbers view it as a more English (30 per cent) or more British (40 per
cent) institution (Curtice and Heath 2000: table 8.15).[5]

What is missing following devolution is not a separate set of institutions
the English can identify with, to sharpen their sense of identity, but a clearer
narrative about the Union and England's place within it. McLean and
McMillan argue in chapter 2 that there is a vacuum in unionism following
the collapse of the primordial and instrumental arguments for it, and Aughey

suggests (chapter 3) that now we need a new narrative of integration, a new ideology of unionism, which restates and justifies the Union and England's place in it. What are the values and interests which bind the nations of the UK together in the twenty-first century? In the past the Union and what it stood for could be taken largely for granted. Following the bout of self-questioning which followed the loss of empire and Britain's economic decline and entry into Europe, a restatement is called for. One might expect the English, as the senior partners in the Union, to lead such an exercise. No English politician has seen the need or risen to the challenge. Typically it has fallen to a Scottish politician, Gordon Brown, in his British Council lecture in July 2004 to initiate a debate on 'the need to celebrate and entrench a Britishness defined by shared values strong enough to overcome discordant claims of separatism and disintegration'.

Institutional answers to decentralising the government of England

The second part of this final chapter considers the answers to the '*English*' version of the English Question, which is about improving the government of England. The main institutional answers to this version of the question are as follows:

- elected regional assemblies;
- administrative regionalism;
- strengthening local government; and
- elected mayors.

As in the first part of the chapter, each solution is assessed in terms of its elite support and mass support, its probability and feasibility. With the exception of city–regions, all the solutions are technically feasible. The real arguments revolve around their probability and the extent to which they present satisfactory answers to the English Question. None is wholly satisfactory; but, to anticipate the argument, the chapter concludes that regionalism is more probable, and offers a more satisfactory set of answers than any of the alternatives based on local government.

Elected regional assemblies

PROBABILITY

At the elite level, elected regional assemblies have been supported by Labour and the Liberal Democrats, but opposed by the Conservatives and by the business community. Mass support has always been much harder to gauge, with opinion surveys producing wildly varying figures caused by low levels of public understanding and large groups of 'Don't-knows' among those canvassed. However the balance of opinion seemed to suggest that a referendum in the North East would be carried, although on a low turnout (Jeffery 2003). This continued to be the expert view until about a month before polling.

Then came the result. In November 2004 the people of the North East voted decisively by four to one to reject the Government's proposals for an elected regional assembly, on a turnout of 48 per cent. There were many possible reasons for the result.[6] The 'No' campaign had argued that the assembly would mean more politicians, more bureaucracy, more council tax, at a time when politicians of all parties are deeply unpopular. The assembly was dismissed as a mere talking shop because of its strategic role and lack of substantive powers. Some of the popular press linked regional policy to Europe, and played upon anti-EU feeling. John Prescott appeared to be the sole champion of the policy, with many of his colleagues hanging back. The Government had insisted on local government reorganisation as a precondition of regional government, risking confusing the electorate and alienating local government. And some voters will simply have voted 'No' because they preferred the status quo.

Following this decisive rejection, it might be assumed that elected regional assemblies are dead. They clearly are, for the time being; but not necessarily for ever. In 1979 the people of Wales voted by four to one against the Labour Government's plans for an assembly, but in 1997 they narrowly reversed their decision, and the Welsh Assembly now seems firmly established. Could such a *volte face* happen in England with regional government? It all depends on the dynamics of devolution. The North East will continue to look enviously across the border at Scotland. Regionalism will not go away, for reasons explained below, and functional regionalism seems likely to continue to grow. Whether further attempts will be made to introduce elected regional assemblies depends on whether regional elites continue to espouse them, and whether mass opinion comes round to support them.

Feasibility

Elected regional assemblies are perfectly feasible. The government offered a blueprint in the 2002 White Paper *Your Region, Your Choice* (Cabinet Office DTLR 2002), and in 2004 published a draft Regional Assemblies Bill setting out their proposed composition, powers and functions. The assemblies were to be slim-line strategic bodies whose main functions would be economic development, strategic land-use planning, transport strategy and housing investment. The functions were criticised as inadequate (Adams and Tomaney

2002; Sandford 2002a), and it is not surprising that they were dismissed by the 'No' campaigners as mere talking shops. If a future government were ever to resurrect the idea of elected regional assemblies it would have to demonstrate more convincingly that they would have a set of powers and functions, and budgets to match, which could really make a difference.

Defeat of the 2004 proposals has raised the bar. Just as in Scotland and in Wales the Government came forward with a stronger set of proposals in 1997 compared with 1979,[7] so a future government would need to strengthen as well as repackage any new proposals for regional government. That would require a degree of leadership and a level of collective commitment from its cabinet that were absent in 2004. A future government might also prefer to uncouple the threat of local government reorganisation from the creation of a new regional tier, in order to retain the support of local government for any new set of proposals.

Functional regionalism

PROBABILITY

If elected regional assemblies seem far, far away, functional regionalism is strongly here and now, for the reasons presented in chapter 9. Mark Sandford described the dense network of policy actors which has gradually grown up in each region around the triumvirate of the GO, the RDA and the regional assembly. From small beginnings these three core institutions have grown significantly in terms of their powers, budgets, influence and effectiveness. Equally significant are the policy networks that have grown up around them, which come together in forums like the sustainable development round tables, regional cultural consortiums, regional health observatories, regional housing forums and regional rural affairs forums, as well as through the business and voluntary sector members of the regional assembly. These fledgling regional institutions have begun to take on a life of their own, and to develop a capacity and focus for policy-making, which suggests that 'bottom–up' regionalism will continue, and continue to grow, despite the rejection of elected regional assemblies.

In chapter 5, Lodge and Mitchell suggested that 'top–down' regionalism also seems likely to continue, thanks to the growing interest of the Treasury in improving regional productivity and reducing the disparities in regional economic performance. Regionalism has permeated Whitehall's thinking, and the thinking of the business community. Business remains strongly opposed to elected regional assemblies, but has become supportive of the RDAs and (to a lesser extent) the existing regional assemblies (also known as regional chambers) in which they are represented among the social and economic partners. The regional assemblies now have budgets and small staffs of their own, and with their mixed composition of local authority leaders and representatives of the private and voluntary sectors, they are defended by their members as 'partnership assemblies' in which the private and the public sector can do business together. Many of them did not want to see elected assemblies, and will not regard it as a setback that they have been rejected. But it is a technocratic form of regionalism, played only by regional elites, in a way which is invisible to the general public.

FEASIBILITY

This technocratic regional tier would be difficult, if not impossible, to abolish, even if the political weather changed. Regional elites have a growing interest in its continuance, and new functions continue to be transferred to the regional level, albeit in an ad hoc and unplanned way. The only limits to this creeping regionalism are those posited by Michael Keating in chapter 7. Keating argued, based on European experience, that a tipping point will come when functional regionalism evolves into political regionalism, because the technocratic structures can not go on as they are. It is not wholly clear in this model whether the push will come from regional elites, who propose electoral legitimacy to give them more effective power; or from regional populations, who demand elections to cure the regional democratic deficit. But we cannot assume there is something inevitable about the shift from functional to political regionalism. The safer prediction for England must be that functional regionalism will continue for some time to come, and possibly for ever.

Strengthening local government and elected mayors

FEASIBILITY

The main alternative advanced as the answer to excessive centralisation is to restore powers and functions to local government. There is no shortage of proposals for strengthening local government. Just in the last ten years there has been the Commission for Local Democracy (1995), the House of Lords report Rebuilding Trust (1996), and recent proposals from the Local Government Information Unit (2002) and the Local Government Association (2004). Most of the proposals are perfectly feasible. What is lacking is any evidence of political will in central government to let go. Local government in turn has lowered its sights in recent years, recognising that New Labour did not usher in a brave new world for local government, but more of the same: more targets, more regulation, more central initiatives, tighter controls. Local government's wish-list for greater freedoms is tightly bounded by the recognition that under

New Labour, as under the Conservatives, local government now dances to central government's tune.

This is not to ignore New Labour's own agenda for reviving local government. This included elected mayors, briefly Labour's 'big idea' for the transformation of local government, with some thirty referenda being held in 2002 by local authorities wishing to introduce elected mayors. In the event only eleven localities voted for elected mayors, and none of those were in large cities (Game 2003; Sandford 2004b). It seems unlikely that the election of mayors will spread fast, and the Government has gone quiet about them.[8] The Government further hopes to reinvigorate local government through the cabinet system (the alternative chosen by most local authorities over that of elected mayors); the new power of general competence conferred by the Local Government Act 2000; and the freedoms conferred on high-performance 'beacon' councils. There is also a review of local government finance (ODPM 2004).[9]

PROBABILITY

The mood music has not changed, however. Freedoms are to be earned, not given to local government. There is little recognition of local government as a sphere of government in its own right, and no talk of restoring the powers and functions lost to local government over the last twenty years. Further powers continue to be removed, some to the regional level. Strategic land-use planning, previously a function of county councils through their structure plans, was given in 2004 to regional assemblies which are to be the new regional planning bodies.

In theory the government of England could be decentralised by a major transfer of powers and functions from central government to local government. In practice, it seems most unlikely to happen. All parties pay lip-service to the importance of reviving local government, but in private both Labour and the Conservatives continue to harbour a deep distrust in the competence of local councillors. If the centre is minded to devolve any of its power, any powers transferred in the future are more likely to devolve on the regional than the local level.

Regionalism emerges as the best answer to the English Question . . .

It is time to sum up. In the final part of the book we stand back from all the institutional answers analysed thus far, eliminate those which seem to be unpromising or non-starters and discuss what is left. We evaluate them against both versions of the English Question: rebalancing England's place in the Union following devolution; and decentralising the government of England.

It will emerge that regional government is the only solution which offers an answer to both versions of the Question. Of those institutional solutions which might rebalance England's place in the Union, none survived the twin tests of probability and feasibility. Three solutions were considered at the beginning of the chapter: English independence; an English parliament; and English votes on English laws. There is no demand for English independence, and it seems unlikely there ever will be. There is a slight demand for an English parliament, but not from any political heavyweights; and, even if demand grows, it is not a feasible solution, because an English parliament would be hugely dominant: it would be as overloaded as Westminster, and would be perceived to be equally remote. The strongest candidate of the three solutions in terms of probability is English votes on English laws, because it commands broad mass and some elite support. But chapter 4 showed how extraordinarily difficult it would be to implement in practice: politically and technically it has to be ruled out as not feasible.

Solutions we have considered to decentralise the government of England have included elected regional assemblies, functional regionalism, strengthening local government and elected mayors. All are perfectly feasible. But most have question marks about their probability. Elected regional assemblies are dead for the time being; strengthening local government and elected mayors seem unlikely to make much headway. But there is a further distinction worth making between regional government and local government, in terms of their capacity to answer the first version of the English Question, about England's place in the Union. Strengthening local government, however desirable it may be in its own right, does not offer much in terms of rebalancing England's place in the Union. For that we have to look to one of the forms of regional government: functional regionalism or, better still, elected regional assemblies.

Regional government in England is the only solution which offers an answer to both versions of the English Question. It could help to give England a louder voice within the Union; and it would help to decentralise the government of England. But it could achieve the first aim, of giving England a louder voice, only if there were elected assemblies with strong powers and functions – the stronger the better. The stronger the powers, the louder would be England's voice within the Union, because those powers would be a closer match for the devolved assemblies in Scotland, Wales and Northern Ireland. And the stronger the powers, the greater would be the decentralisation of England. But the 2004 proposals for elected regional assemblies were about as weak as they could be.

. . . Yet regionalism is not a complete answer

In one respect only would the 2004 proposals come close to rebalancing the regions of England with the smaller nations of the UK. In terms of both population size and territory, regional government in England does approximate to devolution in Scotland, Wales and Northern Ireland. It divides England into eight regions which are broadly similar in terms of population. Scotland has a population of 5.1 million, Wales 2.9 and Northern Ireland 1.7 million. The English regions range in size from the North East, the smallest with 2.5 million population, to the South East, with 8.1 million people. The average population of the 8 English regions is 6.1 million, slightly larger than the population of Scotland.

In other respects, though, regional government in England can never match devolution in Scotland and Wales. Elected assemblies might emerge in some regions but not in others, so long as the policy remains one of devolution on demand. Even if every region eventually had an elected assembly, their leaders could never speak for England with a single voice; but representing a population of several million people, one such leader would have a louder voice than any local government leader; indeed, the regional leader could become a political figure on a par with the mayor of London or the first minister in Scotland and in Wales, though with lesser powers.

In terms of power, the 2004 proposals for regional government were not at all proportionate. Scotland, Wales and Northern Ireland have powers to make laws in their devolved assemblies, and substantial executive powers over major public services such as health, education, local government. English regional assemblies would have had no law-making power, and no executive powers to speak of.

The difference can be seen in their budgets. The devolved bodies have substantial budgets to match their substantial devolved powers: £21 billion for Scotland in 2004–5; £12 billion for Wales. The proposed North-East Assembly, however, would have had a budget of £350 million and a staff of around 200. In proportion to population, its budget would have been thirty times smaller than those of the devolved administrations in Scotland and Wales. The tiny budget reflects its strategic role, shorn of responsibility for any major public service. It would require a revolution in thinking about regional government for it to be granted responsibility for a major public service with a big budget such as health or education. Such responsibilities are not uncommon in the regions of Europe, but they are currently beyond the imagination of politicians in England. Until that mindset changes, the major public services whose operation is devolved to Scotland, Wales and Northern Ireland, in England will continue to be run or supervised by Whitehall.

Aside from the huge differences in terms of power and functions, there is also a different basis in terms of popular support or affinity for the new assemblies. In Scotland and Wales, and, for different reasons, Northern Ireland, there is a connection between national distinctiveness and the new institutions of devolved governance.[10] This is largely missing from the English case. The connection in England between institutions and national identity is to be found at Westminster. Regional identity is less strong, in some English regions non-existent, and so does not provide the same symbolic or affective basis for regional government in England.

How might regionalism develop in the future?

How regionalism develops will depend on the further evolution of the regional structures now in place. They are all still relatively new, and capable of further development. How they will develop can best be assessed by a consideration of the forces now in play. The first three mentioned below talk up the dynamics of regionalism, while the last is a reminder of the powerful forces ranged against it. The first can best be described as incremental change, a continuation of the creeping regionalism described above. The GOs will gradually become better recognised as a regional centre of political power. Local authorities having dealings with Whitehall will increasingly find they can do their business with their GO. The regional director will become a figure of higher profile, more like the *préfet*. The regional assembly will also develop a higher profile through its regional planning responsibilities. The English will slowly become more aware of the regional tier, and of the power and influence exercised at the regional level.

Two factors could help to accelerate this process, and one to retard it. The first, top–down, accelerator would be if the Government decided to throw its weight more strongly behind regionalism (something which might happen under a Brown premiership). The 'Chapter 2 Agenda' in the 2002 White Paper could be extended to strengthen the existing regional assemblies: they could absorb other regional forums and scrutinise the GOs as well as the RDAs (Sandford 2001, 2002a). The Government could decentralise more functions to the GOs, and link that process more explicitly to the relocation of central government functions outside of London.[11] They could renew the attempt to standardise the regional boundaries of the many central government departments and agencies which do not use the standard regions. If they standardised a major public service, such as health, on to the eight standard regions, that would make a big difference (see chapter 10). And if they wanted to prepare for a renewed attempt to introduce elected regional assemblies, they could first introduce unitary local government across the whole of England, as the Conservatives did for Scotland and Wales in 1994, thus blunting the argument about regional government being an extra tier.

The second, bottom–up, set of forces would be more of a slow-burning fuse. It would depend on the constitutional conventions established in five of the English regions not giving up or faltering following the defeat in the North East, but redoubling their efforts in the same way that the Scots doggedly did after 1979. Following the precedent of the Scottish Constitutional Convention, they might decide not to be bound by the Labour Government's proposals, but instead to come forward with their own proposals for a set of powers and functions suitable for the needs of the region. If any of the English constitutional conventions decided to embark on this path, they would need to be prepared for a seriously long march. In Scotland it took 18 years; and although the Scots may not have appreciated it at the time, the 18 years of Conservative rule at Westminster helped to fan the flames of devolution in Scotland. Another prolonged period of Conservative rule could similarly help to rekindle the cause of devolution in the northern regions of England.

Other forces could retard the process of regionalism or obstruct it altogether. Re-election of a Conservative government would stop the process, even if it stored up regional resentment to be exploited in the future. And if the Labour Government continues in office, no one should under-estimate the forces of inertia in Whitehall, or the scepticism of many Labour ministers. Devolution may have released a powerful dynamic, but the machinery of central government has shown an extraordinary capacity to ride above it. Devolution to Scotland and Wales involved relatively clean surgery, hiving off the Scottish Office and Welsh Office. Regional government in England is far messier, requiring sacrifices from most of Whitehall's line departments. It is a fate they have successfully resisted, with the full support of their ministers. First over the proposals for RDAs, and then over regional assemblies, Whitehall departments have strenuously resisted the transfer of any significant functions or budgets. John Prescott found few allies in the Cabinet for the cause of regional government, and the only significant powers offered up for devolution came from his own department. The line-up in any future government would be unlikely to be much different. To overcome ministerial and departmental resistance would require a new Prime Minister to give a very different kind of lead.

Ultimately, only the English can answer the English Question

It is time to sum up one last time. At present the English seem relaxed about devolution to Scotland and Wales, but they do not seem to want devolution for themselves, and they seem not to mind centralisation in the government of England. They do not want an English parliament, and they are not going to get English votes on English laws. But it is a dynamic and fluid situation, in which the most likely outcome is the further development of regionalism in England.

This is not to suggest that the devolution dynamic is irresistible. There is no logic in the process of devolution which requires the English, too, to have devolution. England could remain a gaping hole in the devolution settlement without the system imploding. The devolution settlements already granted to Scotland, Wales and Northern Ireland are not threatened by the lack of devolution in England. Asymmetry does not necessarily make the system unstable.

The UK has always been an asymmetrical state, a political Union in which the different nations are embedded in the State in different ways. The English are part of that Union tradition, which may help to explain why they are so relaxed about Scottish devolution. They are famously pragmatic, and will not seek uniformity for uniformity's sake. For that reason the CEP seems unlikely to get anywhere. The English can live with untidiness, so long as it works.

Whether the system continues to work in English eyes will depend less on the Union question than on the England version of the English Question. Are the English still content with the arrangements for the government of England? Opinion polls have for some time suggested sharply rising levels of discontent, but there is little evidence that the English yet make a connection with their highly centralised system of government. Politicians begin to make a connection, and all parties pay lip-service to the need for decentralisation, but find it extraordinarily difficult to implement once in government.

One of the obstacles is the expectation of equity. The English may not want uniformity in their system of government, but they do have a high expectation of there being equity in the delivery of public services. Pressure to deliver high-quality public services is one of the drivers of centralisation: it leads politicians to impose national standards and national targets and national funding regimes. Politicians, the media and the people of England are trapped in a media–political vortex where every failing in a public service leads to a media outcry which can lead to a political reaction of further centralisation.

England is now the most centralised of all the large countries in Western Europe. Famously insular as well as pragmatic, the English remain unaware of that. They remain equally unaware of the creeping growth of the regional tier. As regionalism slowly becomes more visible, the regional question will come back onto the political agenda. Of all the institutional solutions analysed in this book, regional government offers the best fit in terms of an answer to the English Question. But the English Question does not have to be answered. It is not an exam question which the English are required to answer. It can remain unresolved for as long as the English want. Ultimately only the English can decide if they want to seek an answer to the English Question.

Notes

1 The press questioned the propriety of Scottish MPs voting in 2001 to ban fox-hunting in England, but were silent about the role of Scottish MPs at the next big hunting vote, July 2003. On foundation hospitals, there was big press coverage of Scottish MPs voting on second reading of the Bill in July 2003, but much less (save for the *Daily Mail*) in November. Similarly with tuition fees, where the second-reading vote in January 2004 attracted intense media interest about the contribution of Scottish MPs (because the Government came close to losing), but much less publicity for the issue on the third reading in March. Intriguingly the Scottish press was more assiduous in reporting on the voting behaviour of Scottish MPs on all these votes on English issues than were the UK media based in London. Details of the votes and how they were reported are in the Devolution and the Centre monitoring reports on the Constitution Unit website: www.ucl.ac .uk/constitution-unit/monrep/centre.

2 Discounted to a level of representation about a third below that for England. Scotland is to have 59 MPs following the 2004 boundary review, bringing Scottish representation into line with the English quota; Wales had 40 MPs in 2004, but if Welsh representation were brought into line with the English quota Wales would have around 33 MPs at Westminster.

3 For a discussion of how the Jenkins 'AV+' system would impact on the West Lothian Question see Russell and Hazell (2000: 213).

4 Homepage: www.englishindependenceparty.com; the party also supports an English parliament as a step on the road towards independence.

5 It would be interesting also to ask the English whether the Crown is English or British (the coronation ceremony suggests that it is both). The survey question which asked about Westminster showed that the English are capable of distinguishing between Englishness and Britishness. When asked about other symbols of national identity, the English viewed the Royal Navy and the Union Jack as predominantly British rather than English, but fox-hunting and Guy Fawkes' Night as predominantly English.

6 This commentary is written prior to publication of the report on the North-East referendum commissioned by the Electoral Commission; Rallings and Thrasher's analysis, due in spring 2005, may help identify which of these reasons were the main ones for rejecting the proposals.

7 By removing most of the override powers of the Secretary of State, increasing the powers of the Scottish Parliament, and changing the electoral system to PR, thus reducing the likelihood of Labour domination.

8 City–regions, sometimes linked to elected mayors, never made it on to the political agenda; they are occasionally written about to remind people of the impor-

tance of sub-regional economies, conurbations and travel to work areas, but no one seriously propounds them as units of government: see Harding (2002).

9 See also the subsequent enquiry chaired by Sir Michael Lyons to consider changes to the system of local government funding: www.lyonsinquiry.org

10 Exemplified by Ron Davies's decision to call the Welsh Assembly the National Assembly for Wales.

11 The Lyons review made relatively little connection between relocation and regional policy (HM Treasury 2004d: paras 2.17–18).

Bibliography

Adair, G. (1986). *Myths and Memories*, London: Fontana.

Adams, J. and Tomaney, J. (2002). *Restoring the Balance: Strengthening the Government's Proposals for Regional Assemblies*, London: IPPR.

Adams, J., Robinson, P. and Vigor, A. (2003). *A New Regional Policy for the UK*, London: IPPR.

Alibhai-Brown, Y. (2000). 'Muddled leaders and the future of the British national identity', *Political Quarterly*, 71(1): 26–30.

Alibhai-Brown, Y. (2002). 'The excluded majority: what about the English?', in P. Griffith and M. Leonard (eds), *Reclaiming Britishness*, London: Foreign Policy Centre.

Allen, E. (1966). 'Breakthrough to regionalism', in J. W. House (ed.), *Northern Geographical Essays in Honour of G. H. J. Daysh*, Newcastle upon Tyne: Oriel Press.

Allsopp, C. (2003). *The Allsopp Review: Review of the Statistical Requirements for Monetary and Wider Economic Policymaking*, London, HM Treasury.

Amin, A., Thrift, N. and Massey, D. (2003). *Decentering the Nation: A Radical Approach to Regional Inequality*, London: Catalyst.

Anderson, J. (1992). *The Territorial Imperative: Pluralism, Corporatism and Economic Crisis*, Cambridge: Cambridge University Press.

Anderson, P. (2002). 'Internationalism: a breviary', *New Left Review* (2nd series), 14: 5–25.

Armstrong College (1931). *The Industrial Position of the North-East Coast of England*, Newcastle upon Tyne: North-East Development Board.

Armstrong College (1936). *A Survey of Industrial Facilities of the North-East Coast*, Newcastle upon Tyne: North-East Development Board.

Austrin, B. and Beynon, H. (1994). *Masters and Servants: Class and Patronage in the Making of a Labour Organisation: The Durham Miners and the English Political Tradition*, London: Rivers Oram Press.

Aydelotte, W.O. (1963). 'Voting patterns in the British House of Commons', *Comparative Studies in History and Society*, 5: 134–63.

Aydelotte, W. O. (1967). 'The country gentlemen and the repeal of the Corn Laws', *English Historical Review*, 82: 47–60.

Ayres, S. and Pearce, G. (2004). 'Central government responses to governance changes in the English regions', *Regional and Federal Studies*, 14(2): 187–210.

Bagehot, W. (2001 [1867]). *The English Constitution*, ed. P. Smith, Cambridge: Cambridge University Press.

Bagnasco, A. and Oberti, M. (1997). 'Le trompe-oeil des regions en Italie', in P. Le Galès and C. Lequesne (eds), *Les Paradoxes des regions en europe*, Paris: La Découverte.

Baker, K. (1998). 'Speaking for England', *Spectator*, 1 August, 14–15.

Baldwin, S. (1926). *On England*, London: Philip Allen.

Balls, E. (2000). 'Britain's new regional policy', in E. Balls and J. Healey (eds), *Towards a New Regional Policy: Delivering Growth and Full Employment*, London: Smith Institute.

Balls, E. and Healey, J. (2002). 'The regional economic challenge', in N. Engel (ed.), *Age of Regions: Meeting the Productivity Challenge*, London: Smith Institute.

Barker, E. (1928). *National Character and the Factors in its Formation*, London: Methuen.

Barker, E. (1947). *The Character of England*, Oxford: Clarendon.

Barker, R. (1996). 'Political ideas since 1945, or how long was the twentieth century?', *Contemporary British History*, special issue, 10(1): 2–19.

Barnett, C (2001). 'Prelude to an industrial defeat: from the 1944 Education Act to the 1956 White Paper on technological education', RSA Lecture, 17 October.

Bellamy, R. (1989). 'The peculiarities of the English', *History of European Ideas*, 10(2): 227–30.

Bennett, A. (1997). '"Village greens and terraced streets": Britpop and representations of "Britishness"', *Nordic Journal of Youth Research*, 5(4): 20–33.

Bennett, R. and Payne, D. (2000). *Local and Regional Economic Development: Renegotiating Power Under Labour*, Aldershot: Ashgate.

Benneworth, P. and Tomaney, J. (2002). 'Regionalism in north east England', in J. Tomaney and J. Mawson (eds), *England: The State of the Regions*, Bristol: Policy Press.

Benwell CDP (1979). *The Making of a Ruling Class. Two Centuries of Capital Development on Tyneside*, Newcastle upon Tyne: Benwell Community Development Project.

Berki, R. (1981). *On Political Realism*, London: Dent.

Board of Trade (1963). *The North East: A Programme for Regional Development*, Cmnd 2206 ('Hailsham Report'), London: Stationery Office.

Bogdanor, V. (2001). *Devolution in the United Kingdom*, Oxford: Oxford University Press.

Bogdanor, V. (2002) 'Lions, unicorns and ostriches . . .', *Times Higher Education Supplement*, 8 November, 15.

Borrow, G. (2002 [1862]). *Wild Wales*, Wrexham: Bridge Books.

Borthwick, R. L. (1978). 'When the short cut may be a blind alley: the Standing Committee on Regional Affairs', *Parliamentary Affairs*, 201–9.

Bowling, H. G., Coombes, L. C. and Walker, R. (1958). *The Land of Three Rivers: The Tyne, the Wear and the Tees*, London: Macmillan in association with the North-East Industrial and Development Association.

Bragg, B. (1995) 'Looking for a new England', *New Statesman*, 17 March, 14.

Bragg, B. (1996) 'I *am* looking for a new England', *New Statesman*, 26 July, 14–15.

Braithwaite, W. J. (1957). *Lloyd George's Ambulance Wagon: Being the Memoirs of William J. Braithwaite, 1911–1912*, London: Methuen.

Brown, G. (2001). 'Enterprise and the regions', speech by Gordon Brown to UMIST, 29 January, available at: www.hm-treasury.gov.uk

Brown, G. (2004). British Council Annual Lecture, London, 7 July.

Brown, A., McCrone, D., Paterson, L. and Surridge, P. (1999). *The Scottish Electorate*, Basingstoke: Macmillan.

Buchanan, R. O. (1953). 'Obituary: Professor C. B. Fawcett, BLitt, DSc', *Geographical Journal*, 118: 514–16.

Buruma, I. (1999). *Voltaire's Coconuts or Anglomania in Europe*, London: Weidenfeld & Nicolson.

Cabinet Office (1999). *Modernising Government*, London: Stationery Office.

Cabinet Office/Department for Transport, Local Government and the Regions (2002). *Your Region, Your Choice: Revitalising the English Regions*, Cm 5511, London: Stationery Office.

Cabinet Office–Performance and Innovation Unit (2000). *Reaching Out: The Role of Central Government at the Regional and Local Level*, London: Stationery Office.

Caciagli, M. (1977). *Democrazia Cristiana e Potere nel Mezzogiorno*, Rimini: Guaraldi.

Campaign for an English Parliament (2001). *The Constitutional Case for an English Parliament*, Mansfield: Portshel Industries.

Campaign for the English Regions (2002). 'A good starting point: CfER response to the White Paper *Your Region, Your Choice*', available at: www.cfer.org.uk

Cannadine, D. (1987). 'British history: past, present – and future?', *Past and Present*, 116: 169–92.

Clark, A. (1997). *The Tories: Conservatives and the Nation State 1922–1997*, London: Weidenfeld & Nicolson.

Clark, J. C. D. (1997). 'The strange death of British history? Reflections on Anglo-American scholarship', *The Historical Journal*, 40: 787–809.

Clark, J. C. D. (2003). *Our Shadowed Present: Modernism, Postmodernism and History*, London: Atlantic Books.

Cohen, R. (2000). 'The incredible vagueness of being British/English', *International Affairs*, 76(3): 575–82.

Cole, G. D. H. (1947). *Local and Regional Government*, London: Cassell.

Colley, L. (1992). *Britons: Forging the Nation 1707–1837*, London: Pimlico.

Collini, S. (1985). 'The idea of "character" in Victorian political thought', *Transactions of the Royal Historical Society* (5th series), 35: 29–50.

Colls, R. (1998). 'The Constitution of the English', *History Workshop Journal*, 46: 97–128.

Colls, R. (2002). *The Identity of England*, Oxford: Oxford University Press.

Commission for Local Democracy (1995) (Chair Simon Jenkins). *Taking Charge: The Rebirth of Local Democracy*, London: Commission for Local Democracy.

Commission on the Constitution (1973). *Research Papers 7: Devolution and Other Aspects of Government: An Attitudes Survey*, London: HMSO

Conservative Party (2000). *Strengthening Parliament: Report of the Commission to Strengthen Parliament*, London: Conservative Party.

Conservative Party (2001). *Time for Common Sense: The Conservative Manifesto*, London: Conservative Party.

Constitution Unit (1996). *Regional Government in England*, London: Constitution Unit.

Cooke, P. and Morgan, K. (1998). *The Associational Economy: Firms, Regions and Innovation*, Oxford: Oxford University Press.

Coombes, M. (1996). *Building a New Britain*, London: City Region Campaign.

Coulthard, E. M. (1934). *From Tweed to Tees: A Short Geography of North Eastern England*. Edinburgh: W. & A. K. Johnston.

Cousins, J. M., Davis, R. L., Paddon, M. J. and Waton, A. (1974).'Aspects of contradiction in regional policy: the case of north east England', *Regional Studies*, 8(1): 133–44.

Cowley, P. (2005). *The Rebels: How Blair Mislaid his Majority*, London: Politicos.

Cowley, P. and Stuart, M. (2004). 'When sheep bark: the parliamentary Labour Party, 2001–2003', *British Elections and Parties Review*, 14: 211–29.

Cox, D. (2002). 'At last, the silent people speak', *New Statesman*, 22 April, 12.

Crick, B (1991). 'The English and the British', in B. Crick (ed.), *National Identities: The Constitution of the United Kingdom*, Oxford: Blackwell.

Crick, B. (1995). 'The sense of identity of the indigenous British', in B. Parekh (ed.), *British National Identity in a European Context*, *New Community*, 21(2): 167–82.

Cunningham, H. (1981). 'The language of patriotism, 1750–1914', *History Workshop Journal*, 12: 8–33.

Curtice, J. (1999), 'Is Scotland a Nation and Wales Not?', in Taylor, B. and Thomson, K. (eds), *Scotland and Wales: Nations Again?* Cardiff: University of Wales Press, 1999.

Curtice, J. (2001). 'Hopes dashed and fears assuaged? What the public makes of it so far', in A. Trench (ed.), *The State of the Nations 2001: The Second Year of Devolution in the UK*, Exeter: Imprint Academic.

Curtice, J. and Heath, A. (2000). 'Is the English lion about to roar? National identity after devolution', in R. Jowell *et al.* (eds), *British Social Attitudes: The 17th Report – Focusing on Diversity*, London: Sage.

Curtice, J. and Seyd, B. (2001). 'Is devolution strengthening or weakening the UK?', in A. Park *et al.* (eds), *British Social Attitudes: The 18th Report – Public Policy, Social Ties*, London: Sage.

Daily Telegraph (2002). 'Shires fall to power of the regions', 10 May

Dalyell, T. (1977). *Devolution: The End of Britain*, London: Jonathan Cape.

D'Ancona, M. (2002). 'Why the right must embrace multiculturalism', in P. Griffith and M. Leonard (eds), *Reclaiming Britishness*, London: Foreign Policy Centre.

Davie, G. E. (1961). *The Democratic Intellect: Scotland and Her Universities in the Nineteenth Century*, Edinburgh: Edinburgh University Press.

Davies, N. (1999). *The Isles: A History*, London: Macmillan.

Department of the Environment, Transport and the Regions (2001), *Strengthening Regional Accountability*, Consultation Paper, London: Stationery Office.

Department of Health (1998). *The New NHS: Modern–Dependable*, London: Stationery Office.

Department of Trade and Industry (2001). *Opportunity for All in a World of Change: A White Paper on Enterprise, Skills and Innovation*, London: Stationery Office.

Department for Transport, Local Government and the Regions (2001). *Planning: Delivering a Fundamental Change*, London: DTLGR, available at: www.odpm .gov.uk

Dicey, A. V. (1915 [1885]). *Introduction to the Study of the Law of the Constitution*, 8th edn, London: Macmillan.

Dicey, A. V. and Rait, R. S. (1920). *Thoughts on the Scottish Union*, London: Macmillan.

Dudley, G. and Richardson, J. (2000). *Why Does Policy Change? Lessons from British Transport Policy 1945–99*, London: Routledge.

Dunleavy, P., Margetts, H., Smith, T. and Weir, S. (2001a). 'Constitutional reform, New Labour in power and public trust in government', *Parliamentary Affairs*, 54: 405–24.

Dunleavy, P., Margetts, H., Smith, T. and Weir, S. (2001b). *Voices of the People: Popular attitudes to democratic renewal in Britain*, London: Politicos.

Dunleavy, P., Weir, S. and Subrahmanyam, G. (1995). ' "Sleaze" in Britain: media influences, public response and constitutional significance', *Parliamentary Affairs*, 48: 602–16.

Dyson, K. (1980). *The State Tradition in Western Europe*, Oxford: Martin Robertson.

Eckstein, H. (1959). *The English Health Service: Its Origins, Structure and Achievements*, Oxford: Oxford University Press.

Edwards, K.C. (1966). 'Foreword: academic', in J. W. House (ed.), *Northern Geographical Essays in honour of G. H. J. Daysh*, Newcastle upon Tyne: Oriel Press.

Elton, G. R. (1991). *Return to Essentials: Some Reflections on the Present State of Historical Study*, Cambridge: Cambridge University Press.

Ensor, R. C. K. (1936). *England 1870–1914, Oxford History of England*, vol.14, Oxford: Clarendon Press.

Environment, Transport and Regional Affairs Select Committee (1999). *Regional Development Agencies*, HC 232–1, London: Stationery Office.

Evans, D. F. T. (1986). 'Le Play House and the regional survey movement in British sociology, 1920–1955', unpublished MPhil thesis, City of Birmingham Polytechnic–CNAA.

Fabian Society, 'Regionaliter' (1942). *Regional Government*, Fabian Research Series no. 63, London: Fabian Society–Victor Gollancz.

Fawcett, C. B. (1928). 'North-east England', in A. G. Ogilvie (ed.), *Great Britain: Essays in Regional Geography*, Cambridge: Cambridge University Press.

Fawcett, C. B. (1919). *Provinces of England: A Study of Some Geographical Aspects of Devolution*, Making of the Future series, London: Williams & Norgate.

Fawcett, C. B. (1920). 'A regional study of northeEast England', *Geographical Teacher* 10: 224–360.

Fawcett, C. B. (1934). 'Foreword', in E. M. Coulthard, *From Tweed to Tees: A Short Geography of North Eastern England*, Edinburgh: W. & A. K. Johnston.

Fawcett, C. B. (1961). *Provinces of England: A Study of Some Geographical Aspects of Devolution*, rev. edn, ed. W. G. East and S. W. Wooldridge, London: Hutchinson.

Forbes, R. (ed.) (1992). *Governing Ourselves*, Newcastle upon Tyne: Campaign for a Northern Assembly–Trade Union Studies Information Unit.

Forster, S. (1966). 'Foreword: personal' in J. W. House (ed.), *Northern Geographical Essays in honour of G. H. J. Daysh*, Newcastle upon Tyne: Oriel Press.

Foster, R. F. (1995). *Paddy & Mr Punch: Connections in Irish and English History*, London: Penguin.

Fox, D. J. (1986). *Health Policies, Health Politics: The British and American Experience, 1911–1965*, Princeton, NJ: Princeton University Press.

Freeman, T. W. (1982). 'Charles Bungay Fawcett, 1883–1952', in T. W. Freeman (ed.), *Geographers: Bibliographical Studies 6*, London: Mansell.

Game, C. (2003). 'Elected mayors: more distraction than attraction', *Public Policy and Administration*, 18(1): 13–28.

García Barbancho, A. (1979). *Disparidades regionales y ordenación del territorio*, Barcelona: Ariel.

Gay, O. (2003). 'Evolution from devolution: the impact of devolution on West-minster', in R. Hazell (ed.), *The State of the Nations 2002: The Third Year of Devolution in the United Kingdom*, Exeter: Imprint Academic.

Gellner, E. (1983). *Nations and Nationalism*, Oxford: Blackwell.

Gilmour, I. (1977). *Inside Right: A Study of Conservatism*, London: Hutchinson.

Gilroy, P. (1999). 'A London sumpting dis . . .', *Critical Quarterly*, 41(3): 57–69.

Grainger, J. H. (1986). *Patriotisms: Britain 1900–1939*, London: Routledge & Kegan Paul.

Grant, R. (1998). 'The English tradition in literature', *Salisbury Review*, autumn: 26–31.

Greer, S. L. (2004). *Territorial Politics and Health Policy*. Manchester: Manchester University Press.

Greer, S. L. (2005a). *Nationalism and Self-Government: The Politics of Autonomy in Scotland and Catalonia*, Albany: State University of New York Press (under review).

Greer, S. L. (2005b). 'The politics of health policy divergence', in J. Adams (ed.), *Devolution in Practice II*, London: IPPR.

Grémion, P. (1976). *Le pouvoir périphérique. Bureaucrates et notables dans le système politique français*, Paris: Seuil.

Groom, B. (1999). 'A federal England?', *Financial Times*, 31 March.

Guthrie, R. and MacLean, I. (1978). 'Another part of the periphery: reactions to dev-olution in an English Development Area', *Parliamentary Affairs*, 31: 190–200.

Hacker, J. S. (1998). 'The historical logic of National Health insurance: structure and sequence in the development of British, Canadian, and US medical policy'. *Studies in American Political Development*, 12 (spring): 57–130.

Hadfield, B. (1989). *The Constitution of Northern Ireland*, Belfast: SLS.

Hadfield, B. (2003). 'The United Kingdom as a territorial state', in V. Bogdanor (ed.), *The British Constitution in the Twentieth Century*, Oxford: Oxford University Press.

Hague, W. (1999). *Strengthening the Union After Devolution*, London: Centre for Policy Studies.

Hague, W. (2000). *A Conservative View of the Constitution*, London: Centre for Policy Studies.

Hall, G. (2000). 'Rising to the challenge: the changing agenda for RDAs and govern-ment in building world class regions', in E. Balls and J. Healey (eds), *Towards a New Regional Policy: Delivering Growth and Full Employment*, London: Smith Institute

Ham, C. (2004). *Health Policy in Britain: The Politics and Organisation of the National Health Service*, Basingstoke: Macmillan.

Hands, D. (2000). *Evidence-Based Organisational Design in Health Care: The Contribution of the Health Services' Organisation Research Unit at Brunel University*, Maureen Dixon Essay Series on Health Service Organisation, no. 2, London: Nuffield Trust.

Harding, A. (2002). *Is There a 'Missing Middle' in English Governance?*, London: New Local Government Network.

Harrison, S. and Schulz, R. (1989). 'Clinical autonomy in the United Kingdom and the United States: contrasts and convergence', in G. Freddi and J. W. Björkman (eds), *Controlling Medical Professionals: The Comparative Politics of Health Governance*, London: Sage.

Harvie, C. (1977). *Scotland and Nationalism*, London: Allen & Unwin.

Haseler, S. (1996). *The English Tribe: Identity, Nation and Europe,* Basingstoke: Macmillan.

Haskins, C. (2003). *Rural Delivery Review: A Report on the Delivery of Government Policies in Rural England,* London: DEFRA.

Hazell, R. (2000a). *An Unstable Union: Devolution and the English Question,* London: Constitution Unit.

Hazell, R. (2000b). 'Regional government in England: three policies in search of a strategy', in T. Wright and S. Chen (eds), *The English Question,* London: Fabian Society.

Heath, A. Rothon, C. and Jarvis, L. (2002). 'English to the core?', in A. Park *et al.* (eds), *British Social Attitudes: The 19th Report,* London: Sage.

Heclo, H. (1978). 'Issue networks and the executive establishment', in A. King (ed.), *The New American Political System,* Washington, DC: American Enterprise Institute.

Heffer, S. (1998). *Like the Roman: The Life of Enoch Powell,* London: Weidenfeld & Nicolson–Phoenix.

Heffer, S. (1999). *Nor Shall My Sword: The Reinvention of England,* London, Weidenfeld & Nicolson.

Heffer, S. (2002a). 'The next great exodus', *Spectator,* 30 March, 12–13.

Heffer, S. (2002b). 'The case for anarchy', *Spectator,* 18 May, 14–15.

Heim, C. (1986). 'Inter-war responses to regional decline', in B. Elbaum and W. Lazonick (eds), *The Decline of the British Economy,* Oxford: Clarendon Press.

Herrero de Miñon, M. (1998). *Derechos históricos y constitución,* Madrid: Tecnos.

Hitchens, P. (1999). *The Abolition of Britain: The British Cultural Revolution from Lady Chatterley to Tony Blair,* London: Quartet Books.

HM Treasury (1979). *Needs Assessment,* Report, London: HM Treasury.

HM Treasury. (2000a). *Spending Review 2000: Prudent for a Purpose. Building Opportunity and Security for All,* CM 4807, London: Stationery Office.

HM Treasury (2000b). *Building Long-term Prosperity for All,* Pre-Budget Report, CM 4917, London: Stationery Office.

HM Treasury. (2002). *2002 Spending Review: Opportunity and Security for All – Investing in an Enterprising and Fairer Britain,* London: Stationery Office.

HM Treasury (2004a). *2004 Spending Review: Stability, Security and Opportunity for All – Investing for Britain's Long-Term Future,* London: Stationery Office.

HM Treasury (2004b). *2004 Spending Review: Meeting Regional Priorities,* London: Stationery Office.

HM Treasury (2004c). *Public Expenditure Statistical Analyses 2004,* Cm 6201, available at: www.hm-treasury.gov.uk/media/FC4B2/pesa04_complete_190404.pdf.

HM Treasury (2004d). *Independent Review of Public Sector Relocation,* at: www.hm-treasury.gov.uk/consultations_and_legislation/lyons/consult_lyons_index.cfm#final.

HM Treasury–Cabinet Office (2004). *Devolved Decision Making: 1 Delivering Better Public Services – Refining Targets and Performance Management,* London: Stationery Office.

HM Treasury–DTI (2001). *Productivity in the UK 3: The Regional Dimension,* London: HM Treasury–DTI.

HM Treasury–DTI–ODPM (2003). *A Modern Regional Policy for the United Kingdom,* London: Stationery Office.

HM Treasury–DTI–ODPM (2004). *Devolved Decision Making: 2 Meeting the Regional Economic Challenge – Increasing Regional and Local Flexibility,* London: Stationery Office.

Hogwood, B. (1996). *Mapping the Regions: Boundaries, Co-ordination and Government,* Bristol: Policy Press.

Hogwood, B. and Keating, M. (1982). *Regional Government in England,* Oxford: Clarendon.

House of Commons Library (2003). *Division 280 on Foundation Hospitals,* Standard Note SN/SG/2228, London: House of Commons Library.

House of Lords Select Committee on the Constitution (2003). *Devolution: Inter-Institutional Relations in the United Kingdom,* Second Report of the Session 2002–3, London: Stationery Office.

House of Lords Select Committee on Central–Local Relations (1996). *Rebuilding Trust,* London: Stationery Office.

House, J. W. (1970). 'Regionalism and the sense of community', *Geographical Journal,* 136(1): 6–12.

Howe, S. (1989). 'Labour patriotism 1939–83', in R. Samuel (ed.), *Patriotism: The Making and Unmaking of British National Identity,* London: Routledge.

Hudson, R. (1989). *Wrecking a Region: State Policies, Party Politics and Regional Change in North East England,* Studies in Society and Space, London: Pion.

Hunter, D. J. (1994). 'From tribalism to corporatism: the managerial challenge to medical dominance', in J. Gabe, D. Kelleher and G. Williams (eds), *Challenging Medicine,* London: Routledge.

Innes, J. (2003). 'Legislating for three kingdoms: how the Westminster Parliament legislated for England, Scotland and Ireland, 1707–1830', in J. Hoppit (ed.), *Parliaments, Nations and Identities in Britain and Ireland, 1660–1850,* Manchester: Manchester University Press.

Jackson, A. (2003). *Home Rule: An Irish History 1800–2000,* London: Weidenfeld & Nicolson.

Jaques, E. (1976). *A General Theory of Bureaucracy,* London: Heinemann.

Jaques, E. (1978). *Health Services: Their Nature and Organisation and the Role of Patients, Doctors, Nurses and the Complementary Professions,* London: Heinemann.

Jeffery, C. (2003). *The English Regions debate: What do the English want?,* ESRC Devolution Briefing no 3, Swindon: ESRC.

Jeffery, C. (2005). 'Devolution and social citizenship: which society, whose citizenship?' in S. L. Greer (ed.), *Territory, Justice and Democracy,* Basingstoke: Palgrave Macmillan.

Jeffery, C., Hough, D. and Keating, M. (eds) (2003). Multilevel Electoral Competition: Elections and Parties in Decentralized States, *European Urban and Regional Studies,* special issue, 10(3).

Jeffery, C. and Reilly, A. (2002). 'The regional question in the west midlands: initial report on focus group research on public attitudes', available at: www.cfer.org.uk

Jenkins, S. (2002). 'Save the counties, not compass-point regions', *The Times,* 10 May, 22.

Jenkins, S. (2004). *Big Bang Localism: A Rescue Plan for British Democracy,* London: Policy Exchange.

Johnson, B. (2004). 'England expects . . . a fairer deal', *Daily Telegraph,* 10 June.

Johnson, N. (2000). 'Then and now: the British Constitution', *Political Studies*, 48(1): 118–31.

Jones, J. B. and Wilford, R. A. (1986). *Parliament and Territoriality: The Committee on Welsh Affairs 1979–1983*, Cardiff: University of Wales Press.

Jones, M. (2001). 'The rise of the regional state in economic governance: "partnerships for prosperity" or new scales of state power?', *Environment and Planning C*, 33: 1185–211.

Joseph Rowntree Reform Trust (2004). 'State of the Nation' poll 2004: summary of main findings, available at: www.jrrt.org.uk/findings.pdf

Judge, David (2004). 'Whatever happened to parliamentary democracy in the United Kingdom?', *Parliamentary Affairs*, 57(3): 682–701.

Kearney, H. (2000). 'The importance of being British', *Political Quarterly*, 71(1):, 15–26.

Keating M., Loughlin, J. and Deschouwer, K. (2003). *Culture, Institutions and Economic Development: A Study of Eight European Regions*, Aldershot: Edward Elgar.

Keating, M. and Bleiman, D. (1979). *Labour and Scottish Nationalism*, London: Macmillan.

Keating, M. J. (1975). 'The role of the Scottish MP in the Scottish political system, in the United Kingdom political system and in the relationship between the two', unpublished PhD thesis, Glasgow College of Technology.

Keating, M. (1982). 'The debate on regional reform', in B. Hogwood and M. Keating (eds), *Regional Government in England*, Oxford: Clarendon Press.

Keating, M. (1988). *State and Regional Nationalism: Territorial Politics and the European State*, London: Harvester Wheatsheaf.

Keating, M. (1998). *The New Regionalism in Western Europe: Territorial Restructuring and Political Change*, Aldershot: Edward Elgar.

Keating, M. (2001). *Plurinational Democracy: Stateless Nations in a Post-Sovereignty Era*, Oxford: Oxford University Press.

Kellas, J. G. (1975). *The Scottish Political System*, Cambridge: Cambridge University Press.

Kidd, C. (1993). *Subverting Scotland's Past: Scottish Whig Historians and the Creation of an Anglo-BritishIidentity*, Cambridge: Cambridge University Press.

Kipling, R. (1898). 'The bridge builders', in *The Day's Work*, quoted in E. Stokes, '"The voice of the hooligan": Kipling and the Commonwealth experience', in N. McKendrick (ed.), *Historical Perspectives: Studies in English Thought and Society in Honour of J. H. Plumb* (1974), London: Europa Publications.

Kitson-Clark, G. (1950). *The English Inheritance: An Historical Essay*, London: SCM Press.

Klein, R. (2000). *The New Politics of the NHS*, 4th edn, London: Longman.

Klein, R. (2003). 'Governance for NHS foundation trusts: Mr Milburn's flawed model is a cacophany of accountabilities', *British Medical Journal*, 326 (25 January): 174–5.

Klein, R. (2004). 'The first wave of NHS foundation trusts: low turnout in elections sends a warning signal', *British Medical Journal*, 328 (5 June): 1332.

Knowles, M. (2004). 'It's only fair for England to be given a parliament of its own', *Herald*, 9 January.

Knox, M. T. (2000). 'Terence O'Neill and the crisis of Ulster Unionism, 1963–1969', unpublished PhD thesis, University of Ulster.

Kohn, H. (1940). 'The genesis and character of English nationalism', *Journal of the History of Ideas*, 1: 69–94.

Kumar, K. (2003). *The Making of English National Identity*, Cambridge: Cambridge University Press.

Labour Party (1995). *A Choice for England: A Consultation Paper on Labour's Plans for English Regional Government*, London: Labour Party.

Langford, P. (2000), *Englishness Identified: Manners and Character 1650–1850*, Oxford: Oxford University Press.

Liaison Committee (2003). Evidence Presented by the Rt Hon. Tony Blair MP, Prime Minister, on Tuesday 8 July 2003, HC 334–ii, Q281, London: House of Commons.

Liberal Democrat Party (2004). 'Cleaning up the mess: Liberal Democrat policies for constitutional reform', Policy Briefing no. 42, London: Liberal Democrat Party.

Light, A. (1991). *Forever England: Femininity, Literature and Conservatism Between the Wars*, London: Routledge.

Lloyd, J. (2002). 'The end of multiculturalism', *New Statesman*, 27 May, 12–14.

Local Government Association (2004). *Independence, Opportunity, Trust: A Manifesto for Local Communities*, London: LG Connect.

Local Government Information Unit (2002). *Free to Differ: The Future of Local Democracy*, London: Local Government Information Unit.

Lodge, G. (2003a). *Devolution and the Centre Quarterly Monitoring Report*, August 2003, London: Constitution Unit, available at: www.ucl.ac.uk/constitution-unit/monrep/centre/centre_august_2003.pdf

Lodge, G. (2003b). *Devolution and the Centre Quarterly Monitoring Report*, November 2003, London: Constitution Unit, available at: www.ucl.ac.uk/constitution-unit/monrep/centre/centre_november_2003.pdf

Lodge, G. (2004). *Devolution and the Centre Quarterly Monitoring Report*, February 2004, London: Constitution Unit, available at: www.ucl.ac.uk/constitution-unit/monrep/centre/centre_february_2004.pdf

Lodge, G., Russell, M. and Gay, O. (2004). 'The impact of devolution on Westminster: if not now, when?', in A. Trench (ed.), *Has Devolution Made a Difference? The State of the Nations 2004*, Exeter: Imprint Academic.

Loebl, H. (1987). *Government Factories and the Origins of British Regional Policy: A Case Study of North East Trading Estates Ltd*, Aldershot: Avebury.

Loebl, H. (2001). *Outside In: Memoirs of Business and Public Work in the North East of England, 1951–1984*, Newcastle upon Tyne: Fen Drayton.

Lovejoy, J. (2000). *The Deculturisation of the English People*, Kings Lynne: Athelney.

Lovering, J. (1999). 'Theory led by policy: the inadequacies of the "new regionalism"', *International Journal of Urban and Regional Research*, 23(2): 379–95.

Lynch, P. (1998). 'Reactive capital: the Scottish business community and devolution', *Regional and Federal Studies*, 8(1): 86–102.

Mackinder, H. (1947 [1907]). *Britain and the British Seas*, 2nd edn, Oxford: Clarendon Press.

MacLaren, A. A. (1974). *Religion and Social Class: The Disruption Years in Aberdeen*, London: Routledge.

Marquand, D. (1995). 'After Whig imperialism: can there be a new British identity?', in B. Parekh (ed.), *British National Identity in a European Context*, *New Community*, special issue, 21(2): 167–82.

Marquand, D. (1997). *The New Reckoning: Capitalism, States and Citizens*, London: Polity Press.

Marquand, D. and Tomaney, J. (2000). *Democratising England*, London: Regional Policy Forum.

Massie, A. (2002). 'Maddest of tribunals', *Times Literary Supplement*, 9 August.

Masterman, R. and Hazell, R. (2001). 'Devolution and Westminster', in A. Trench (ed.), *The State of the Nations 2001: The Second Year of Devolution in the United Kingdom*, Exeter: Imprint Academic.

Matthew, H. C. G. (1999). *Gladstone 1809–1898*, Oxford: Oxford University Press.

Mawson, J. and Spencer, K. (1997). 'The government offices for the English regions: towards regional governance?', *Policy and Politics*, 25(1): 51–4.

McEwen, N. (2002). 'State welfare nationalism: the territorial impact of welfare state development in Scotland', *Regional and Federal Studies*, 12(1): 66–90.

McKenzie, R. T. and Silver, A. (1968). *Angels in Marble: Working Class Conservatives in Urban England*, London: Heinemann.

McLean, I. (1970). 'The rise and fall of the Scottish National Party', *Political Studies*, 17: 357–72.

McLean, I. (1995). 'Are Scotland and Wales over-represented in the House of Commons?', *Political Quarterly*, 66(4): 250–68.

McLean, I. (2001). *Rational Choice and British Politics*, Oxford: Oxford University Press.

McLean, I. (2003a). 'Devolution bites', *Prospect*, March, 20–1.

McLean, I. (2003b). *Identifying the Flow of Domestic and European Expenditure into the English Regions*, London: Stationery Office.

McLean, I. (2004). 'Financing the Union – Goschen, Barnett and beyond', in W. L. Miller (ed.), *Anglo-Scottish Relations Since 1900*, London: British Academy.

McLean, I. (no date). 'The machinery of government reform: principles and practice', available at: www.nuff.ox.ac.uk/politics/whitehall/Machinery.html.

McLean, I. and McMillan, A. (2003a). 'The distribution of public expenditure across the UK regions', *Fiscal Studies*, 24(1): 45–71.

McLean, I. and McMillan, A. (2003b). *New Localism, New Finance*, London: New Local Government Network.

McLean, I. and McMillan, A. (2005). *State of the Union*, Oxford: Oxford University Press.

McLean, I. *et al.* (2003). *Identifying the Flow of Domestic and European Expenditure into the English Regions*, Oxford: Nuffield College; London: ODPM, available at: www.local.odpm.gov.uk/research/expnder.htm.

McMillan, J. (1999). 'Remind me who I am again . . .', *New Statesman Scotland*, 5 July.

Meller, H. (1990). *Patrick Geddes: Social Evolutionist and City Planner*, London: Routledge.

Mess, H. (1928). *Industrial Tyneside: A Social Survey made for the Bureau of Social Research for Tyneside*, London: Ernest Benn.

Milburn, A. and Corrigan, P. (1989). 'The case for regional government', Discussion Paper, Northern Region Labour Party.

Miller, W. (1981). *The End of British Politics? Scots and English Political Behaviour in the Seventies*, Oxford: Clarendon Press.

Milward, A. S. (2002). *The Rise and Fall of a National Strategy, 1945–1963*, London: Whitehall History Publishing–Frank Cass.

Mitchell, J. (1996). *Strategies for Self-Government: The Campaigns for a Scottish Parliament*, Edinburgh: Polygon.

Mohan, J. (2002). *Planning, Markets and Hospitals*, London: Routledge.

Moore, B. (1978). *Injustice: The Social Bases of Obedience and Revolt*, White Plains, NY: M. E. Sharpe

Moran, M. (1999). *Governing the Health Care State: A Comparative Study of the United Kingdom, the United States and Germany*, Manchester: Manchester University Press.

Moreno, L. (1988). 'Scotland and Catalonia: the path to home rule', in D. McCrone, and A. Brown (eds), *The Scottish Government Yearbook 1988*, Edinburgh: Unit for the Study of Government in Scotland.

Morgan, K. O. (1984). *Labour in Power 1945–1951*, Oxford: Oxford University Press.

Morgan, K. O. (1991). *Wales in British Politics 1868–1922*, Cardiff: University of Wales Press.

Morgan, K. (2002). 'The English Question: regional perspectives on a fractured nation', *Regional Studies*, 36(7): 797–810.

MORI (2003). 'Regional government in England 2003: a synthesis of research undertaken by MORI', available at: www.mori.com.

Myles, J. and Pierson, P. (2001). 'The comparative political economy of pension reform', in P. Pierson (ed.), *The New Politics of the Welfare State*, Oxford: Oxford University Press.

Nairn, T. (1977). *The Break-Up of Britain: Crisis and Neo-Nationalism*, London: NLB.

Nairn, T. (1981). *The Break-Up of Britain: Crisis and Neo-Nationalism*, 2nd edn, London: Verso.

Nairn, T. (2000). *After Britain: New Labour and the Return of Scotland*, London: Granta Books.

Nairn, T. (2002). *Pariah*, London: Verso.

NEPC (1966). *Challenge of the Changing North*, Newcastle upon Tyne: Northern Economic Planning Council.

NHS Management Inquiry (1983). Letter to the Rt Hon. Norman Fowler, MP, Secretary of State for Social Services, 6 October.

Nunning, V. (2001). 'The invention of cultural traditions: the construction and deconstruction of Englishness and authenticity in Julian Barnes's *England, England*', *Anglia*, 119: 58–76.

Oakeshott, M. (1948). 'Contemporary British politics', *Cambridge Journal*, 1: 474–90

Oates, W. (1999). 'An essay on fiscal federalism', *Journal of Economic Literature*, 37: 1120–49.

ODPM (2003). *Your Region, Your Say*, London: Stationery Office.

ODPM (2004), *Balance of Funding Review*, chaired by Nick Raynsford, MP, July, available at: www.local.odpm.gov.uk/finance/balance/report.

ODPM Select Committee (2003). *Reducing Regional Disparities in Prosperity*, 9th Report of the Session 2002–3, HC 492–I, London: House of Commons.

Ohmae, K. (1995). *The End of the Nation State: The Rise of Regional Economies*, New York: Free Press.

Orwell, G. (2001). *Orwell's England*, ed. P. Davison, Harmondsworth: Penguin.

Orwell, G. (1957). *Inside the Whale*, Harmondsworth: Penguin.

Page, A. and Batey, A. (2002). 'Scotland's other Parliament: Westminster legislation about devolved matters in Scotland since devolution', *Public Law*, autumn: 501–23.

Parekh, B. (2000). 'Defining British identity', *Political Quarterly*, 71(1): 4–15.

Park, A., Curtice, J., Thomson, K., Jarvis, L. and Bromley, C. (2003). *British Social Attitudes: The 20th Report – Continuity and Change Over Two Decades*, London: Sage.

Pasquier, R. (2003). 'From identity to collective action: building political capacity in French regions', in J. Bukowski, S. Piattoni and M. Smyrl (eds), *Between Europeanisation and Local Societies: The Space for Territorial Governance*, Oxford: Rowman & Littlefield.

Pastori, G. (1980). 'Le regioni senza regionalismo', *Il Mulino*, no. 2 (March–April): 204–16.

Paton, C. (2005). 'The state of the health care system in England', in S. Dawson and C. Sausman (eds), *Future Health Organizations and Systems*, London: Palgrave–Macmillan.

Paxman, J. (1998). *The English: A Portrait of a People*, London: Michael Joseph.

Pepler, G. and MacFarlane, P. W. (1949). *The North East Development Plan*, Report to the Minister of Town and Country Planning.

Percy, E. (1939). 'Introduction', in C. Headlam (ed.), *The Three Northern Counties of England*, Gateshead upon Tyne: Northumberland Press.

Percy, E. (1958). *Some Memories*, London: Eyre & Spottiswoode.

Pimlott, B. (1985). *Hugh Dalton*, London: Cape.

Pimlott, B. and Rao, N. (2002). *Governing London*, Oxford University Press: Oxford.

Pocock, J. G. A. (1999). 'Enlightenment and counter-enlightenment, revolution and counter-revolution: a eurosceptical enquiry', *History of Political Thought*, 20: 125–39.

Pocock, J. G. A. (2000). 'Gaberlunzie's return', *New Left Review* (2nd series), 5: 41–52.

Political Quarterly (1998). 'Commentary: and so to England . . .', *Political Quarterly*, 69(1): 1–3.

Pollitt, C. (1993). *Managerialism and the Public Services*, 2nd edn, Oxford: Blackwell.

Powell, E. (1995). 'Commentary', in B. Brivati and H. Jones (eds), *What Difference Did the War Make?*, London: Leicester University Press.

Powell, J. E. (1994). *The Evolution of the Gospel: A Commentary on the First Gospel, with Translation and Introductory Essay*, New Haven, CT: Yale University Press.

Powell, M. (1997). *Evaluating the NHS*, Milton Keynes: Open University Press.

Procedure Committee (1999). *The Procedural Consequences of Devolution*, House of Commons Procedure Committee, 4th Report of the Session 1998–99, HC 185, 19 May, London: House of Commons.

Pugh, M. (1985). *The Tories and the People 1880–1935*, Oxford: Blackwell.

Putnam, R. (1993). *Making Democracy Work: Civic Traditions in Modern Italy*, Princeton, NJ: Princeton University Press.

Rallings, C. and Thrasher, M. (2001). *British Electoral Facts 1832–1999*, Aldershot: Ashgate.

Regional Policy Commission (1996). *Renewing the Regions: Strategies for Regional Economic Development*, Sheffield: Sheffield Hallam University.

Rhodes, R. A. W. (1995). 'Introducing the core executive', in R. A. W. Rhodes and

P. Dunleavy (eds), *Prime Minister, Cabinet and Core Executive*, London: Macmillan.

Rich, P. (1988). 'British imperial decline and the forging of English patriotic memory, c.1918–1968', *History of European Ideas*, 9(6): 659–80.

Rich, P. (1989). 'A question of life and death to England: patriotism and the British intellectuals, c.1886–1945', *New Community*, 15(4): 491–508.

Richard Commission (2004). *Report of the Richard Commission on the Powers and Electoral Arrangements for the National Assembly for Wales*, Cardiff: National Assembly for Wales.

Rintala, M. (2003). *Creating the National Health Service: Aneurin Bevan and the Medical Lords*, London: Frank Cass.

Rivett, G. (1998). *From Cradle to Grave: Fifty Years of the NHS*, London: King's Fund.

Robinson, P. (2000). 'Does the Government really have a regional policy?', unpublished paper, London: IPPR.

Rose, R. (1980). *Politics in England*, 3rd edn, London: Faber & Faber.

Rose, R. (1982). *Understanding the United Kingdom: The Territorial Dimension in Government*, London: Longman.

Royal Commission (1937). *Local Government in the Tyneside Area*, Cmd 4502, London: HMSO.

Royal Commission on the Constitution (1973). *Royal Commission on the Constitution 1969–1973*, Cmnd 5460, London: HMSO, vol. 1.

RSA (2001). *Labour's New Regional Policy: An Assessment*, Seaford: RSA.

Runnymede Trust (2000). *The Future of Multi-Ethnic Britain: The Parekh Report*, London: Profile Books.

Russell, M. and Hazell, R. (2000). 'Devolution and Westminster: tentative steps towards a more federal Parliament', in R. Hazell (ed.), *The State and the Nations: The First Year of Devolution in the UK*, Exeter: Imprint Academic.

Salisbury, Third Marquess of (1884). 'The value of redistribution: a note on electoral statistics', *National Review*, 4: 145–62.

Sanders, W. S. (1905). *Municipalisation by Provinces*, New Heptarchy Series no. 1, Fabian Tract 125, London: Fabian Society.

Sandford, M. (2001). *Further Steps for Regional Chambers*, Constitution Unit: London.

Sandford, M. (2002a). *A Commentary on the Regional Government White Paper 'Your Region, Your Choice'*, London: Constitution Unit.

Sandford, M. (2002b). *The Inclusiveness of Regional Chambers*, London: Constitution Unit.

Sandford, M. (2004a). 'The governance of London: strategic government and policy divergence', in A. Trench (ed.), *Has Devolution Made a Difference? The State of the Nations 2004*, Exeter: Imprint Academic.

Sandford, M. (2004b). 'Elected mayors I: political innovation, electoral systems and revitalising democracy', *Local Government Studies*, 30(1): 1–21.

Schöpflin, G. (2000). *Nations, Identity, Power: The New Politics of Europe*, London: Hurst.

Schulz, R. and Harrison, S. (1984). 'Consensus management in the British National Health Service: implications for the United States', *Milbank Quarterly*, 62: 657–81.

Scott, A. (1998). *Regions and the World Economy: The Coming Shape of Global Production, Competition and Political Order*, Oxford: Oxford University Press.

Scott, P. (1996). 'The worst of both worlds: British regional policy, 1951–64', *Business History*, 38(4): 41–64.

Scottish Conservative and Unionist Party (1997). *Fighting for Scotland*, Edinburgh: Scottish Conservative and Unionist Party.

Scottish National Party (2003). 'Salmond proposes English affairs committee and financial independence for Scotland', Press Release, 4 December, SNP.

Scruton, R. (2000). *England: An Elegy*, London: Chatto & Windus.

Seaward, P. and Silk, P. (2003). 'The House of Commons', in V. Bogdanor (ed.), *The British Constitution in the Twentieth Century*, Oxford: Oxford University Press.

Sharpe, L. J. (ed.) (1993). *The Rise of Meso Government in Europe*, London: Sage.

Shils, E. (1972). *The Intellectuals and the Powers and Other Essays*, Chicago, IL: University of Chicago Press.

Sisson, C. H. (1992). 'An English perspective', *Salisbury Review*, September: 51–3.

Smailes, A. E. (1960). *North England*, London: Nelson.

Smith, D. (1970). *An Autobiography*, Newcastle upon Tyne: Oriel Press.

Snape, S., Ashworth, R., Aulakh, S., Dobbs, L. and Moore, C. (2003). *The Development of Regional Scrutiny*, available at: www.emra.gov.uk/publications /documents/development_of_regional_scrutiny.pdf.

Special Areas Commissioners (1934). *Reports of Investigations into the Industrial Conditions in Certain Depressed Areas of: I Cumberland and Haltwhistle; II Durham and Tyneside; III South Wales and Monmouthshire; IV Scotland*, Cmd 4728, London: HMSO.

Stapleton, J. (1999). 'Englishness, Britishness and patriotism in recent political thought and historiography', *British Journal of Politics and International Relations*, 1(1): 119–30.

Stapleton, J. (2001). *Political Intellectuals and Public Identities in Britain Since 1850* Manchester: Manchester University Press.

Stevens, C. (2004). 'English regional government', in M. O'Neill (ed.), *Devolution and British Politics*, Harlow: Pearson.

Stevens, S. (2004). 'Reform strategies for the English NHS', *Health Affairs*, 23(3): 37–44.

Stewart, A. T. Q. (1967). *The Ulster Crisis*, London: Faber & Faber.

Stoker, G. (2000). 'Is regional government the answer to the English Question?', in T. Wright and S. Chen (eds), *The English Question*, London: Fabian Society.

Storper, M. (1997). *The Regional World: Territorial Development in a Global Economy*, New York and London: Guildford Press.

Straw, J. (1995). *A Choice for England*, London: Labour Party.

Straw, J. (1996). *A New Voice for England's Regions*, London: Labour Party.

Street, A. and AbdulHussain, S. (2004). 'Would Roman soldiers fight for the financial flows regime? The re-issue of Diocletian's edict in the English NHS', *Public Money and Management*, 24(5): 301–8.

Surridge, P. and McCrone, D. (1999). 'The 1997 Scottish referendum vote', in B. Taylor and K. Thomson (eds), *Scotland and Wales: Nations Again?*, Cardiff: University of Wales Press.

Tarrow, S. (1998). *Power in Movement: Social Movements and Contentious Politics*, 2nd edn, Cambridge: Cambridge University Press.

Taylor, A. J. P. (1977). *Essays in English History*, London: Book Club Associates.

Times Books (1974). *Guide to the House of Commons October 1974*, London: Times Books.

Thompson, E. P. (1963). *The Making of the English Working Class*, London: Gollancz.

Thompson, E. P. (1978). *The Poverty of Theory and Other Essays*, London: Merlin Press.

Thompson, E. P. (1993). 'The making of a ruling class', *Dissent*, 40(3): 377–82.

Thomson, P. (2001). 'New dawn for England?', *Salisbury Review*, winter: 48–9.

Tomaney, J. (1999). 'In search of English regionalism: the case of the north east', *Scottish Affairs*, 28: 62–82.

Tomaney, J. (2000a). 'The regional governance of England', in R. Hazell (ed.), *The State and the Nations: The First Year of Devolution*, Exeter: Imprint Academic.

Tomaney, J. (2000b). 'Democratically elected regional government in England: the work of the North-East Constitutional Convention', *Regional Studies*, 34(4): 383–8.

Tomaney, J. (2001). 'Reshaping the English regions', in A. Trench (ed.), *The State of the Nations 2001: The Second Year of Devolution in the United Kingdom*, Exeter: Imprint Academic.

Tomaney, J. (2002). 'The evolution of regionalism in England', *Regional Studies*, 36(7): 721–31.

Tomaney, J. (2003). 'Governing the region: past, present and future', Inaugural Lecture, University of Newcastle upon Tyne, 20 March.

Tomaney, J. and Hetherington, P. (2001). *Monitoring the English Regions*, London: Constitution Unit.

Tomaney, J. and Hetherington, P. (2003). 'England arisen?', in R. Hazell (ed.), *The State of the Nations 2003: The Third Year of Devolution in the United Kingdom*, Exeter: Imprint Academic.

Tomaney, J. and Hetherington, P. (2004). 'English regions: the quiet revolution?', in A. Trench (ed.), *Has Devolution Made a Difference? The State of the Nations 2004*, Exeter: Imprint Academic.

Tomaney, J. and Humphrey, L. (2002). *Regional Government in North East England*, vol. 1: *Main Report*, Newcastle: CURDS.

Tomaney, J. and Mawson, J. (2002). *England: The State of the Regions*, Bristol: Policy Press.

Trade and Industry Select Committee (1995). *Regional Policy*, 4th Report of the Session 1994–95, HC 356, London: House of Commons.

Travers, T. (2004). *The Politics of London: Governing an Ungovernable City*, Basingstoke: Palgrave.

Trench, A. (ed.) (2005). *Devolution and Power in the UK*, Manchester: Manchester University Press.

Trigilia, C. (1991). 'The paradox of the region: economic regulation and the representation of interests', *Economy and Society*, 20(3): 306–27.

Tuohy, C. H. (1999). *Accidental Logics: The Dynamics of Change in the Health Care Arena in the United States, Britain and Canada*, Oxford: Oxford University Press.

Tyneside Fabian Society (1966). *Regional Government for North-East England*, Newcastle upon Tyne: Co-operative Printing Society.

Vacher Dod (1997, 2003). *Dod's Parliamentary Companion*, London: Vacher Dod.

Vansittart, P. (1998). *In Memory of England*, London: John Murray.

Voegelin, E. (1953). 'The Oxford philosophers', *Philosophical Quarterly*, 3(11), quoted in N. O'Sullivan (ed.) (2004), *European Political Thought Since 1945*, London: Macmillan.

Wald, K. D. (1983). *Crosses on the Ballot: Patterns of British Voter Alignment Since 1885*, Princeton, NJ: Princeton University Press.

Watson, G. (1973). *The English Ideology: Studies in the Language of Victorian Politics*, London: Allen Lane.

Watt, N. and Carvel, J. (2004). 'NHS puts squeeze on private medicine', *Guardian*, 3 July.

Webster, C. (1988). *The Health Services Since the War*, vol. 1: *Problems of Health Care: The National Health Service Before 1957*, London: HMSO.

Weight, R. (1999). 'Raise St George's Standard high', *New Statesman*, 8 January.

Weight, R. (2002). *Patriots: National Identity in Britain 1940–2000*, Basingstoke: Macmillan.

Wilkinson, E. (1939). *The Town that Was Murdered: The Life Story of Jarrow*, London: Gollancz–Left Book Club.

Wilson, H. (1971). *The Labour Government, 1964–1970: A Personal Record*, London: Weidenfeld & Nicolson.

Winetrobe, B. K. (1995). 'The West Lothian Question', House of Commons Library Research Paper 95/96, London: House of Commons.

Winetrobe, B. K. (2001). 'Counter-devolution? The Sewel convention on devolved legislation at Westminster', *Scottish Law and Practice Quarterly*, 6: 286–92.

Worsthorne, P. (1998). 'England don't arise!', *Spectator*, 19 September.

Worsthorne, P. (1999). 'Only a federal Europe can stop the abolition of Britain', *Spectator*, 4 September.

Wright, T. (2000). 'England, whose England?', in T. Wright and S. Chen (eds), *The English Question*, London: Fabian Society.

YouGov (2004). YouGov Telegraph Poll, *Daily Telegraph*, 14 February, available at: www.telegraph.co.uk.

Young, G. M. (1947). 'Government', in E. Barker (ed.), *The Character of England*, Oxford: Clarendon Press.

Index

Abse, Leo (Labour MP) 80
Act of Union (1534) (union of England and Wales) 15
Act of Union (1800) (union of UK and Ireland) 15, 27–8, 30
Acts of Union (1707) (union of England and Scotland) *see* Treaty of Union
Alibhai-Brown, Yasmin 61
Armstrong, Hilary (Labour MP and minister) 109, 189
asymmetrical devolution 4, 66, 89, 97–8, 128, 221, 239
Attlee, Clement (UK Prime Minister 1945–51) 37, 196–7, 199

Baldwin, Stanley (UK Prime Minister 1923, 1924–29, 1935–37) 24
Balls, Ed (Labour MP) 111, 114
Bank of England 162, 165
Belgium
federalism 146
Flanders 147, 149–50
regional government and policy 144–5, 147
Bevan, Aneurin (Labour MP and minister)
instrumental unionism 37, 39–40
NHS 199
Beveridge, William 37
Beveridge Report (1942) 199
Blair, Tony (UK Prime Minister 1997–) 9, 11, 13, 51, 54, 73, 172, 189, 218
Board of Trade 162, 167–9
see also Department of Trade and Industry
Bogdanor, Vernon 63, 82

Bonar Law, Andrew (UK Prime Minister 1922–23) 29, 33, 35–6
Book of Common Prayer (1928) 82
Britishness 15, 16, 24–5, 50–1, 54, 60, 63, 229–30
British Social Attitudes survey (BSA) 120–1, 123–8, 134
British solidarity 13, 51, 149, 156
Brown, Gordon (Chancellor of the Exchequor 1997–)
Britishness 230
regional agenda 11, 114, 180, 224, 237
see also Treasury
use of tax and benefits regime as tool of social policy 42
Bulpitt, J. 217
Burke, Edmund 103
business
regionalism 11, 114, 127, 144, 148, 153–6, 169, 172, 176–8, 183–7, 230–3
Butler, R. A. (Conservative MP and minister) 37, 167
Byers, Stephen (Labour MP and minister) 112

Cabinet, the 13, 98, 102, 232, 238
Cabinet committees 113, 176
Cabinet Office 102, 110–12, 178–9
Caborn, Richard (Labour MP and minister) 107, 109
Campaign for an English Parliament (CEP) 3, 5–7, 13
Campaign for the English Regions (CFER) 5, 8–9
Campaign for a Scottish Parliament 224

Canada
  asymmetric/symmetric devolution
    142
  pressure for decentralisation 196
  Quebec 142, 149
Charles I (King of England and
    Scotland 1625–49) 26
Charles II (King of England and
    Scotland 1660–85) 26
Church of England 34
Churchill, Winston (UK Prime Minister
    1940–45, 1951–55) 36
city–regions 3, 107, 174, 188, 191,
    223, 230
civil society 152, 183, 185
civil war *see* English Civil War
committees *see* Westminster Committees
Confederation of British Industry (CBI)
    153
Conservatism (1980s) 50
  see also Thatcherism
Conservative Party
  Commission to Strengthen
    Parliament (Norton
    Commission) 7, 14, 17, 90–1
  decline in the periphery of the UK
    37, 76
  electoral reform 92
  English nationalism 54
  English parliament 14, 120, 224
  'English votes on English laws' 14,
    16, 73, 78, 83–8, 120, 224–6
  Home Rule for Ireland (late 19th and
    early 20th centuries) 28–9, 34–6,
    76
  instrumental unionism 37–8
  lack of Welsh MPs 102
  local government 234, 238
  NHS 199, 209, 210, 217
  October 1974 general election 38
  policy on devolution 38–9, 41,
    43
  poll tax 80
  regional policy 4, 146–7, 153, 159,
    168, 183, 186, 190, 192, 230,
    238
  split with the Northern Ireland
    Unionists 78
  Welsh disestablishment 81–2
  West Lothian Question 68, 70–3,
    79–81, 83, 227
Conservative and Unionist Party *see*
    Conservative Party

Cook, Robin (Labour MP and minister)
    68, 87, 103
core executive 102, 114, 117
Cornwall
  Constitutional Convention 186
  County Councils' Network 125
Criminal Justice (Mode of Trial) Bill
    2000 71
Cromwell, Oliver 26
Cross of St George 48, 52, 59, 61–3

Daily Mail 73
Daily Telegraph 73
Dalton, Hugh
  regional policy 166–7
Dalyell, Tam (Labour MP) 7, 70, 85–6
  see also West Lothian Question
Davis, David (Conservative MP) 14
Daysh, Henry 159, 162–4, 170, 172
democratic deficit (in England) 59, 107,
    233
Department for Constitutional Affairs
    (DCA) 113
Department for Culture, Media and
    Sport (DCMS) 66, 110, 112–13,
    115, 179, 181
Department for Education and
    Employment (DfEE) 99, 107–9
Department for Education and Skills
    (DfES) 66, 97, 100, 112, 115,
    117–18
Department for the Environment, Food
    and Rural Affairs (DEFRA) 100,
    112, 115
Department of the Environment,
    Transport and the Regions
    (DETR) 97, 99, 107–12, 116,
    179, 181
Department of Health 66, 68, 100,
    115, 118, 178, 196, 200–8,
    211–15
Department of Trade and Industry
    (DTI) 97, 105, 107–9, 111–17
Department for Transport, Local
    Government and the Regions
    (DTLR) 110, 112
Department for Work and Pensions 42,
    97, 100, 112, 115
devolution
  budgets of devolved bodies 119, 236
  Callaghan government 39
  culture 149–51
  effects on Westminster 7, 64–92

effects on Whitehall 17, 42, 66,
    96–118
electoral systems 227
English opinion of 120, 128–9, 143,
    228
English Question 1–20, 51, 89, 96,
    107, 117–18, 119–38, 143, 150,
    157, 158, 168, 170, 174, 176,
    189, 215, 224, 228, 231–2,
    235–9
implementation (in 1999) 40, 42, 64,
    82
referendums (1979) 39
    comparing (1979) with (1997) 231
West Lothian Question see West
    Lothian Question
devolution (Northern Ireland) 42, 51,
    64, 92, 113, 117, 157, 176,
    235–7, 239
devolution (Scotland)
    block grant 86, 104
    Conservative opposition 41, 84
    general elections (1974) 38–9
    reasons for demand for 120–1, 238
    tax-varying power 40, 42, 44
    votes at Westminster (prior to 1979)
        78
devolution (Wales)
    Bevan's opposition 37
    English support for extending powers
        129
    general elections (1974) 39
Dicey, A. V.
    classical unionism 27
    Home Rule 29–30, 98
    parliamentary sovereignty 29
    primordial unionism 33
Disraeli, Benjamin (UK Prime Minister
    1868, 1874–80) 33
Dobson, Frank (Labour MP) 72
dual state 217
Duncan, Peter (Conservative MP) 87

East of England
    Constitutional Convention 186
    public opinion toward devolution 124
    regional chamber–RDA conflict 181
    scrutiny of RDA 182
East Midlands
    East Midlands Assembly 186
    integrated regional strategy 180
    public opinion towards devolution
        167

scrutiny of RDA 181
elected mayors 2–3, 6, 10, 107,
    189–90, 221, 230, 233–6
elections
    European Parliament election (2004)
        41
    London mayoral election (2000) 13
    UK general election (1874) 28
    UK general election (1885) 28, 76
    UK general elections (1910) 76
    UK general election (1915) 29
    UK general election (1918) 30
    UK general election (1959) 83
    UK general election (1964) 227
    UK general election (1966) 78
    UK general election (1970) 38
    UK general elections (1974) 38–9,
        78, 227
    UK general election (1979) 217
    UK general election (1992) 209
    UK general election (1997) 10, 41,
        51, 106
    UK general election (2001) 4, 9, 11,
        14, 112, 211, 226
    UK general election (2005) 87
English backlash against devolution
    39–40, 229
English Civil War 26
English common law 47
English independence see independence
    for England
English Independence Party 8, 228
English National Party see English
    Independence Party
Englishness 1, 15–16, 24, 40, 45–6,
    48, 51–4, 56–62, 131, 133, 229
    Baldwin, Stanley 24
    class-based nature of 57–9, 62
    conservative Englishness 16, 4–7,
        52–63
    elegiac Englishness 16, 53, 56–7,
        59–60, 62
    exceptionalism 45–9, 57, 63
    as exemplar 46–7, 57–8, 63
    Kipling, Rudyard 25
    Orwell, George 24, 49, 58
    radical Englishness 16, 47, 50, 52,
        57–62
    universal and particular versions 46–7,
        49–52, 57–8
    see also narrative of disintegration;
        narrative of integration; national
        identity; regional identity

English parliament (proposed) 2–3, 5–6, 14, 16–17, 19–20, 65, 84, 88–92, 120–3, 128, 130–3, 160, 220–4, 228–9, 235, 239
English Question, the
as elite or mass-level question 4–5
English and UK versions 2–4, 221
static and dynamic views of 4
'English votes on English laws' 2–4, 6–7, 14–16, 20, 62, 65, 73, 77, 83–9, 92, 120, 123, 128, 132, 134, 221, 224–6, 228, 235, 239
see also West Lothian Question, 'in and out' solution
Environment Agency 11, 188
European Community
UK's accession 15, 230
European countries
comparing Britain to 18–19, 47, 49, 58, 142–4, 152–3, 155, 156–7, 194, 236, 239
regionalism in 148, 150, 155, 233
European integration and Englishness 15–16, 41, 46, 50–1, 56, 58–9, 61
European Parliament
UK Independence Party election to the 41
European Union, the
British expectations of 50
effect on Whitehall departments 97–8, 99–100
English nationalism 8, 41, 46, 53–4, 58–9, 61
'new regionalism' 148–9, 176, 231
pressure for withdrawal from 8, 54, 228
regional distribution of expenditure 43
structural funds 116, 185

Fabians, the 159–60, 168, 170
Fawcett, C. B. 159–61, 164, 166, 168, 170
federalism
Belgium 146, 148
France 146
Germany 143, 145, 150
number of sub-national units in federal constitutions 195
in the UK 6, 8, 89, 160, 221–4
financing devolution 104
Barnett formula 39–40, 43

block grants 86, 104, 178, 236
convergence of per capital public spending 40
regional disparities in public expenditure 14, 40
territorial needs assessment (1979) 39
flag, English *see* Cross of St George
Foreign and Commonwealth Office 66
Forth, Eric (Conservative MP) 14
foundation hospitals 14, 72–3, 86–7, 212–14, 216, 218
France
alliance with Scotland (17th–18th century) 27
De Gaulle, Charles 145–6
French model of the nation-state 27, 143
French Revolution 27
Jacobin concept of democracy 27, 143
Pompidou, Georges 146
regional tier of government 18–19, 144, 151, 154, 185, 218

Geddes, Patrick 160–1
General Strike (1926) 166
George III (King of United Kingdom 1760–1820)
veto of catholic emancipation legislation 28
George IV (King of United Kingdom 1820–30)
visit to Edinburgh (1822) 32
George V (King of United Kingdom 1910–36)
Home Rule 36
Germany
Basic Law (1949) 146, 224
federalism 143, 145–6, 150–1
Länder 151
Prussia 224
regional economies 150
socially-embedded capitalism 154
Gladstone, William (UK Prime Minister 1868–74, 1880–85, 1886, 1892–94) 2, 16, 28, 30, 32–3, 35, 41
Government of Ireland Act (1920) 36
Government of Ireland Bill (1886) 28–9
Government Offices for the Regions (GOs) 9–12, 17, 105–6, 108, 110, 112, 127, 146, 155, 176–9, 182–3, 185–6, 203, 232

Greater London Authority (GLA) 8, 107, 119, 164, 174, 177, 181, 189
Greater London Authority Bill/Act (1999) 17, 87–8
Greater London Council (GLC) 105, 188
Green Papers
  Modern Regional Policy for the UK, A (2003) 116

Hague, William (Conservative Party leader 1997–2001) 4, 14, 84, 120, 226
Hailsham, Lord (minister for the North East) 168–9
Health and Social Care (Community Health and Standards) Bill (2003) 72, 86
Heath, Edward (UK Prime Minister 1970–74) 78
Heclo, Hugh 184
Heffer, Simon 8, 45, 54
Higher Education Bill (2004) 72, 85–6, 225
Hinchcliffe, David (Labour MP) 72
HM Treasury *see* Treasury
Home Office 110–12, 115, 179
Home Rule Bill (1886) 28, 76–7
Home Rule Bill (1893) 77
Home Rule Bill (1914) 29
Home Rule for Ireland (late 19th–early 20th century debates) 2, 15–16, 24, 28–36, 43, 75–7, 82, 89, 91, 98, 158, 160
  see also Gladstone, William
House of Lords *see* Westminster
Howard, Michael (Conservative MP, minister and leader) 84, 226

identity *see* national identity, regional identity
independence for England 2, 6–8, 54–5, 59, 62, 221–2, 227–8, 235
  see also Heffer, Simon; Nairn, Tom; Weight, Richard
Ireland
  British Empire 31–2
  Catholicism 27, 35
  dominion of British Empire 36
  independence (1921) 24, 30, 36, 161
  Irish disestablishment 34–5
  national identity 24

nationalists' success in 1885, 1892, 1910 elections 76
periphery of UK 33–4
Republic of Ireland established (1949) 39
security threat to England in seventeenth century 27
  see also Home Rule for Ireland
Irish Party 28–31
Irish Union (1800–1) 28
  see also Act of Union (union of UK and Ireland)
Italy
  asymmetric devolution 142
  constitutional barriers 87–8
  Democratici di Sinistra 147
  'in and out' rule 16, 77–8, 85–8, 92
  Lega Nord (Northern League) 146
  political barriers 87
  regional government and policy 144–7, 151, 218
  technical barriers 85–7

Jacobite rising (1745–46) 31
James II (King of England and Scotland 1603–25)
Johnson, Boris 49, 61–2

Kilbrandon Commission *see* Royal Commission on the Constitution
Kipling, Rudyard 25, 30, 53

Labour Party
  devolution to Scotland, Wales, Northern Ireland 1, 39–40, 51, 70, 231
  English Grand Committee 91
  'English votes on English laws'/'in and out' solution 14, 71–3, 75, 83–8, 225, 227
  hunting with dogs 70
  instrumental unionism 37–9
  local government 233–4
  multiculturalism 61
  National Health Service 199, 211–12, 216
  nationalists' challenge (1960s–70s) 38
  New Voice for England's Regions, A (1995 policy document) 176
  North East 159, 162, 166, 169–72
  party of the periphery (late 19th–early 20th centuries) 33
  populist Englishness 60, 62

rebelliousness among Labour MPs
    (since 1997) 70–3, 84
regional committees (Westminster) 91
regional policy 1, 4 , 9–12, 106–17,
    144–5, 147, 154–5, 159, 166–7,
    169–72, 174–92, 224, 230, 238
Renewing the Regions (1995 policy
    document) 176
strength in Scotland, Wales, the
    periphery 33, 37–8, 70, 80–1,
    83, 92, 226–7
West Lothian Question 71–3, 75, 83,
    227
see also West Lothian Question
laissez-faire economics 162, 164
Learning and Skills Council (LSC) 109,
    117, 178, 182
Liberal Democrats
    'English votes on English laws' 89
    local income tax proposal 42
    regional committees (Westminster) 91
    regional policy 230–1
Liberal Party
    party of the periphery (late 19th–early
        20th centuries) 33
Lloyd George, David (UK Prime
        Minister 1916–22) 31, 37, 89, 91
local government
    alternative to regionalism 190–2,
        233–4
    business 154
    Comprehensive Performance
        Assessment 190
    Department of the Environment,
        Transport and Regions 97, 99
    Fawcett, C. B. 160
    financing of 42
    NHS 197, 199, 200–1, 205–6, 207,
        214–15
    in the North East 168–9
    pressures to decentralise 11
    reform of
        in Britain 144, 147, 166, 190
        in France 144, 146–7
    Regional Development Agencies
        (RDAs) 155, 177–8, 181, 184
    regionalism 127, 147, 153, 155, 180,
        187, 231–2
    strengthening it as a solution to
        English Question 2, 5–6, 10,
        107, 127, 190–2, 221, 230,
        233–4, 235
    unitary local government 190, 238

Local Government Act (2000) 10, 190,
    234
London
    Greater London Authority *see* Greater
        London Authority
    mayor of London 13, 187–9, 236
    North–South divide 3, 11, 18
    resentment against London as spur to
        devolution 3, 18, 135

Major, John (Prime Minister 1991–97)
    9, 17, 41, 79, 84, 105–6
Marshall-Andrews, Bob (Labour MP) 71
mayors *see* elected mayors
median voter theory 33
metropolitan countries 105, 190–2
Milburn, Alan 172, 211, 224
Miners' Strike (1984–85) 155, 172
Ministry of Agriculture, Fisheries and
        Food (MAFF) 99–100, 110, 179
Ministry of Defence 66
multiculturalism 53, 55, 61

Nairn, Tom
    the break-up of the UK 7–8, 16
    narrative of disintegration 50–1
    nationalism 53
    radical Englishness 58
narrative of disintegration 15–16, 46,
    49–51, 55
narrative of integration 15, 45, 46–51,
    230
National Assembly for Wales 39, 72, 76,
    82, 85, 89, 174, 121, 127–9, 231
National Health Service (in England)
    18, 37, 86, 194–218
    centralisation/decentralisation
        194–218
    consensus management 205–6, 208
    district general hospitals 203–4
    district health authorities (DHAs)
        205, 207, 210–11
    functional and territorial logics 194,
        196, 204, 206–7, 210, 214–15,
        217–18
    Hospital Plan (1962) 202–4
    internal market 209–11, 216
    local/regional autonomy 194–7, 199,
        201, 204–7, 209–10, 215,
        217–18
    monopsony 197
    NHS Management Executive 208,
        210

Payment by Results 213, 217
professional autonomy 194, 196,
    199, 204–7, 218
strategic health authorities (SHAs)
    211–14
structure (1948–74) 199–204
    local health authorities 200
    regional hospital boards 200–1
structure (after 1974) 204–7
    area health authorities (AHAs) 201,
        205, 207
    hospital management committees
        204
    primary care trusts (PCTs) 203,
        211–13, 218
    regional health authorities (RHAs)
        18, 200–1, 205
    reorganisation during Blair
        governments 211–14
    reorganisation during Thatcher and
        Major governments 207–11
    waiting lists 214
national identity (English) 1, 8, 16,
    49–63, 120, 128, 131–3, 138,
    196, 228–9, 237
nationalism, English 6, 8, 15–16, 25,
    48, 51–63, 128, 228
    see also Britishness; Englishness
nationalism, general 50
nationalism, Scottish 24, 38, 43
nationalism, Welsh 24, 38, 43
neo-liberalism 147, 152
network governance 145, 148, 151–2,
    156
network governance in the English
    regions 10–11, 18–19, 156,
    174–5, 182–9, 192, 196, 232
network governance in the NHS 207,
    214
New Labour 10–11, 51, 106, 109, 169,
    175, 233–4
    see also Labour Party
new localism 212
Norman, Montagu (Governor of the
    Bank of England, 1920–44) 162,
    165
North East
    backlash against devolution to
        Scotland 39
    campaign for a Northern Assembly
        172
    Constitutional Convention 12,
        172

history of regionalism 19, 158–73,
    163–4
North East Development Board 19
public awareness of receiving lower
    public spending than Scotland 13
regional assembly referendum
    (November 2004) 4–5, 9, 12,
    19–20, 113, 117, 119, 124, 175,
    177, 191, 231
regional chamber (unelected) 136
rejection of English Parliament idea
    19
unemployment 161, 165–6, 168–9
Northern Economic Planning Council
    (NEPC) 163, 169–70
Northern Ireland
    britishness 50
    creation of 30, 36
    health service 196, 201
    paramilitarism 35
    public expenditure 43
    religion 35
    special procedures at Westminster 65,
        76–9
    Stormont 76–8, 83, 226
    true home of primordial unionism 35
Northern Ireland Act (1974) 78
Northern Ireland Office 96, 102
North West
    Constitutional Convention 12, 186
    Labour's divisions on establishing a
        directly-elected assembly in the
        region 9
    North West Regional Assembly
        180–1, 186
    public opinion towards devolution
        124
    referendum on establishing an elected
        assembly 9, 124, 177
    regional culture and identity 156
Norton, Philip (Lord Norton of Louth)
    7, 90
Norton Commission see Conservative
    Party

Oakeshott, Michael 48–9, 52
Office of the Deputy Prime Minister
    (ODPM) 43, 66, 100, 102,
    111–17, 179
Orwell, George 24

Parekh Report 61
Parliament Act (1911) 29

parliamentary sovereignty 15, 50
  Home Rule for Ireland 29–30
  Powell, Enoch and the threat of EC
    membership to 41
  see also Powell, Enoch
  Union with Scotland 27
Parnell, Charles Stewart (Irish Party
  leader) 28
Paxman, Jeremy 45, 55, 63
Plaid Cymru
  by-election victory in Carmarthen
    (1966) 24, 38
Pocock, J. G. A. 46, 62–3
policy communities (around regional
  government institutions) 11
policy divergence (since devolution) 99,
  104, 174
policy networks *see* network governance
policy spill-over 104
poll tax (and Anglo-Scottish conflict) 80
Poor Law hospitals 206
popular sovereignty 53, 59, 143
post-war consensus 199
Powell, Enoch (Conservative and Ulster
  Unionist MP 1950–87) 36,
  40–1, 45, 52–3, 202, 204
Prescott, John (Deputy Prime Minister
  1997–) 5, 9, 107, 109, 112–14,
  117, 172–3, 224, 231, 238
Primrose League 34
proportional representation 37, 92,
  227
public expenditure
  higher level in Scotland, Wales,
    Northern Ireland 13
  see also financing devolution
Public Health Act (19th century) 206
public opinion (England)
  perception of effects of devolution
    128–9, 136
  perception of impact of regional
    institutions 136–7
  reasons for low support for
    constitutional change in England
    128–38
  regional pride 134–5
  toward devolution in Scotland/Wales
    4, 129–31
  towards the English Question and
    possible solutions 11–13, 14–20,
    73, 85, 121–8, 132, 134, 224–5,
    228–9
public opinion (Scotland) 14, 85

Raynsford, Nick (Labour MP and
  minister) 189–90
referendums
  directly elected mayors 9, 189–90,
    234
  France (1969) 145
  Home Rule for Ireland (late 19th and
    early 20th centuries) 29
  North East regional referendum
    (November 2004) 4–5, 9, 12,
    19–20, 113, 117, 119, 124, 177,
    175, 191, 231
  regional devolution referendums
    (general) 9, 107, 124–6, 177,
    185
  Scottish devolution referendum
    (1979) 39
  Welsh devolution referendum (1979)
    39, 231
regional assemblies (elected) 2–6, 8–9,
  17, 20, 88, 117–19, 122–7, 132,
  136, 172, 174–6, 183, 185–6,
  188–9, 192, 220–1, 223–4,
  230–2, 235–8
Regional Assemblies (Preparation)
  Bill/Act (2003) 9, 17, 86
regional chambers (unelected) 8–12, 18,
  107, 119, 127, 136–9, 153, 167,
  174, 176–88, 180, 182, 186,
  188, 232–4, 237
regional constitutional conventions 9, 12
Regional Co-ordination Unit (RCU)
  110, 112, 177, 179
Regional Cultural Consortiums 181–2,
  232
Regional Development Agencies
  (RDAs)
  budgets (including 'single pot'
    funding) 10, 108, 111–12,
    114–15, 177–9, 238
  business 187, 232
  Conservative Party views on 183,
    190–1
  establishment of (1999) 8–10, 19,
    107–8, 119, 172–3, 177
  influence of 108–9, 114
  role in policy networks 183–4, 232
  scrutiny by regional chambers 10,
    153, 179, 181–2, 237
Regional Economic Planning Boards
  (REPBs) 105, 145
Regional Economic Planning Councils
  (REPCs) 19, 105, 145

Regional Housing Forums 19, 182, 232
regional identity (English) 18, 134–5,
    138, 144, 149, 151, 153–4, 159,
    161, 163, 170, 180, 188, 192,
    237
regionalism
  administrative decentralisation 3, 106,
    113–14, 230
  capacity building 19, 14, 174–5,
    179–80, 182, 232
  city-regions 3
  'creeping regionalism' 11, 178, 233,
    237, 239
    Environment Agency 11
    Fire and Rescue Service 11
  culture 149–50, 155, 176
  dominance of London and South East
    3
  economic crisis 161–7
  economic development 148–9, 152
  economic disparities/uneven growth
    3, 12
  economies of scales 11, 179, 191,
    196
  functional regionalism 2, 6, 9–10, 19,
    101, 105–6, 117, 142–6, 148,
    151–7, 176, 221, 223, 231–3,
    235
  historic nations 4, 6, 150, 221–2
  long history 3, 19, 158–73
  new regionalism 148–53, 184
  North–South divide 3, 11, 107, 119
  party politics 147, 150
  path dependency 150
  political regionalism 9, 18, 142–4,
    146–9, 153, 161, 169, 170, 217,
    233
  regional assemblies see regional
    assemblies (elected) and regional
    chambers (unelected)
  as response to elite rather than public
    opinion 11, 12
  social capital 152
  strategic functions of regional bodies
    5, 101, 115, 153, 174, 178–88,
    191–2, 231, 234, 236
  trade unions 144, 148, 150, 154,
    169, 172
Regional Observatories 179, 181–2, 232
regional planning 19, 105, 115, 122,
    144–6, 148, 153, 160, 162,
    164–5, 167–9, 171, 175,
    179–80, 183, 231, 234, 237

Regional Planning Guidance 179
Regional Policy Commission 107
regional referendum see referendums;
    North East
Regional Selective Assistance (RSA) 108
regional skills partnerships 117
regions see names of particular regions
Reid, John (Labour MP and minister)
  appointment as Health Secretary
    (2003) and related controversy
    13, 68, 103
Royal Commission on the Constitution
    (Kilbrandon Commission) 85–6,
    88, 101, 125, 138, 158, 170
Rural Development Service 177–8
Rushdie, Salman 52

Salisbury, Lord (UK Prime Minister
    1885–86, 1886–92, 1895–1902)
    28, 33–4, 37, 41
Salisbury Review 55
Schöpflin, G. 58–9
Scotland
  British Army 31
  British Empire 30–1
  civil war (17th century) 26
  Conservative party 37–8, 41, 73,
    79–80, 87, 103
  health service 42, 104, 194, 196, 198
  independence 7–8, 43–4
  knock-on effects of English legislation
    17
  Labour Party 38–9, 70, 80, 83, 87
  legal system 79, 80, 83
  Liberal Democrats 87
  national identity 24, 48–51, 54
  nationalism 38, 50, 60, 168, 171
  over-representation at Westminster
    13, 37, 39, 65
  poll tax 80
  public expenditure 13, 39–40, 43
  religion 26–7, 35, 42
  romantic Scotland 33
  security threat to England 26, 31
  special procedures at Westminster
    79–81, 83–8, 90–1
  Union with England (1707) 15,
    25–8, 43, 79
  unionism 33–5, 167
  West Lothian Question see West
    Lothian Question
Scotland Act (1998) 42
Scotland Bill (1977) 171

Scotland Office *see* Scottish Office
Scotland and Wales Bill (1977) 39
Scotsman 73
Scott, Sir Walter 32
Scottish Constitutional Convention 5,
    238
Scottish Enlightenment 32
Scottish National Party (SNP)
    fall of Callaghan Government (1979)
        39
    Hamilton by-election victory (1967)
        38
    policy of not voting on English
        legislation 86
    success in UK general elections
        (February and October 1974) 38
Scottish Office 67, 81, 96, 103, 118,
    158, 238
Scottish Parliament
    English Parliament 5–6, 89, 120–1,
        224
    English regions 174
    federalism 89
    public opinion (England) 228
    public opinion (Scotland) 127–9
    rise of Scottish nationalism (1960s,
        1970s) 38–9
    Sewel convention 85
    West Lothian Question 68, 70, 72,
        76, 84, 89
Scottish Social Attitudes Survey 127
scrutiny
    in regional government 8, 10, 153,
        179, 180–2, 187, 237
    at Westminster 65, 78, 216
Scruton, Roger 56–9, 62
Secretary of State for Health 216
single pot *see* Regional Development
    Agencies
Sinn Féin 30
Skinner, Dennis (Labour MP) 214
Smith, T. Dan 155, 159, 169, 171–2
social capital 152
Solemn League and Covenant 26
solidarity among the four nations of the
    UK 13
South East
    economic dominance of England 3, 11
    growing divide with northern regions
        11, 18
    public opinion towards devolution
        123–4
    scrutiny of RDA 181

South East England Regional
    Assembly 180
South West
    Constitutional Convention 12, 186
    scrutiny of RDA 181
South West Regional Assembly 180–1
Spain
    Andalucia 215
    asymmetrical devolution 4
    Basque Country 4, 146–7
    café para todos 142
    Catalonia 4, 146–7, 149–50, 215
    devolution and regionalism after
        Franco 4, 142, 145, 146–7, 151,
        194, 218
    Galicia 4
    regionalism in the late 19th and early
        20th centuries 147
Speaker's Conference on Devolution
    (1919) 19, 91, 158, 160
Special Areas Acts (1934 and 1937)
    162, 165–6
stakeholders (in the English regions)
    10–11, 180, 184, 186–8
St George's Cross *see* Cross of St George
Straw, Jack (Labour MP and minister)
    11, 107
Strengthening Regional Accountability
    (consultation paper 2001) 179
subsidiarity 147, 205
Sustainable Development Round Tables
    19, 181–2, 232

Taylor, A. J. P. 46–7
Thatcher, Margaret (UK Prime Minister
    1979–91) 39, 51, 80, 105, 172,
    207–8
    abolition of regional institutions 105
Thatcherism
    anglocentric integration 50
    North East 172
Third Reform Act (1884) 37
Thompson, E. P. 57–8, 61
Tory Party 33
    see also Conservative Party
trade unions
    regionalism 144, 148, 150, 154, 169,
        172
Treasury
    Barnett formula 39
    financing devolution 39–40, 43, 104
    local government finance 42–3
    Public Service Agreements (PSAs) 116

regional policy 11–12, 17, 102, 111,
113–17, 145, 162, 165, 168,
174, 180, 191–2, 232
Scottish ministers 67
Spending Review (2000) 108, 111
Spending Review (2002) 12, 115–16
Spending Review (2004) 12, 177,
188
territorial politics 102
Treaty of Union (1707) (union of
England and Scotland) 15, 25–7,
30, 32, 75

Union of Crowns (1603) 25–6, 79
unionism
classical unionism 27
see also Dicey, A. V.
'English votes on English laws' 16
ideology of unionism 15
instrumental unionism 36–9
Attlee Government 37
Wilson Governments 37–8
loss of Ireland 31
Northern Irish Unionists 29, 36, 77–8
parliamentary sovereignty 15, 27, 30,
40–1, 48, 50, 229
passionate or primordial unionism 15,
28–30, 32–8, 40–1, 43
United Kingdom Independence Party 41

Victoria (Queen of United Kingdom
1837–1901)
opposition to Home Rule 28
unionism 32–3
voluntary sector (and regional
governance) 10–11, 19, 155,
180, 183–4, 187, 232–3

Wales
Act of Union with England 15
British Army 31
British Empire 31
Conservative Party 37, 41, 73, 101–2
health service 42, 86, 104, 194, 196,
198
independence 7–8
knock-on effects of English legislation
17
Labour party 39, 70, 81
national identity 24, 48–51, 82
nationalism 38, 50, 60, 168
over-representation at Westminster
13, 37, 65

public expenditure 13, 39
religion 81
see also Welsh disestablishment
special procedures at Westminster
81–2, 87, 90–1
unionism 33–4, 167
Wild Wales 33
Wales Office see Welsh Office
Weight, Richard 8, 59–60, 62
Welsh Assembly see National Assembly
for Wales
Welsh disestablishment (and English
MPs blocking of, 1880–1914)
16, 35, 81–2
Welsh Disestablishment Bill 82
Welsh Life and Times Survey 127
Welsh nationalism see nationalism,
Welsh; Plaid Cymru
Welsh Office 82, 96, 158, 191, 205,
238
West Lothian Question 7, 43, 69–76,
84, 89, 91–2, 107, 142, 226–7
Commons votes on fox-hunting
(2000) 14, 70
creation of foundation hospitals
(2003) 14, 72–3, 86–7
'in and out' solution 16, 77–8, 85–9,
92
see also 'English votes on English
laws'
Irish Home Rule debates 16
limiting access to jury trials in
England 71
long history 75
university top-up fees 14–15, 72, 85
West Midlands
Constitutional Convention 12, 186
public ignorance of regional
institutions 12
West Midlands Government Office 12
West Midlands Regional Assembly 12
Westminster
changing roles of Scottish and Welsh
MPs since devolution 64, 66–9
distinct territorial structures and
procedures (England) 82–3,
90–2, 224, 228
distinct territorial structures and
procedures (general) 7, 64–6,
75, 79, 83
distinct territorial structures and
procedures (Ireland/Northern
Ireland) 76–9

Westminster (*cont.*)
  distinct territorial structures and
      procedures (Scotland) 79–81,
      83, 90
  distinct territorial structures and
      procedures (Wales) 81–2
  House of Lords 29, 34, 37, 71–2,
      81–2, 103, 158
  Irish representation 77
  over-representation of Scotland,
      Wales, Northern Ireland 13, 37,
      39, 65, 226
  procedural change as answer to
      English Question 84, 89–92
  proxy for English Parliament 7, 43,
      224
    see also 'English votes on English
      laws'
  rebelliousness among Labour MPs
      (since 1997) 70–3, 84
  territorial extent and territorial
      application of legislation 85–6,
      225
  territorial tensions 64, 70–6, 83, 88
    see also 'English votes on English
      laws'; West Lothian Question
Westminster Committees (House of
      Commons)
  Agriculture Committee 81
  Committee of the Nations and the
      Regions 113
  English Grand Committee (proposed)
      91
  Liaison Committee 73
  membership of select committees by
      location of constituency 68
  Procedure Committee 7, 14, 17, 90
  regional committees 91
  Scottish Affairs Select Committee 80
  Scottish Grand Committee 80, 90–1
  Scottish MPs' representation on
      standing committees 81
  Scottish Standing Committee 80
  select committee for the North East
      191
  Standing Committee on Regional
      Affairs 7, 65, 91
  Trade and Industry Select Committee
      106
  Welsh Affairs Select Committee 80,
      82
  Welsh Grand Committee 82, 91

Whitehall
  devolution's impact 97–9
  English dimension 96–101, 104
  English regional dimension 97,
      101–18
  European dimension 99–100
  functional rather than territorial
      organisation 17–18, 42, 96, 98,
      101–2, 105–6, 109, 117, 196,
      210, 214–15, 217–18
  Government Offices for the Regions 9
  joined-up government 102, 108
  London-centric character 3, 119, 128,
      237
  opposition to devolving powers to
      regional bodies 5, 17, 107, 113,
      238
  regional turn (1999–2004) 111
  territorial breakdown of Whitehall
      departments 66, 100
  territorial secretaries of state 13
    see also individual department names
White Papers
  Modernising Government (1999)
      109–11
  *Productivity in the UK 3: The
      Regional Dimension* (2001) 111,
      114
  Your Region, Your Choice (2002) 10,
      110–13, 170, 177, 185–7, 192,
      231, 237
Wilson, Harold (UK Prime Minister
      1964–70, 1974–76)
  'in and out' rule 16
  instrumental unionism 37–8
  Northern Irish MPs voting rights at
      Westminster 77–8, 83
  regionalism 91, 169
  Royal Commission on the
      Constitution (Kilbrandon
      Commission) 38
  territorial tensions 79
Wright, Tony (Labour MP) 51–2

Yeo, Tim (Conservative MP) 72
Yorkshire & Humber
  Constitutional Convention 12, 186
  public opinion towards devolution
      124
  referendum on regional devolution
      (2004) and its cancellation 9,
      177, 185